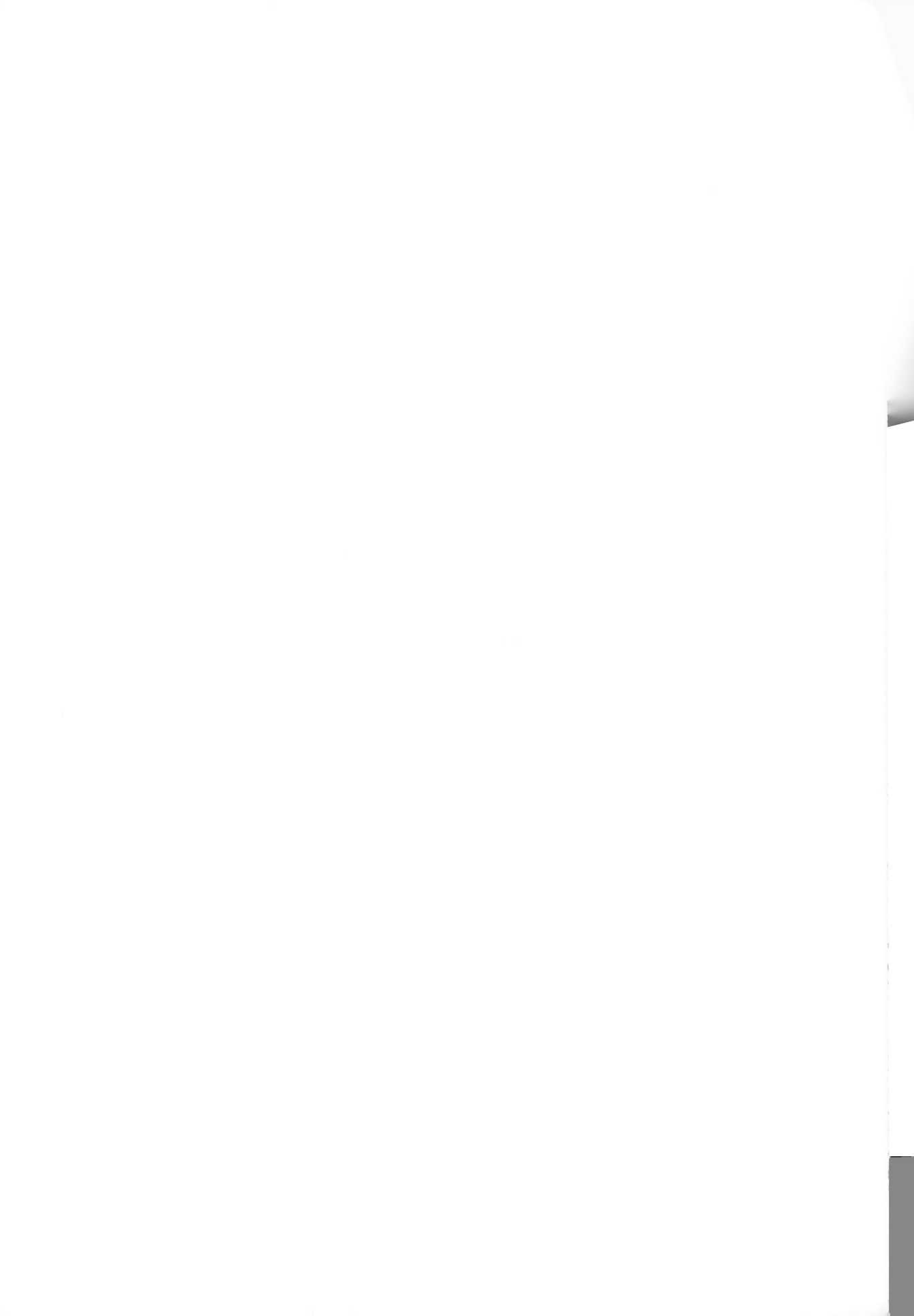

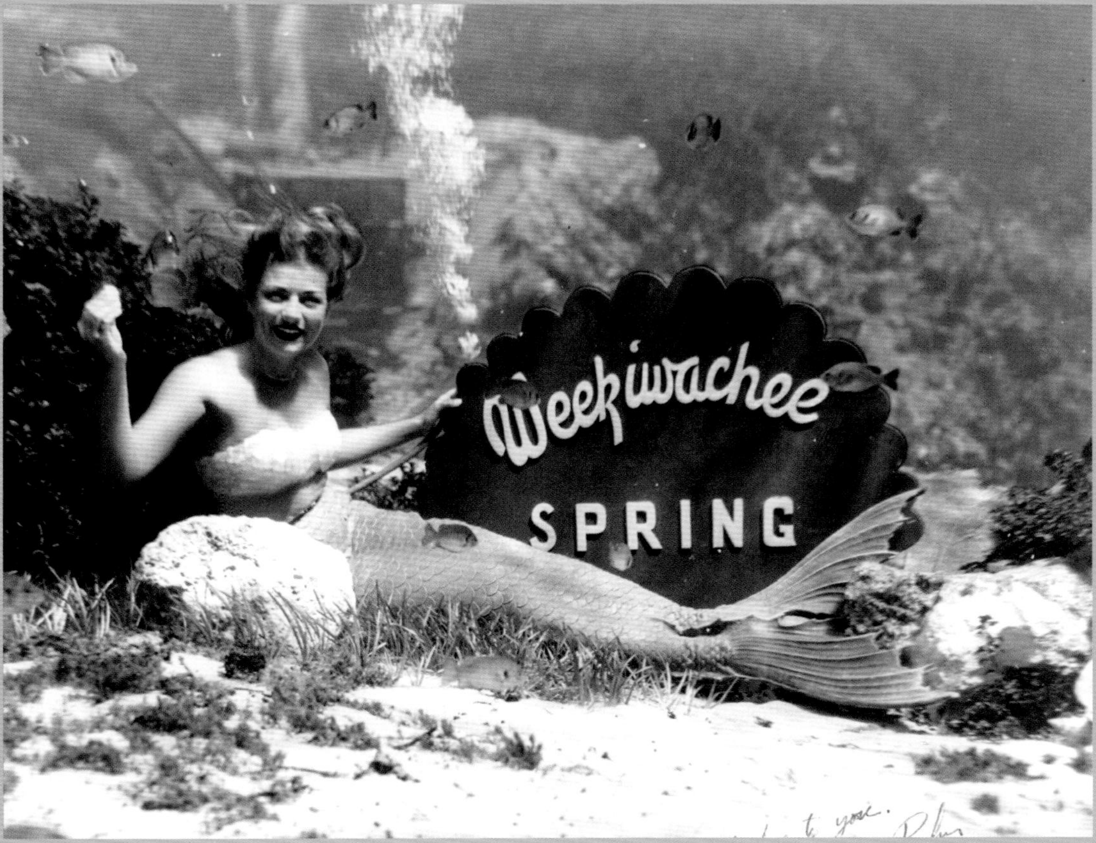

UNIVERSITY PRESS OF FLORIDA

Florida A&M University, Tallahassee
Florida Atlantic University, Boca Raton
Florida Gulf Coast University, Ft. Myers
Florida International University, Miami
Florida State University, Tallahassee
New College of Florida, Sarasota
University of Central Florida, Orlando
University of Florida, Gainesville
University of North Florida, Jacksonville
University of South Florida, Tampa
University of West Florida, Pensacola

Weeki Wachee Mermaids

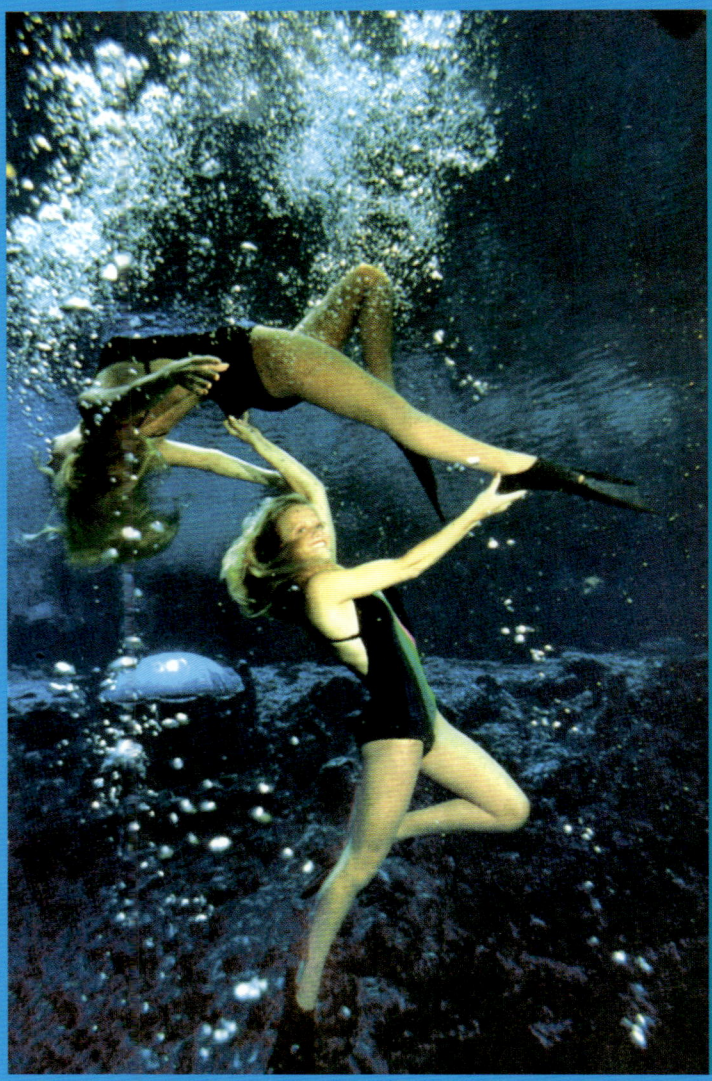

University Press of Florida

Gainesville · Tallahassee · Tampa · Boca Raton · Pensacola · Orlando · Miami · Jacksonville · Ft. Myers · Sarasota

Thirty Years of Underwater Photography

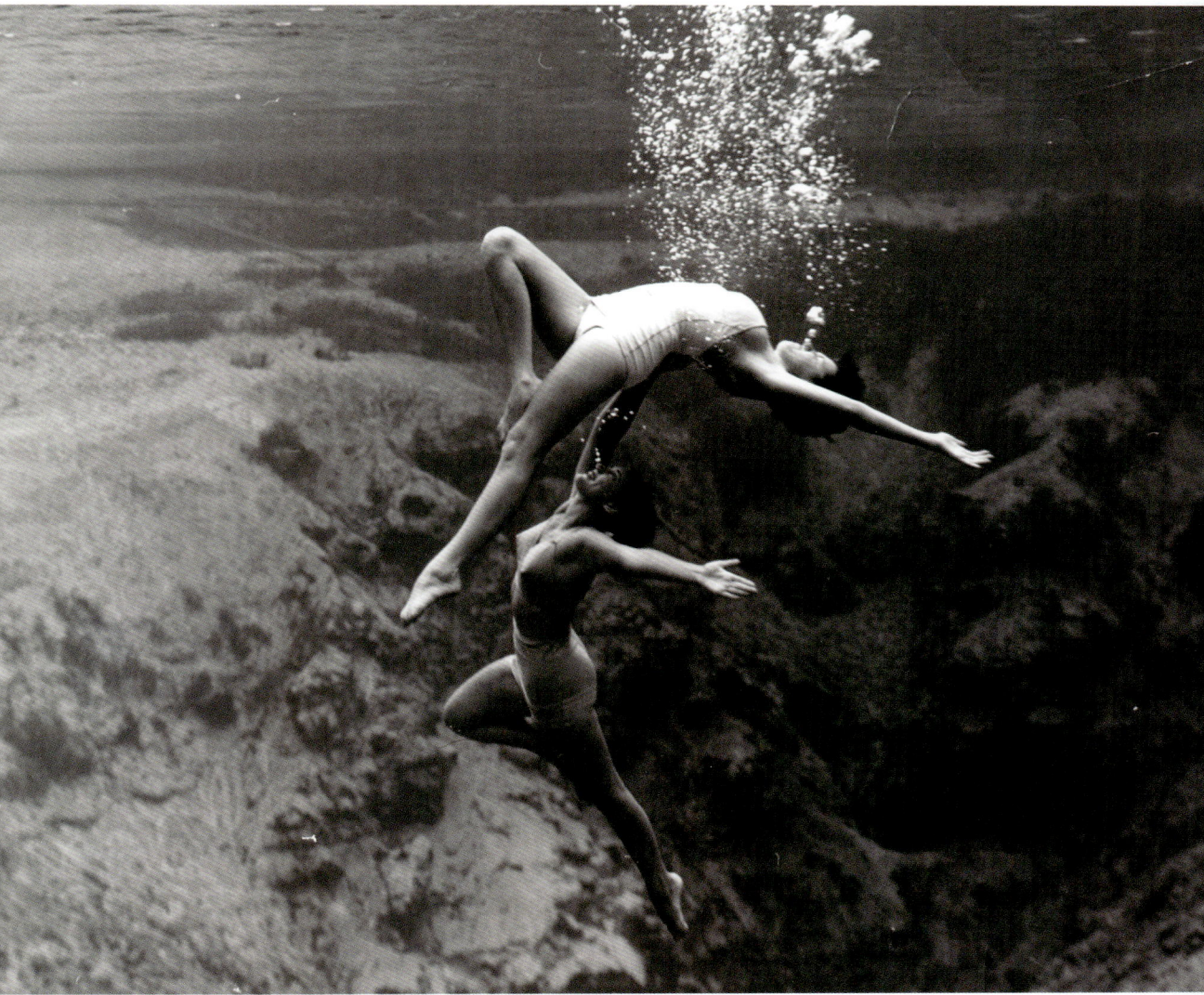

Lu Vickers and Bonnie Georgiadis

17   16   15   14   13   12   6   5   4   3   2   1

A record of cataloging-in-publication data is
available from the Library of Congress.
ISBN 978-0-8130-4430-9

University Press of Florida
15 Northwest 15th Street
Gainesville, FL 32611-2079
http://www.upf.com

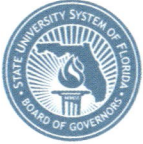

Introduction

The photographs of the mermaids and occasional mermen in this book were taken between 1946 and 1977 at Weeki Wachee Springs, Florida's one-of-a-kind roadside attraction, the Spring of Live Mermaids. Never mind that the performers rarely wore tails—they breathed underwater. We're talking Weeki Wachee mermaids here, the kind that perform adagios and knee-back dolphins, the kind of mermaids that eat bananas and drink soda—all beneath the surface of the nation's deepest spring. The images range from dreamy black-and-white candids of mermaids and mermen performing effortlessly underwater to the brightly colored and elaborately staged photos reenacting scenes from shows such as *Alice in Waterland* and *Snow White*. The latter shots were taken after ABC acquired the attraction in 1959, built a million-dollar theater, and began staging shows "just like a Broadway musical . . . underwater!" Max Weldy of Sarasota's Ringling Brothers Circus designed the props, and the mermaids were fully accessorized—decked out in fiberglass costumes as Tweedle Dum and Tweedle Dee or sporting rubber ears as Snow White's dwarves. They even began wearing sequined mermaid tails. However, no matter what the subject—pure underwater ballet, a kitschy underwater tribute to John F. Kennedy's birthday, or an underwater production of *Mermaids on the Moon*—nearly all the photographs collected here were shot for publicity and either sent to newspapers, used in brochures, or printed up as postcards with messages like this one scrawled across the back: "Just seen a good show here. Having a swell time."

According to Jean Marbella, Florida, more than any other state, "can trace its history through its postcards. This land of palm trees and flamingos, and beaches and bikinis has always lent itself to being reduced to a brightly colored, 3 × 5 image." By *always,* she meant the nineteenth century, when the very first postcards were dropped into the mail, although one might argue that in naming the state *Pascua Florida*, Ponce de Leon reduced it to a "brightly colored image" that stuck. Although the flamingos and Weeki Wachee mermaids that made up the quintessential Florida vacation came later, Ponce de Leon has long been described as Florida's first tourist. Historian Tracy Revels explains:

According to the legend, Florida's first tourist sought a vacation in paradise, the trip of a lifetime that would literally renew his life. But history is rarely as entertaining as fable. There is no credible evidence that Ponce de Leon was seeking anything more than the usual land and treasure.

Ponce de Leon might not have discovered the Fountain of Youth—he might have not even been looking for it—but it certainly discovered him. The mythical fountain associated with Ponce de Leon may well be Florida's first Authentically Fake attraction. As Michael Garvey points out—using the myth as his yardstick—Ponce de Leon and the founders of Weeki Wachee weren't that different from each other:

> Weeki Wachee was a hauntingly beautiful crystalline natural spring in West Florida, the sort of place Ponce de Leon was looking for when he was searching for the Fountain of Youth. Its discovery and exploration by [Newton] Perry and [Ricou] Browning began the weirdest chapter of its evolution from backwater Eden to cracker amusement park to national tourist destination to American Broadcasting Company asset to . . . well, to Authentically Fake Florida relic perhaps.

Garvey's phrase *Authentically Fake* originated with Joel Achenbach, a Florida native and columnist, who defined Authentically Fake Florida as being largely

> composed of vanishing tourist attractions that were popular long ago, like roadside alligator wrestling stands, the Cypress Knee Museum, the Citrus Tower, Spook Hill, the glass-bottomed boats at Silver Springs, and so forth. . . . You will instantly know if you are in Authentically Fake Florida. For example, you might find yourself in an underground amphitheater staring through a huge glass window at women swimming in a deep freshwater spring, wearing bikini tops and mermaid-fin bottoms, smiling, doing spins and flips and occasionally sucking on air hoses to stave off drowning. This would be Weeki Wachee Springs, a.k.a. "the Spring of Live Mermaids," about 45 miles north of Tampa. I called to make sure the spring is still open—you never know with businesses that depend heavily on underwater air hoses.

*   *   *

By 1874, over 50,000 tourists had visited Silver Springs, Florida's first "backwater Eden," and many sent home photos of cypress swamps, alligators, and steamboats. William Henry Jackson, whose 1871 photographs of Yellowstone led to its becoming a national park, visited Florida in 1892; his exquisite black-and-white photographs of Silver Springs were sent to

Detroit, where they were hand colored and made into penny postcards, the U.S. Postal Service's nod to the growing tourism industry. As historian Charlotte Porter points out, the print shop workers who had only heard of Florida "selected the bright colors and omitted both insects and shadows in these durable images of Florida." These enhanced images of Florida's natural beauty bought by Florida tourists then sent back home "popularized the Florida tourist trail." It's no surprise, wrote Hampton Dunn, that the "development of the tourist industry in Florida coincides with the development of the picture postcard trade." And what a development it was. Florida went from being a wild place where tourists could steam down the Ocklawaha taking potshots at alligators to a place where, at Gatorland, they could amble through the open jaws of a giant concrete alligator head, sit in bleachers, and watch them do the Gator Jumparoo.

By the mid-1940s, visitors to Florida were sending home 30 million postcards a year. A Florida postcard was the ultimate souvenir in those halcyon days. "Persons shop for postcards just as they would deliberate over buying a tie, a dress, or a pair of shoes," reported Russell Kay, the secretary of the Florida Press Association, of the 1940s-era tourists. "Bok Tower is number one . . . runners up are cards showing a pretty girl with fruit in a citrus grove or decorated with a pelican." The fact that postcards sold so well and that they advertised both the attractions and the state was not lost on those early attraction owners, as Kay pointed out later:

> Florida can thank the amazing growth of her tourist business over the years largely to the faith, enterprise and effort of her attraction promoters. . . . without them, millions who now know and love the state, in all probability would have never heard of it. The publicity experience and "know-how" possessed by such men as Dick Pope of Cypress Gardens, Bob Eastman of Marine Studios, Pete Schall of Silver Springs, and Newt Perry of Weekiwachee Springs has brought this state more priceless advertising than it has gained from all other mediums combined.

The years captured in the photos and postcards collected here—from the monochrome 1940s to the colorful Photochromed 1970s—were the wonder years, not just for Weeki Wachee, but for all of Florida's attractions, the years that began when, as historian Gary Mormino points out, a "flood of postwar tourists spawned a commercial creativity that survives to this day." No other state can lay claim to such creativity. By the late 1940s, Florida had more gardens, jungles, monkeys, and parrots than a tourist could snap with a Brownie Hawkeye. But only one place had banana-eating mermaids, and that was Weeki Wachee. As an anonymous caption writer wrote beneath one of the thousands of photographs to come out of Weeki Wachee featuring a group of teenaged mermaids playing on an underwater playground, "It took Florida to come up with this stunt."

Russell Kay singled Newt Perry out for his originality, praising him for "getting away from the glass-bottom boat or diving bell as a means of presenting the springs" by creating an underwater theater "where the humans are caged and the fish are free." Kay might have stolen his praise from Monkey Jungle, which advertised itself as the place "where humans are caged and monkeys run wild," but he was right. As Perry said a couple of years later, sinking a theater in a spring and then putting on mermaid shows took a bit of nerve: "Many people said I was crazy when I told them I could present floor shows, ballets and the like underwater." Even after he proved he could do just that, people still had a hard time believing what they were seeing. Scuba was still in its infancy, so watching people perform underwater was akin to watching the first moon landing on television. Countless mermaids have told stories about audience members who thought the show was faked.

Nancy Tribble Benda, one of the first mermaids to perform at Weeki Wachee, said that sometimes tourists would go to irrational lengths to explain away what they were actually seeing. "One time this woman was sitting right in the front row and of course the turtles were there and the fish were there and the ducks were there and this turtle just happened to float through the scene and this woman just let out this squeal and said 'Look at that, look at that. I didn't know turtles could fly.' The water was so clear and I guess there are some people who aren't swimmers that just couldn't comprehend what they were looking at."

The disbelief did not diminish over the years. Terry Hamlet, who performed as a mermaid in the 1960s, explained how one man refused to believe the mermaids were underwater. He was convinced that fans were blowing their hair up—who knows what he believed allowed the mermaids themselves to float. He didn't relent, Terry said, until she took him into the tube room after a show and let him watch the mermaids climb out of the porthole dripping wet from head to toe.

The otherworldly images of women surrounded by fish while hula dancing or eating bananas or playing football underwater are so wholly original that they almost do seem faked. When Newt Perry sent his photo of teenaged mermaids playing on a swing set sunk fifteen feet into the spring to newspapers in 1948, editors across the country debated whether the mermaids were indeed underwater. The staff at the *Evening Independent* came to Perry's defense: "They look as though they were in a school playground," claimed one northern newsman.

"They sure wouldn't enjoy half drowning that much."

"They ain't in no school yard. They're underwater," the harassed *Independent* men insisted. "And they love it. And they are not half drowning. Perry teaches them to stay underwater by starting them off with a hose to breathe through—or something."

The argument went back and forth until one observant person noticed the bubbles rising from the girls' mouths—that and the fact that their feet weren't on the ground. Disbelief was then replaced with the notion that the photos couldn't have been made anywhere *but* the City of Mermaids: "Florida kids take to the water like ducks in the underwater playgrounds [at Weekiwachee Springs] North of St. Petersburg, Florida." But these images do indeed have their underwater predecessors, just as the Weeki Wachee mermaids themselves do—and Newton Perry had a hand in popularizing both.

The *idea* of a performer diving into a pool of water and acting out scenes before an audience actually originated much earlier than 1946. In the late 1800s, a vaudeville performer named Blatz the Human Fish climbed into a water-filled tank, played a trombone, read newspapers, and apparently napped underwater. In the early 1900s, the "Australian mermaid," Annette Kellerman, made a career of performing underwater by swimming with fish and eels at the Melbourne Exhibition Aquarium, and, later, by performing underwater in films such as *Siren of the Seas* (1911), *Neptune's Daughter* (1914), and *A Daughter of the Gods* (1916). Kellerman wore the first "swimmable mermaid costume" in *Sirens of the Sea* and was the first major actress to go nude in *A Daughter of the Gods,* the first million-dollar film made by a studio.

By 1917, when she returned to the "stage" (a giant aquarium at the New York Hippodrome equipped with tunnels for her water sprite co-stars to disappear into), Kellerman was the best-paid woman in vaudeville. By performing water ballet as the first "aquatic glamour girl," she made "mermaid" a household word and paved the way for the development of synchronized swimming as well as for future aquatic stars like Esther Williams and Newton Perry.

Homer Gramling of the *Miami Herald* described Perry's incomparable contributions to Florida's underwater history best: "Hollywood may be the movie capital of the world; and Broadway's claim to the legitimate theater is undisputed. But for underwater show business, Florida is 'Stage

One.' . . . The history of the underwater show is also the life history of one man: Newton A. Perry."

Perry began his underwater journey at Silver Springs in 1924, just a few years after he arrived in Florida, when he took a job as a lifeguard. His immersion in this unbelievably beautiful underwater landscape changed his life. Silver Springs had become famous for its underwater vistas when, in 1878, Hullam Jones fitted a piece of glass in the bottom of a boat. Phillip Morrell later built his own version to ferry paying tourists over the spring. A booklet published in the late 1800s by the Marion County Chamber of Commerce describes how, "seen through the glass-bottom boat," fish seem "suspended in mid-air" and the effects of sunlight are "truly magical."

In retrospect, given the transformative effect of looking into a spring through the glass bottom of a boat, it seems inevitable that the boat would eventually evolve into a theater sunk into a spring. Newt Perry would be the one to do it. Gazing into the spring held a huge appeal for tourists, whose interest, as historian Wendy Adams King points out, "was not unlike the interest that the Space Shuttle launches and IMAX movies possess for many tourists today." Carl Ray and Shorty Davidson, then co-owners of the park, capitalized on that appeal, King writes, creating brochures that touted the virtues of "Florida's Subaqueous Fairyland":

> The underwater scenery is as gorgeous and varied as terrestrial plant and animal life is multiple; for here at Silver Springs Nature has drawn aside the curtain of mystery that shrouds other waters and revealed the living panorama of a world unknown to those who have never seen beneath its surface.

In 1916, one visitor seemed to foresee Weeki Wachee's underwater theater when she floated over the spring head—and she wasn't even in a glass bottomed boat:

> There the transparent depths of the water gave one the impression the boat had turned itself into a flying machine and that we were moving through the air. Every pebble and every aquatic plant stood out so clear as if it were on the shore instead of at the bottom of a lake. Even the fish and alligators swimming about seemed to be in an aquarium or at least in a tank behind a glass plate.

The water was that transparent. Glass-bottom boat guides would point out sites such as the "DEVIL'S KITCHEN with its interesting imageries of pop-corn roasting and boiling pots," the "Catfish Hotel" (with a private bath in every room), and the "POT O' PEARLS, a basin of pearl-like shells." Word of the underwater fairyland at Silver Springs spread fast—and it was only a matter of time before the newly established newsreel companies sent crews down to Florida for a look. What they found kept them coming back again and again. "Paramount News came down from New York," Perry told an interviewer in 1974, explaining how he came up with the idea for Weeki Wachee. "They asked Shorty Davidson if he would go out and eat a banana underwater, which he did. . . . They asked me if I would swim back and forth before the camera, which I did. That's how I got my start in 1924 swimming underwater for the camera when I was 14 years of age." *British Pathé* newsreel has preserved the film of Shorty Davidson eating his banana, the favored snack of the Weeki Wachee mermaids yet to come. There he is in grainy black and white, a fireplug of a man plunging deep into the water, wearing a black swimsuit with two white Ss for Silver Springs emblazoned over his chest. He squats in the sand eating a banana, his face screwed up; clearly he hasn't mastered the art of appearing at ease underwater.

But Newt Perry did, and the underwater world became his stage: first at Silver Springs, then at Wakulla, and finally at Weeki Wachee. Delee Perry, Newt's youngest daughter, who still runs the Perry Swim School her father started in 1955, said that just a couple of years after her father swam back and forth in front of Paramount's camera, filmmaker Grantland Rice asked him to set up a table for an underwater picnic. Thinking all the eating and drinking had to be done in one shot, he inadvertently set a world record for holding his breath underwater. By 1928, Perry was an old pro in the submarine environment, sitting at a café table underwater for a photo that appeared in the *Atlanta Constitution's* Gravure Pictorial section. In 1929, he caught 50 turtles in one hour as "champion turtle catcher" in *Crystal Champions*, one of the short Grantland Rice films, which also launched the film career of one of Perry's friends, Olympic swimming champion Johnny Weissmuller. The film also set up Silver Springs to become the underwater movie capital of the world. Within the next two years, nearly every film company in the United States had visited Silver Springs, Davidson told a reporter, drawn "by the remarkable clarity" of the water. Johnny Weissmuller, who had donned a loin cloth to become Tarzan, persuaded MGM to head to Silver Springs, where they made *Tarzan Finds a Son*. The studio was impressed with what it found. "We've spent fortunes in Hollywood for huge tanks," an MGM spokesperson said, "and have planted fresh vegetation in them every shooting day. We've installed expensive filtration machinery, and hired the best engineers None of them has produced what we could term photographically clear water. But in Florida's springs we have the ideal set up."

Filmmakers couldn't seem to get enough of the novelty of the underwater landscape. By the late 1930s, 90 percent of all underwater movies and newsreels were made at the spring, and Newton Perry had a hand in quite a few of them. In fact, he so rarely seemed to come up for air that in 1932 Grantland Rice made a short film about Perry called "The Human Fish." In this short film, Perry demonstrated some of the moves he later taught the Weeki Wachee mermaids, including the elevator, the knee-back dolphin, and the pinwheel.

Perry wasn't the only person in his family to perform underwater. His sisters Eileen and Martha, his cousin Newton Fiveash, and his first wife Margaret Carman (whose cousin Claude starred as Jody in *The Yearling*) also performed underwater for newsreels. Eileen Perry Hogshead, Newt's oldest daughter (and her aunt's namesake), has a collection of photos depicting this family of underwater performers from as early as the 1920s at springs from Silver to Wakulla to Weeki Wachee. One especially beautiful photo depicts her mother and two aunts posing underwater at Silver Springs while feeding fish—an activity the Weeki Wachee mermaids would make famous twenty years later. Her Aunt Eileen was fourteen when she began performing underwater at Silver Springs; in 1933, she and Newt appeared together in an underwater "magic carpet ride" in *Silver Springs*, a film short. Whenever Eileen appeared in newsreels and still photos, she was always swimming, always underwater. An Irish paper dubbed her "Mermaid of the Springs." Newt's other sister, Martha Dent Perry, also performed at the springs, both for newsreels and film—she doubled in some scenes for Maureen O'Sullivan, who played Jane to Weissmuller's Tarzan.

Other women performed underwater at Silver Springs as well. A 1935 *American Weekly* newspaper featured photos of professional wrestlers Dolly Dalton and Dixie Taylor duking it out surrounded by fish alongside an image of Christine Lamb belting out a tune—all of them underwater, of course. The writer explained why: "The best place in America to get underwater photographs is Silver Springs, Florida, and the spot is a magnet for cameramen as it is for expert swimmers who are good at submarine maneuvers." Showing great appreciation for the skill it takes to perform underwater, the writer noted that the photos were made while "the amphibious subjects were only a few feet below the surface, but anyone who never has tried wrestling—or merely sitting down—in the

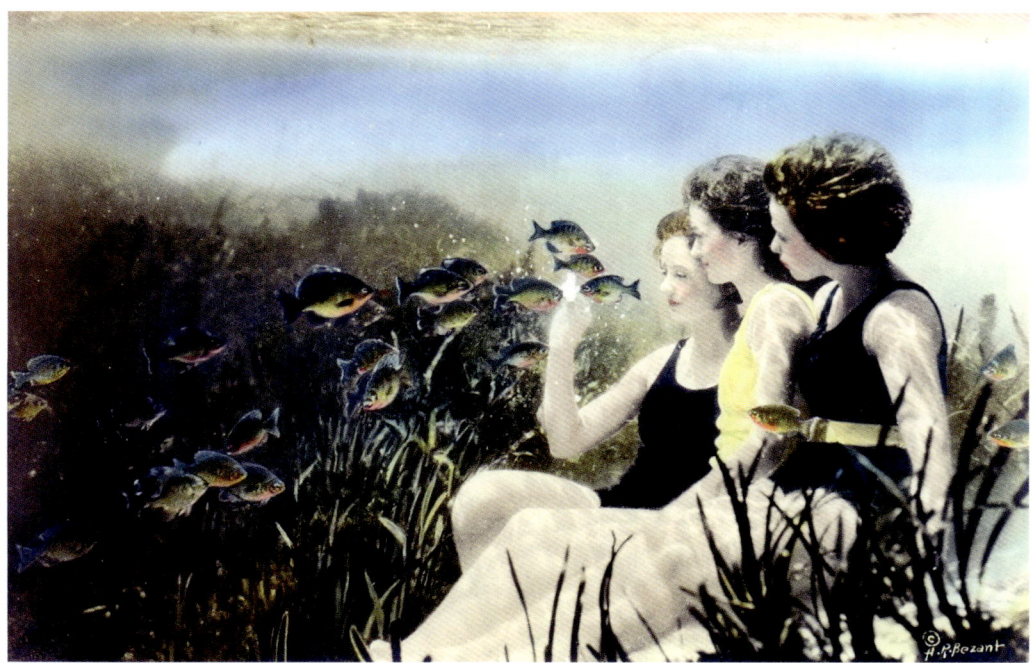

Eileen Perry Hogshead said this photo of her aunts and her mother was the first under-water photo made for a postcard at Silver Springs, circa 1928. *From left*, Eileen Perry Waddington, Margaret Jarman Perry, and Martha Dent Perry. Photo by H. P. Bezant. By permission of Eileen Perry Hogshead.

natural environment of a fish cannot appreciate what a job it is to fully enjoy the facilities of this unusual playground." One expert swimmer who showed up to use the underwater facilities at Silver Springs was Annette Kellerman. She dove into the spring in 1936 to film scenes for a series of fairytales; stills of the Australian swimmer made it into the papers. She could have passed for a Weeki Wachee mermaid.

It was inevitable that Eileen Perry Hogshead would become a Weeki Wachee mermaid herself, the youngest to perform continuously at the attraction. "I should've been born at Silver Springs," she said, "but my mother got sick when she was seven months pregnant and had to go home to Tennessee to have me. We moved back to Ocala when I was six months old." It was 1935. For about a year, the family lived on and managed a farm owned by financier Ed Ball, who had recently purchased Wakulla Springs.

It was the beginning of a spectacular and unique Florida childhood. While Ross Allen and her father wrestled alligators and anacondas for cameramen, Eileen and Ross's daughter Betty swam in the Silver River, played with poisonous snakes, and steered clear of the rhesus monkeys who liked to jump on tourists. When the crew for a Tarzan movie came to town, Eileen rode an elephant and her mother doubled for Jane. Meanwhile, her father continued to develop his underwater theatrics.

In 1936, just ten years before he would break ground at Weeki Wachee, Newt and his sister Eileen starred in the prophetic *Neptune's Scholars,* a short film about a mermaid school. Ms. Perry told a reporter about the difficulties of posing underwater for the cameramen, who at that time were encased in a steel box with a window: "The ordinary diver breathes deeply, plunges in, and rises immediately through his own buoyancy. But I must exhale completely so as to stay under long enough for the camera to get into action . . . The hardest thing is keeping one's expression. It's not easy to 'look natural' while under the strain of holding one's breath." The same point would be made twenty five years later in *Care and Feeding of a Mermaid,* a short film made at Weeki Wachee about the training that mermaid wannabes undergo. While Thea, the "seasoned performer," displays "ease and confidence" when she removes her mask to smile underwater, Bonita, the mermaid in training, grimaces. Nancy Tribble Benda recalled one of the techniques she used to make herself grimace-free: "I would squint my eyes," she said, "then close them very, very tightly to get air bubbles out—and then they'd be more open underwater." She also pointed out that the mermaids had more to think about than how they looked. When training new mermaids to "feel and look relaxed underwater," she said, "we also had to warn them, if they had on flippers, not to kick up sand, not to thrash around because that would cloud the water up."

Those who made it through the intensive training looked so natural underwater that audience members believed the mermaids could see them through the glass, sitting in the theater waving—even though, as anyone who has ever opened their eyes underwater knows, all the mermaids really see is a blur. One mermaid revealed their secret: mermaids simply look toward where they think the audience is.

Images of people acting underwater intrigued reporters. Six years after *Neptune's Scholars* played in theaters, the writer of "Wonders of Under-Water Movies," a photo-essay published in *Popular Mechanics,* commented on the underwater set that featured desks, a chalkboard, and a smoking fireplace, wondering how "such movie magic is achieved." He continued, "best qualified to answer these questions is Newton Perry, who for 12 years at Silver Springs, Florida, . . . has been acting, directing and writing scripts for underwater films." The article described how Perry trained his underwater actors and actresses, teaching them to "bob" to the surface for a great gulp of air and then descend and exhale, an exercise they would perform 100 times in a row to begin with, then for an hour and a half each day during the weeks leading up to a film. He also taught his performers "to swim in unison as if they were ballet dancers." He would later use both techniques to train the most famous mermaids of all—those at Weeki Wachee.

Perry and his crew did everything underwater, from dancing, wrestling, playing trombones, eating Thanksgiving dinner, riding bicycles, and smoking cigarettes. Perry even staged an underwater circus. In a grainy copy of the short film titled simply *Underwater Show,* Newt Perry, posing as "Muscleofsky," a strongman, hoists a girl in each hand effortlessly, occasionally letting them float above his palm. In another scene, young women walk across a tightrope on their hands and are then carried back by Perry, balancing on the ends of a long pole while trying not to float away. Many of these scenes were also captured in still photographs—and so in addition to the typical postcard images of glass-bottom boats, beaches, and palm trees, tourists began sending home depictions of underwater sword fights, hula dances, and bouts of tug-of-war, all staged on the sandy bottom of Silver Springs. A couple that looks like Perry and his sister Eileen posed for one such postcard; she wears a hula skirt and he stands next to her in a swimsuit, apparently trying to dance along.

"One Way to Take Your Best Girl for a Ride," an essay published in 1938, featured Ross Allen hanging onto an alligator like an underwater cowboy while Florence Bogar clung to his back. The photographs had the desired effect of attracting attention, and in 1939, a *New York Times* travel writer declared that Silver Springs was Florida's "best known inland attraction, made famous by the underwater mermaid scenes in sports motion pictures." Clearly the mermaid theme had taken hold, tail or no tail.

On his way to Miami in 1938, photographer Bruce Mozert stopped in Ocala to get some shots of Johnny Weissmuller filming *Tarzan Finds a Son.* It was a stop that would change the photographer's life. "There was only a barrel with a piece of glass in it and there was only room for one cameraman and he was in it," Mozert said. "There was no way I could get my photos." Undeterred, he sought out Wilton Martin for permission to use the shop, built a housing for his camera, dove into the water, and began his career as an underwater photography pioneer. Mozert worked at Silver Springs for over 50 years photographing underwater models doing everything from watching television to riding bicycles to golfing. His favorite model was Ginger Stanley Hallowell, who began her underwater career as a Weeki Wachee mermaid before later moving to Silver Springs.

Ginger said that Newt Perry made an indelible mark not just on her but on all underwater photography at Silver Springs. "Newt's influence is what gave everybody else the idea to do them," she said. "I think he influenced all these underwater stories; he did it in the beginning and everybody thought it was neat and copied it."

With the publication of Gary Monroe's *Silver Springs: The Underwater Photography of Bruce Mozert*, Bruce's work has been getting the attention it deserves. When asked about his influences, Bruce also brought up Newt Perry. "Newt was actually the forerunner in underwater photography and directing," Bruce said. "He was it. There was nobody else, so when Hollywood came, they would hire Newt. When other companies came later to film *The Yearling*, they hired Newt because he knew all the locations; he knew the people; he knew the underwater."

The underwater landscape at Silver Springs had always been a draw, but in 1938, the owners added a new twist to the glass-bottom boat. To let tourists get even closer to the underwater flora and fauna and provide better access to the "photographically clear water," they brought in a precursor to the underwater theater: a couple of "Scenic Photo Subs," boats equipped with an underwater compartment complete with portholes. Ernie Pyle, the famous war-correspondent-turned-roving-journalist, popped in at Silver Springs in 1939 for a ride. "Instead of looking down through glass, you descend into the deep bottom of the boat, sit down and look out horizontally through underwater portholes," he wrote. "This ride tickled us to death. People without heads would swim past. We could see their bodies underwater, but the surface of the water makes a ceiling and you can't see up through it." Two years later, when MGM filmed a scene for *Moon over Miami* at Silver Springs, they included a shot just like the one Ernie Pyle described: Betty Grable and her costar take a ride on the photo sub—and who else should swim by but Newt Perry and a group of kids?

Perry had made such a name for himself as the person studios went to if they were interested in doing underwater film that when an Englishman wrote a letter addressed to "the man who swims underwater somewhere in the United States," it reached him. "It was delivered to me at Silver Springs," Perry said, "'cause they couldn't figure but one place in the country was doing underwater work—and that was at Silver Springs."

Word of Perry's exploits had obviously traveled to North Florida because once Ed Ball had purchased Wakulla Springs and built a lodge, he summoned Perry in 1941 to manage and promote the lodge. The Perry family moved into the rooms above the kitchen. "I could get whatever I wanted," said Eileen Perry Hogshead. Because it was wartime, the park was crammed with soldiers, and Eileen got her first taste of performing underwater. "They used to go down on the long pier and dive off. It was probably seven feet deep—the bathing suits had pockets and their money would fall out and I would swim down and fan the bottom to get it. Then they started throwing money out for me."

Meanwhile, her father enlisted the Tarpon Club, a group of swimmers at the Florida State College for Women, to put on synchronized swim shows for the servicemen who flocked to the spring from nearby Camp Gordon Johnston during wartime. He and his sister Martha Dent Perry were also responsible for steering the group into performing for newsreels in films such as *Campus Mermaids,* a short produced by Grantland Rice. Perry and Johnny Weissmuller were such good friends that Tarzan followed Perry to Wakulla as well, even though MGM was scheduled to film another movie at Silver Springs. "Just as good as Silver Springs," Weismuller announced when he saw the deep blue spring. "I hope we can make the Tarzan picture here; I like it." And so they did. The MGM crew descended on Wakulla for two films. Johnny Weissmuller would alarm tourists staying at the lodge by throwing open the windows and bellowing for his breakfast. Eileen said her mother, Margaret, got in on the action as well: when the glass-bottom boat circled the spring head, she would dive down to the ledge where a giant hollow log rested, then swim in one end and out the other, all while waving at the tourists.

Perry continued devising ways to work underwater at Wakulla, and filmmaker Grantland Rice continued counting on him to help with "gags we want to work out." In February of 1941, his producer, Jack Eaton, wrote Newt asking for his assistance in making a "reel on how underwater movies are made . . . Russ [Erwin] mentioned the proposed hole in the water that you are building. Is this ready?" The hole in the water was a contraption Newt designed that would enable a cameraman to stand upright in a submerged compartment to film underwater. Another of his inventions, one he would later use at Weeki Wachee, was the underwater air lock. He placed two of these deep in the spring at Wakulla. One writer described the postbox-shaped contraptions as "swimmers' filling stations." Filled with compressed air and big enough for four people, these "traps," he added, were particularly useful at Wakulla because it is "a thriving center of underwater photography," and the swimmers could save energy by re-fueling in the airlock instead of swimming to the surface.

As he had at Silver Springs, he trained a group of young men and women—mostly kids from the local high schools—to perform underwater at Wakulla. The group included Ricou Browning, Sis Meyers, and Nancy Tribble Benda, all of whom would assist Perry when he went to open Weeki Wachee. Nancy and Ricou Browning (who would go on to have an illustrious film career of his own, most famously as the person who created *Flipper*) both recalled swimming for Perry. "Very early, Newt started using just a group of us from Leon High," said Nancy. "Most of the work he did with us was in the wintertime because the springs weren't busy and theater people liked to come to Florida in the winter." Perry would drive a truck loaded with blankets to Tallahassee on Saturday mornings to pick up a crowd of teenagers to haul to Wakulla, where he would teach them how to hold their breath underwater for long periods. "Sometimes a crew from Grantland Rice would be down," said Nancy, "and he would stage picnics, and Thanksgiving dinners underwater, and the short films would run in movie theaters."

"We had a beauty contest at Wakulla too," Nancy said, "and that was probably paid for by the State under the Florida Attractions Association because each of us represented some attraction. I represented Killearn Gardens and of course the Miss Wakulla Springs won. That was Doris Underwood." The voiceover in the film announces, "From Wakulla Springs comes this bit of nautical nonsense." One bit of nonsense—besides beauty queens parading underwater in high heels—was a shot of Nancy chewing bubble gum then blowing a big bubble—underwater. For the crowning of the "swamp angel," Newt Perry appears on screen wearing a suit and bowtie, nonchalantly smoking a pipe. Somehow he convinced ordinary people to do extraordinary things. One of his protégés, Mary Anne Hartwell, was featured in an underwater photo in *National Geographic* above the following caption: "What's the use of putting on lipstick at the bottom of a lake?"

"I just happened to be there, going swimmin'," Hartwell told a WCTV reporter in 2003 when the image was reprinted in a special issue of *National Geographic* featuring 100 years of swimsuits. "Newt Perry, who managed the Springs, asked me and this other girl if we'd just swim down there and sit on a log," Mary Anne said.

Only Newt Perry could have casually asked a young woman to dive into a spring and "swim down there and sit on a log." That he could do so is testimony to the confidence he instilled in his young swimmers. Not only could they sit on logs and apply lipstick underwater, they could eat, drink, fence, play records, dance, cook hot dogs, eat them, and then smoke cigarettes. One of the reasons they were able to perform underwater so freely was that Perry had taught them to breathe from an air hose he had developed. Nancy Tribble Benda said the original air hose was tricky to use. "It was literally just an old hose, and the deeper you got, the less pressure you had from that air, and you'd have to bite the end of the air hose so that the air would build up, and then you could get a breath when you let it go."

Despite these limitations, the teenagers Perry trained to use the air hose were able to swim circles around the servicemen who came to Wakulla to be trained in underwater maneuvers by Perry. Nancy said that at that time the military still outfitted its divers with heavy metal dive helmets and Perry couldn't convince them that they could breathe unencumbered with his air hoses, so, as Nancy said, "he put all the mermaids swimming around all underwater with just these air hoses."

Ricou recalled the servicemen as well. "They wore the full rig," he said. "They had strung a cable underwater and the divers would go out and get ahold of the cable and then go down to the first stage, and then the second stage, and then down to the bottom. While they were doing this us kids would take the air hose and swim down next to them and they thought we were out of our minds. There they were in these big rigs and here we are with just air hoses in our mouths."

Wakulla was Perry's last stop before he finally fulfilled his life's dream by finding a spring he could call his own and where he could stage his own mermaid shows. He was helped along in this direction by an old friend, Walton Hall Smith. The two men met up in 1939 at Wakulla and discussed the possibility of developing an attraction, but the war intervened. Ed Carmichael, who'd originally developed Silver Springs, had told Smith about a couple of springs on the west coast of Florida, one of which was called "Weekly Washing, or something like that." Smith finally located the spring, but discovered it was nearly inaccessible. However, by the time 1946 rolled around, the Gulf Coast Highway extended into the state and Perry and Smith decided to make their move and take the underwater business to the next level. Forget the glass-bottom boat and the photosub; when they arrived in St. Petersburg in June of 1946 to pitch their plan to develop Weeki Wachee into a roadside attraction, they told the St. Petersburg city council they planned to construct a "'submarine photo lounge' . . . with submerged portholes to allow visitors to make underwater photographs in the crystal clear waters and to view spectacular underwater ballets." That the theater was conceived as a "submarine photo lounge" wasn't just a matter of using 1940s-era parlance; given Perry's long history with underwater performance and filmmaking, he probably couldn't imagine an audience *without* cameras. So of course the theater would be a "submarine photo lounge."

Perry wrote a note to friends on stationery headed with the exclamation "The Mountain Underwater!" announcing that he had "joined a group to develop the most unusual spring in the world. . . . 'The Mountain Underwater' is viewed from our so-called 'Underwater Theater,' the only thing like it in the world. From the Underwater Theater you will also see hundreds of fish, turtles, and best of all a bevy of beautiful girls who will enact an underwater ballet."

By the time Weeki Wachee opened in 1947, Perry "had spent almost as much of his life in water as on dry land" and had swum over 5,000 miles—400 of them underwater and quite a bit of them in front of a camera. Mr. Underwater bragged that he could do anything that could be done on land underwater—even cooking. These weren't empty promises. John Reese reported, "He can produce photos and refer to movies showing him roasting a hot dog over an underwater fire." It was all true. If any one person is responsible for igniting and then fanning the flames of the craze for underwater photography in Florida, it has to be Newt Perry.

When Perry arrived at Weeki Wachee to create his submarine photo lounge/underwater theater, cameras like Kodak's Brownie Hawkeye and the aptly named "Tourist" belonged to practically everyone who crossed the Florida state line. Amateurs would snap photos of orange groves, flamingoes, and beaches and—if Newt Perry had his way—they would also begin to snap photos of "The Mountain Underwater."

But first Ricou Browning had to clean the spring. "I couldn't believe the beauty of the spring," Ricou said in an interview, "but with one exception. It was full of old automobiles and bedframes, mattresses and mattress springs, you name it: it was full of junk." He spent one whole month cleaning the springs, diving down with an air hose and a rope, hooking things to it so the construction crew could haul it up.

Nancy Tribble Benda also went down to Weeki Wachee that summer to help Newt open Weeki Wachee. "That whole first summer we did lots of the promotional shots, including the one that was on the first brochure. And then we started feeding the fish and getting them to come around us and Newt also built the air stage there for us to breathe."

That first brochure featured the image of Nancy and Sis Meyers in swimsuits, Nancy holding Sis aloft as they seemingly float through space over the submarine landscape. "The Mountain Underwater!" the brochure exclaims, ignoring the floating women as if they were an everyday occurrence. Beneath the photo is a drawing of a mountain surrounded by fish overlaid with the words "A NEWLY DISCOVERED PHENOMENON IN THIS WORLD." Despite the uppercase letters, the eye is drawn not to the "newly discovered phenomenon" of the "underwater mountain" but to the apparently weightless figures of the women. A second look at the image reveals the secret: silver bubbles rise from their mouths—they are indeed underwater.

"That photograph was taken long before the stage or the theater was in place," Nancy said. "We took it over and over again, Sis Myers and I. It was hard to balance it so that one person didn't lean too far one way or the other. Sis was a good deal taller than I but she was the one on top; that pose was very hard to control." But control it they did. The photograph, made from Newt Perry's famous "hole in the water," was taken by Ted Lagerberg, who owned the Modern Photographers Studio of New Port Richey. Lagerberg, along with Russell Peterson and J. R. Yagel, was among the handful of photographers who were on hand to snap photographs of the mermaids in those early days.

In spite of the numerous underwater photos and newsreels made over the years at Silver Springs and Wakulla then sent to newspapers or played in theaters, the image of Nancy and Sis suspended in space startled the viewer. Up until this point, there really had not been a photo like this. The images that came out of Silver Springs had largely been staged on the sandy ground, albeit underwater. The models in those photos seemed somehow anchored. The image of Nancy and Sis drifting untethered over the cavernous depth of the spring defied convention.

Inside the brochure was another arresting scene: a black-and-white photograph featuring four young women suspended in space over the underwater canyon, their shapely legs pointing upward toward the surface of the spring. Beneath the photograph, the caption invites the tourist-to-be to

Take Pictures Like This Yourself
of the
UNDERWATER BABE'S BALLET
Seen from the World's ONLY
UNDERWATER THEATRE

The group of young women in this photo were members of the Aqua Belles, a synchronized swim troupe from St. Petersburg whom Perry recruited to perform as soon as he arrived at Weeki Wachee. Dianne Wyatt

McDonald recalled Perry coming over to St. Petersburg to ask the group whether they would put on a "water show on top of the water." The surface show was great for the tourists outside near the edge of the spring, said Dianne, but it wasn't so great for the audience in the theater. So Dianne and her friends Martha Barnes and Judy Cholomitis went back to St. Petersburg and began making drawings of poses they could perform underwater. "We did not use air hoses," said Dianne in an interview, "and we did not use masks or fins—but we dove down 35–40 feet and did underwater poses. Another girl and I originated the adagio pose, which I am very proud of; it has become a symbol of Weeki Wachee. We swam every weekend at Weeki Wachee. We got no pay but we received bathing suits and we got our meals and a lot of publicity. When you're 17 to 18 years old, that publicity was better than any pay you can get, believe me."

The Aqua Belles began performing regularly at the spring doing both synchronized swimming on the surface and underwater ballet, and they, too, attracted the attention of professional photographers. Mary Dwight Rose and her sister Fran drifted upward through the spring holding the adagio pose for *Look* magazine, then participated in yet another *Look* photo shoot along with their fellow Aqua Belles Dianne Wyatt McDonald and Judy Cholomitis. Much to their delight, the result of the eight-hour photo shoot was a two-page spread.

Apparently, everyone wanted to get in on the underwater craze. Before Weeki Wachee officially opened, a reporter for the *St. Petersburg Times* wrote, "Florida will soon be known as the 'Underwater State' . . . the reason is a rash of underwater theaters now being planned." He cited Weeki Wachee, Rainbow Springs, Silver Springs, and Nature's Fish Bowl at Homossassa, where the "fish will serve as actors." But in the end there was to be only one true theater devoted to underwater performances, and that was Weeki Wachee. The mermaids turned out to be much more entrancing than the snook that swam into view at the fish bowl in Homosassa. As Claire Lui wrote in a review of the book, *Weeki Wachee, City of Mermaids*, which featured photos from the attraction, "There is an ethereal beauty to old photographs of mermaids leaping underwater and a sense of wonder in pictures of teenagers guzzling soda pop while sitting on the bottom of the [spring]."

One of these teenagers was Eileen Perry Hogshead, Newt's oldest daughter. By the time Newt founded Weeki Wachee, he and Eileen's mother, Margaret, had divorced, but every summer Eileen and her little brother Newton Jr. would trek to Florida to spend time with their father.

Eileen finally got the chance to become an underwater star when she was thirteen. "I swam three shows a day," she said in an interview, "and the current was strong where the airlock was. I tried to look beautiful but it was hard." She remembered what all of the original mermaids remember: eating, drinking, doing the deep dive and floating up using the adagio pose. "My mother only let me swim if I promised not to do the deep dive," she said. "I couldn't stand not doing it and one day I went down with the air hose. It was wonderful; fish were swimming around me and it was so quiet. I'm so glad I did it that one time." She waited until she was 60 years old to tell her mother she'd done it. "She was very uncomfortable—it was pretty deep down there."

The depth of Weeki Wachee was so impressive, particularly when a mermaid descended into its cavernous darkness, that the park later billed itself as the Underwater Grand Canyon. The images coming out of Weeki Wachee were spectacular and, not surprisingly, caught the attention of people such as Toni Frissell, the famous fashion photographer. Frissell was the first photographer to "take fashion models out of the studio and into nature." Weeki Wachee wasn't her first stop in Florida. In 1941, "in search of a new viewpoint," she ventured down to Florida's Marine Studios "where, as a photographic experiment, she choreographed an elaborate fantasy around a white evening dress." Wearing what looks like a string of giant silver pearls, the model swam into the porpoise tank and struck a pose. The image is lovely, but not as strikingly beautiful as Frissell's iconic photograph of a woman wearing a white gown and floating just beneath the surface of the water at Weeki Wachee. The image was published in *Harper's Bazaar* in 1947, then reprinted by *Sports Illustrated* in 1960 in a two-page spread with the following caption:

> Only once has a young lady drifted, ethereal as Ophelia, past the underwater window in her nightie; not part of her act, it was done by Kay Jones so a photographer could take this lovely hot-weather picture.

Despite what the caption said, Kay Jones, now Kay Finney, said she was not Frissell's model. She was eleven years old at the time and had not become a mermaid yet. Still, there was no shortage of young ladies drifting through the spring. Or young men. Mary Darlington Fletcher and her brother Ed and his friends Ned Stevens and Ed Edwards were the first locals to take Perry's swim test to determine if they could perform. That meant swimming across the spring, Mary said. "And if we made it, and we all did, we were all mermaids, all of a sudden." Although Ed, who passed away in 2008, claimed he just went along for the ride, hauling mermaids up to Weeki Wachee in his Model A, he loved being a merman. He made underwater history:

> For the first time in the history of the attraction, Newton Perry and four of his star performers, Mary Darlington, Ed Darlington, Mary Ann Zeigler, and Ed Edwards, cut and ate a juicy watermelon ten feet beneath the surface of the springs.

Ed and Mary both returned to the underwater stage in 1997, donning their tails after 50 years to join a group of former mermaids in a retro-show. The "formers," as they refer to themselves, had staged a fiftieth anniversary reunion show that year, and the show was such a hit that it became an institution. Ed's presence in the show was a reminder of all the men who swam at Weeki Wachee over the years, often overshadowed by their lovely mermaid counterparts.

Despite their second billing, their lives, just like those of the mermaids, were changed by performing in the spring. Ricou Browning, who helped train mermaids before the park even opened, stayed in the water—he doubled as the Creature in the *Creature of the Black Lagoon*, wrote the screenplay for *Flipper*, and headed up Florida's Ivan Tors Studio, which produced television shows like *Flipper* and *Seahunt*. He was inducted into the Florida Artist's Hall of Fame in 2012. Some mermen found love in the spring. Dick Woolery, who had been Newt Perry's assistant, ended up marrying a mermaid, Shirley, who happened to be Ricou's sister. Bud Boyett married mermaid Patsie Hadley; a newspaper reported that the centerpiece at Patsie's bridal shower was a "replica of Weekiwachee Spring, depicting a ballet routine in pipe cleaners." Rudy Halabuck was married to mermaid Thelma.

Some of the men did the deep dive like Marvin Kimbrough or performed one or two acts in the demonstration shows like Ed Edwards and Ed Darlington. Sometimes they simply posed for photo shoots like the one of Bud taking aim at a fish with a rifle underwater or the one that features Dick, Bud, and Rudy playing cards underwater while their disgruntled mermaid wives look on. Chuck Walls drove Wiley Willy, a sea dragon. Some of the men, like Roy Smith, Lavurne Enfinger, Governor Campbell, Bill Moran, Doug Hopkins, and Allen Scott, worked as underwater boys, supplying the mermaids with air tanks and bananas, cleaning the windows, and arranging lighting. "The underwater boys didn't perform in shows at that time," said Allen. "They used us for help in commercials, magazine pieces, and other special events." Sometimes the underwater boys helped when the unexpected occurred, like the time Doug Hopkins and Allen Scott saved mermaids Karen Dutcher and Susan Sweeney from drowning in 1970. Doug ended up marrying Susan. Allen found himself back in the water after the 1997 reunion show—at first repairing air hoses, valves, and speakers, and later actually performing. Record of the identities of some male performers has sometimes been lost to time only to resurface at their deaths in obituaries. Charles Robert Sims and Ronald Gene Robison were both described as "retired mermen."

Once the park opened, Perry got a call from Universal-International studios wondering whether he knew a good place to make a movie about a mermaid. Sure, he said: Weeki Wachee. The crew of *Mister Peabody and the Mermaid* showed up and cameras began rolling. Perry had to teach star Ann Blyth how to swim underwater, but most of the underwater scenes featuring the mermaid were handled by doubles, including Mary Darlington Fletcher and Nancy Tribble Benda. Nancy flew out to California, where she was fitted with the tail—once she got back to Weeki Wachee, Newt, of course, had her ham it up for the cameras wearing the tail. The caption of one photo reads: "Tired of feeding fish, Mermaid Tribble captures a nice garfish and reclines on a sandy couch for a snack." Mary had a turn in the tail as well. According to the local paper, she got a chance to coach the actress on the finer points of swimming in a fish tail.

Despite the intriguing publicity coming out of Weeki Wachee, Perry wasn't able make enough money to satisfy the stockholders, so, after four years, he made the decision to leave. He wrote a letter to one of the main investors: "To say that my heart is crushed is putting it very mild." His old friend Grantland Rice wrote, reminding Perry that he considered him the "Father of Underwater Swimming . . . and we hope that it will be our pleasure to continue to make Grantland Rice Sportlight Films on the new underwater routines you are constantly working up." Newt Perry may have had to leave Weeki Wachee, but his mark on the spring remained, a fact that is evident even today. Every time the mermaids perform the adagio or the swan or the show-stopping deep dive, they evoke his spirit. Every time they feed bread to the fish, or drink soda, or eat bananas, they pay homage to his creativity and to his more than three decades of teaching people to perform for an audience in extraordinary circumstances—fifteen feet underwater.

Despite Weeki Wachee's early brochure's suggestion that "You can take photos like these," the reality is that taking those underwater photographs wasn't as easy as it looked. Sparky Schumacher, ninety, who was hired along with Claude Long by Ted Lagerberg, and who stayed on as head photographer at Weeki Wachee from 1961 to 1976, remembered taking photographs from inside the original theater. "The tourists would use flash, then they'd get a big glare," he said in an interview, referring to the windows of the theater. "Either that or they didn't have cameras strong enough to take underwater pictures. Those Brownie cameras wouldn't work underwater, they wouldn't let enough light in. If they had a good 35mm they could take them, but not many people had those."

By the time Sparky got settled in as head photographer, ABC purchased the spring and set out to "make Weeki Wachee one of the foremost tourist attractions in the state." That meant building a million-dollar theater, hiring choreographers, and upgrading the shows from ones the mermaids simply improvised, using various moves like the swan, the knee-back dolphin or the arabesque, to launching full-scale productions worthy of Broadway, like *The Underwater Circus*, *Alice in Waterland*, and *Mermaids on the Moon*. ABC also doubled the number of mermaids.

Lauretta Jefferson, who had formerly worked with the Billy Rose Aquacade and the Ringling Brothers' Circus before coming to Weeki Wachee, was the first choreographer to produce a show in the new facility. Given her circus background, it was not surprising that the first show included the "Butterfly Ballet, the Strong Man act, the Underwater tightrope act, the Spangled Tails, and the famous Living Mermaids." She also added a sea dragon named Wiley Willy; he would be "the only man in the show." However, despite the million-dollar theater and despite those intriguing new acts, a *New York Times* reporter was still taken with the basics that Newt Perry had introduced nearly two decades earlier:

> The performers are masters of the art of controlled breathing, and are aided by compressed air fed to them through hoses. Those who have seen the acts marvel when a girl eats a banana under water or opens her mouth and smiles without taking in water.

Marilyn Nagle Cloutier and her husband at the time, Jack, came aboard next. For their first show, *Yellow Bird*, they stuck with the circus theme. The *Miami News* gave an account of the pyrotechnics involved in their production:

> You blink your eyes at girls flitting with precision through underwater acrobatics to the strains of "The Yellow Rose [sic]," . . . see a fiery sea serpent chasing mermaids . . . gasp at the girl who tumbles from a trapeze and catches herself by the heels, . . . then add three underwater seahorses, a clown, and mermaids garbed in dazzling sequined costumes and tails (fish, not "white tie").

Even though the swimmers at Weeki Wachee had always been referred to as "mermaids," they did not wear tails in the shows until the Nagles arrived. "There was a tail around," said Bonnie Georgiadis, who worked at Weeki Wachee from 1953 until 1989, thirteen or so of those years as a mermaid, seven as a producer and choreographer. "I think it was Ann Blyth's tail from *Mister Peabody and the Mermaid*. We had a tail in house."

Bonnie said the first tails the Nagles created had a bib that came up around the mermaids' necks, but those were replaced with tails that were fitted to the mermaids' waists with zippers up each side. "The base of the material was sewn out of a canvassy cloth," said Genie Young, who swam from 1961 to 1965, then supervised mermaids for the next 14 years. "Then they hand-stitched metallic green and blue sequins all over it. They were extremely expensive and they only would last about a month."

Terry Hamlet wore the tail-with-a-bib for a photo shoot. In the color photo, she lies on a bed of eel grass holding a tulip to her nose, her eyes closed as if she were intoxicated by the scent. Terry posed for so many underwater photo shoots, she said she couldn't remember posing for particular ones, but she did remember posing deep in the spring as decidedly unglamorous work. "We froze our butts off," she said, referring to the icy cold water. "It was hell on our sinuses and ears. I remember diving in, flipping my hair back, wiping the bubbles from my face and arms so they wouldn't show up in the photographs. I would take a deep breath of air from the hose, and then someone would pull the hose away. I hit the pose fast. Then the flash would go off. It took many many shots to get the one. One of the hardest things was getting fish into the picture. The water was so clear, people wouldn't believe the shot was made underwater unless a fish was in the frame."

She couldn't remember actually making that photograph of herself reclining on a bed of eel grass wearing the tail, but said that in looking at it she could imagine the difficulty she must've had creating such a relaxed pose. "Tank up on air, give the signal, then exhale everything you've got, then try to keep from floating upward while pretending to smell a flower."

Once ABC bought the park, the black-and-white images of mermaids doing ballet over the mouth of the spring were a thing of the past, as were the mermen. The roles for men were limited to "underwater boys," like Allen Scott and Chuck Walls to handle props and perform other jobs, like putting a stash of bananas underwater for the mermaids. Although there were still photos of mermaids performing the adagio pose and eating bananas and drinking soda—no one ever tired of those images—most of the new images coming out of Weeki Wachee featured mermaids riding

Bubbles the Seahorse, mermaids doing battle with Captain Hook, or mermaids disguised as the Mad Hatter. These images were printed with the brightly colored inks of Chrome postcards that filled the racks at roadside attractions across the country. Dawn Douglas, who swam from 1970 to 1973, and who organized the first former mermaid reunion show in 1997, said that these photos would often require two or three mermaids. "The more people the more difficult the task became," she said. "Imagine: you aren't wearing a mask, so you can't see very clearly; you are in cold water and not moving very much and you quickly get cold and you have to drop or hide your air hose, then smile at the camera in unison, hold your breath, wait for the camera flash. Then you have to retrieve your air hose without running into one another, take a few breaths and begin again."

"We sold half a million dollars of souvenirs a year," Sparky said of those days. "On a busy day we'd sell a hundred dollars' worth of nickel postcards. We had a whole big wall of nothing but postcards—Weeki Wachee and other places in Florida like Cypress Gardens and Silver Springs. We'd trade with some—they'd sell ours and we'd sell theirs. If they didn't want to trade, we'd buy them and sell them anyway." This of course was a period when a typical vacation activity was buying and mailing postcard back home.

> A collection of scenic cards is also a convenient way of recording a trip, and, when pasted in a scrapbook or mounted with gummed photographic corners, makes a souvenir worth saving. With captions underneath each scene, the tourist can relive his travels at will. Quite frankly, the pictures are often much better than those taken of the same scenes by amateur snapshooters.

Weeki Wachee's publicity machine kicked into high gear. "We'd send the photos out once a week or every two weeks," Sparky said, referring to himself and to photographer Claude Long, who came on board to keep up with ABC's demands. "They kept me busy trying to keep up with the ideas. I had a lot of freedom there. They were very interested in publicity. We tried to get the pictures to represent something particular, so the papers would use them. We'd mail out a hundred copies to papers all over the country. I had fun making all that stuff." All that "stuff" included props like a giant camera, a giant hot dog, a giant cutout of Elvis or James Garner as "Brett Maverick," a character from a popular television western. "Posing with Maverick was fun," said Vicki Smith, who swam from 1957 to 1961, "but I thought posing with a cutout was sort of dorky!" Dorky or not, it made a memorable photo, as did an image of Vicki sitting in an

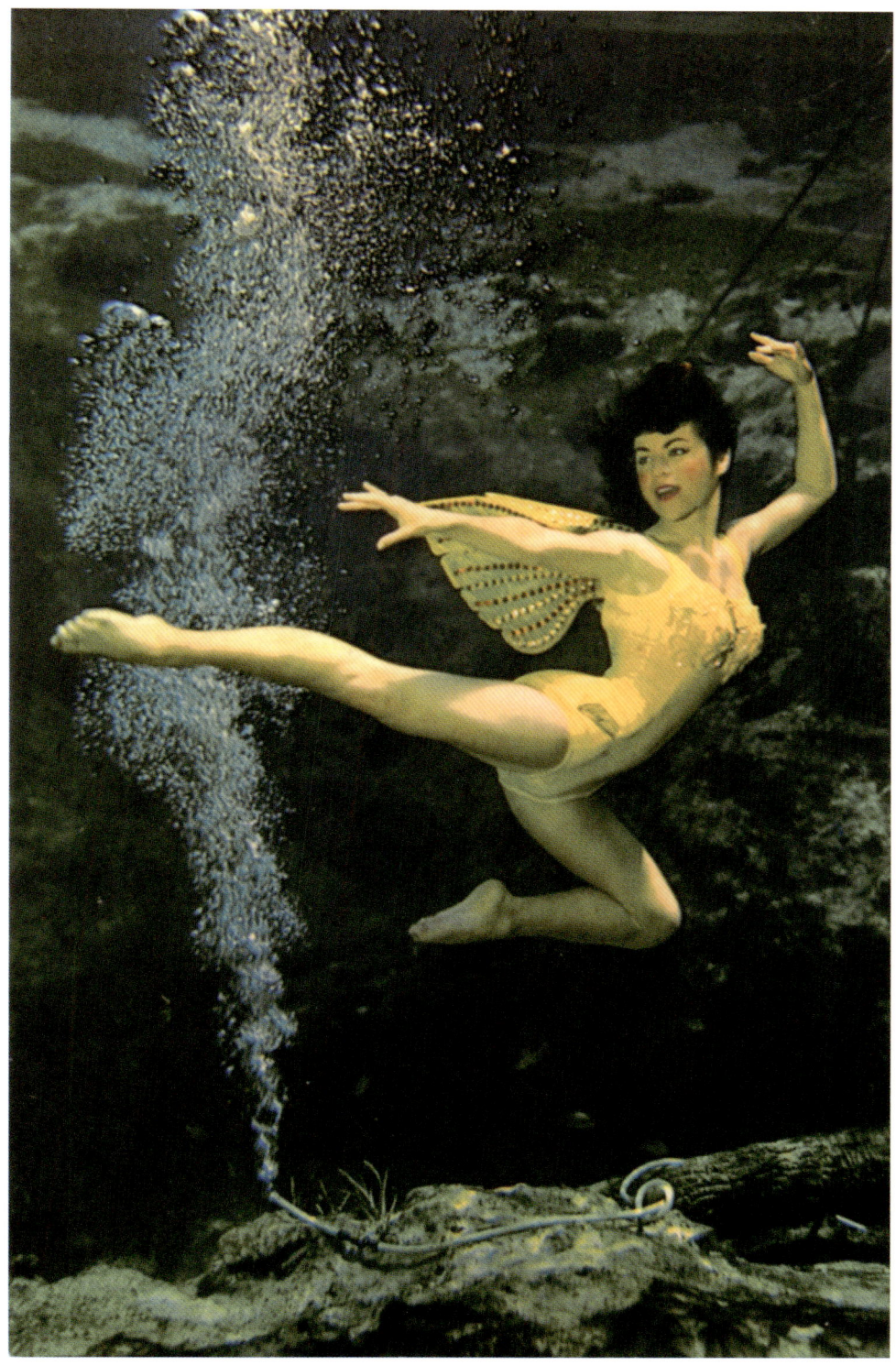

Vicki Smith performs a perfect leap, 1960.
Photo by Ted Lagerberg. By permission of
Bonita Colson.

underwater mermaid school with Terry Hamlet. "Betty Stoneburner (we called her 'Hotrocks') was the instructor," said Vicki. She explained why this pose was easier than most. "Anytime you could take a deep breath of air and had something to hold on to, you could hold your breath longer and therefore hold your pose longer. The 3 Bs offered this ease of posing."

Sometimes, Vicki added, a bit of serendipity is involved. "My yellow bird leap is a great example of the photographer catching the perfect pose at exactly the right time and right angle. Not a hair or bubble is out of place. Anyone could have performed this leap, I'm just thrilled it happened to be me on this lucky day."

In order to hit pay dirt with the wire services—and get publicity for Weeki Wachee, Sparky and Claude were constantly capitalizing on events, like George Washington's birthday, and holidays, like Easter. Bonnie Georgiadis was one of Sparky's favorite models. She said the mermaids did more than pose for photos. "Claude and Sparky developed their pictures here," she said. "The mermaids, as much as they grumbled about it, would sit and paste the little blurbs on the picture and they were mailed to newspapers all over the country."

Little did the newspapers know, the fun shots were sometimes overshadowed by fear. "The one promotional pose I will never forget is the Easter Parade pose where they decked me out in Easter finery along with black patent three-inch heels," said Vicki. Once she jumped into the water, she found that her ability to swim was seriously impeded by her Easter finery. "Much to my great shock . . . I could not tread water with heels on! Kicking did not keep me on the surface and by the time I realized I was losing the battle, I started to sink. Well, voila! That's what mermaids are good at. So even though my lungs were dying for air, I calmly let myself sink, walked over in my three-inch heels, and picked up my ding-bat air hose. Meanwhile, a bunch of people watching the photo shoot from inside the theater were holding their sides laughing, thinking it was all a stunt. To this day, I do not like to wear anything on my feet underwater except fins." And she means that.

Those images of mermaids celebrating Easter or Ragweed Week, or fighting Wiley Willy or Captain Hook, or performing the adagio *one more time*, were effectively the last images created at Weeki Wachee during its heyday before Disney came along and changed everything. With the exception of a few stills made for dwindling brochures after ABC sold the attraction in 1984, the owners seemed to lose interest in promoting the park via postcards or publicity shots generated in-house. This loss of interest was likely caused not just by the Disney empire, but also by the dwindling page space in newspapers, and the fact that, by the 1980s, post-cards were no longer the first souvenir a tourist bought. By the late 1990s, Brownie Hawkeye cameras were collecting dust in junk stores, replaced by digital cameras that made it possible for everyone to make beautiful photos of the mermaids. Today's tourists have even better cameras, along with cell phones with cameras, so they can point and shoot and e-mail the images almost simultaneously. Unlike their 1940s-era counterparts, tourists don't have to worry about convincing their friends that the mermaids are underwater. And it's not just because of Photoshop. The mermaids still perform reality-defying stunts—like becoming a human water wheel to Michael Jackson's *Earth Song*—but the spring is no longer the tabula rasa it was when Newt Perry dove into it in 1946. It has changed: it is no longer timeless, having been aged by all the development around it over the last seventy years. The eel grass is gone and the white sandy floor of the spring is blanketed with algae. The spring itself, once transparent as air, is now tinged a bluish green. It looks like water.

The vintage photographs and postcards that still exist tell more than the story of a park's rise to prominence. They represent a unique piece of Florida's history: the history of a spring, the history of the underwater performance that began the day Newt Perry dove into a crystal clear spring. Nothing says *Florida* quite like the image of a Weeki Wachee mermaid.

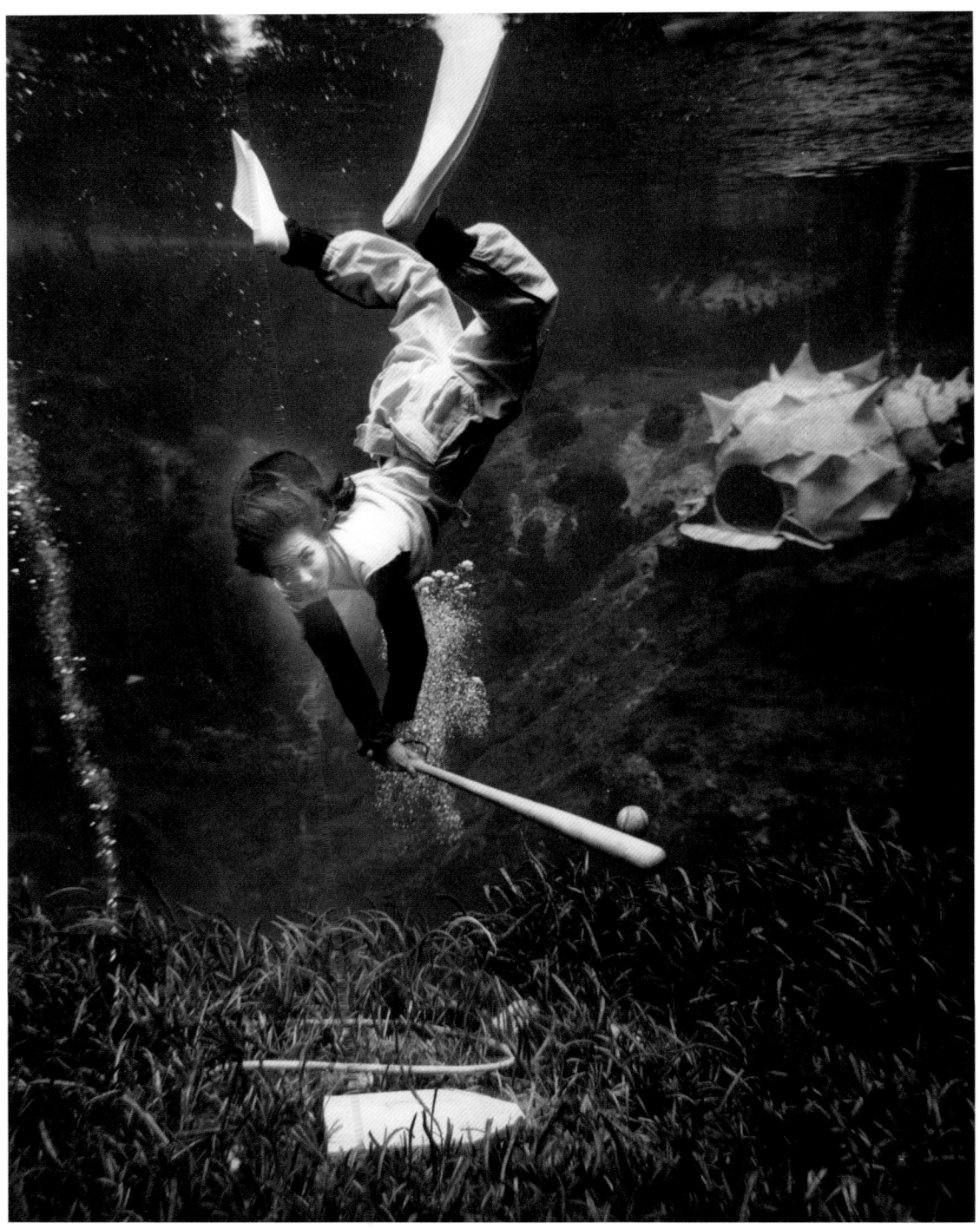

Bonnie Georgiadis proves you don't have
to stay in the batter's box to hit a baseball
when playing underwater, 1960. Photo
by Sparky Schumacher. By permission of
Bonnie Georgiadis.

What the Mermaid Saw

Bonnie Georgiadis, *former Weeki Wachee mermaid*

Esther Williams, the famous swimmer turned movie star, was my idol. I'd seen her in the movies performing synchronized swimming on the water surface and below. She was a ballerina in my eyes, an underwater ballerina. Back when I was a kid, I swam at Wall Springs, south of Tarpon Springs, Florida, my hometown. Pretending to be Esther, I'd slip below the surface of the water and smile and do all kinds of tricks. In my imagination, I would line up a row of my classmates on the roof of the dressing rooms that ran parallel to the swimming pool; then, we would peel off, diving into the water wearing flowered bathing caps and sparkling bathing suits. Of course this never happened, but I sure dreamed it did.

I was in the seventh grade at Tarpon Springs Junior High in 1947 when Weeki Wachee opened. My sister, Marti, was a senior when she drove us the 30 miles up U.S. 19 to see the show. A number of kids in her class were among the original performers. We walked down a set of stairs into what looked like a long steel submarine with three rows of wooden benches where we sat and looked out windows into the spring. We were actually sitting six feet underwater. We looked out and watched our friends, Ed and Mary Darlington, Mary Ann Ziegler, and Ned Stevens, as they ate bananas and drank bottles of Grapette while breathing from air hoses. They also fed the little blue-gilled bream bread right from their hands.

It was hard to believe they were performing underwater, because the water was as clear as air and their hair (at least the girls' long hair) flowed with their movements as if windblown. They carried hoses that constantly streamed air bubbles, and when they nonchalantly put the hoses in their mouths and inhaled a breath of air, they made the act of breathing underwater look simple.

The best part was when one of them made the deep dive for the grand finale. The girl swam directly down into the boil of the spring, deeper and deeper, until she went out of sight. Another mermaid pulled her air hose away so she HAD to hold her breath. Did she rush back to the air chamber? No. As she ascended toward the surface of the spring, she performed ballet for what seemed like a very long time before finally swimming to the chamber for a breath.

These boys and girls were the talk of Tarpon Springs High School. Admiring glances followed them through the halls. They were just like movie stars. After watching them, I knew that's what I wanted to do. I knew I was born to be a Weeki Wachee mermaid! I told my Aunt Margi, who snidely replied, "You could NEVER do that!" That's all she had to say. I HAD to do it. Four years later, when I was seventeen, I applied to be a mermaid.

I called to make an appointment. The person on the phone told me to bring a swimsuit and towel as I would be getting wet during a water test. The day I arrived I got in the water with the mermaid supervisor, Peggy Nunn. She wanted to see if I could relax underwater, if I could smile without "making a face," if I could hold my breath and not panic. There had actually been people try out who didn't even know how to swim! I thought I did pretty well.

When they told me I was accepted, I was so excited I could barely sleep! I had nightmares about being underwater and needing to get air but the spring's surface was covered with snakes. The following week when I began training the bad dreams went away. Part of training was to take a written exam on the dangers of water and air pressure and their effects on the human body. I learned of the possibility of air embolisms and other dangers when performing deep in the spring. As divers know, air expands as your body rises through the water, so if you don't exhale as you ascend, you could burst your lungs.

I practiced three times a day in the public swimming area until Peggy thought I was ready to swim to the big spring where the shows are performed. The very first time I swam over the actual spring and looked down through my face mask, I experienced vertigo. I thought I was going to fall! I was floating over a miniature Grand Canyon, gazing into the abyss. But I had to regain my equilibrium; we had work to do. I was there to be trained. Peggy said, "Follow me," then made a surface dive. I swam after her. On land she had told me that should my face mask suddenly get tight, it meant that I might have inadvertently inhaled through my nose. She told me to exhale through my nose to relieve the pressure. As I dove down, perhaps fifteen feet to an air chamber that looked like a long iron box on legs, sure enough, my face mask tightened. So I exhaled. If I hadn't known what to do I could have burst the capillaries in my eyes.

I swam deeper, following Peggy into the air chamber, also known as the stage. Once inside, we stood on wooden flooring. From our waists up we were in air; from our waists down in water. Now, I encountered a new problem. I felt a weighty pressure on my ear drums that was very uncomfortable. Peggy told me to hold my nose closed and blow gently to force air through the sinuses and behind the eardrums to equalize the pressure. After hearing a high pitched squeal, I felt normal again. "Okay, what's next?" I asked eagerly.

"Try this," Peggy said, as she ducked down below the water line and pushed out of the stage with her legs. I watched her through the glass pane that faced the spring. She performed a slow motion ballet arabesque, then arched back into a knee back dolphin and ended in a swan position. She made it look so easy. But then she'd also given me a list of things to remember while executing the moves:

1. Keep your head back
2. Arch your back
3. Keep your elbows locked straight
4. Keep your fingers together: don't scull. Never scull. It looks like you're waving to someone.
5. Make slow circular pulls with your arms.
6. Keep the instep of your foot beside your knee.
7. Point your toes and force your foot outward so it doesn't turn in.
8. Lock the knee of your straight leg.
9. Do all of these things at the same time.

Performing these moves underwater is about as easy as learning to play golf; swinging a club might look easy, but the pros know there is art to swinging that club right. The same goes for performing arabesques and swans. We mermaids have to constantly think about every part of our anatomy because every ballet position has its own rules.

Peggy's next lesson for me was how to breathe from the air hose. I'm real good at breathing (been breathing for years), but in the spring, I had to learn to keep my lips around the end of the air hose to keep the water out and prevent myself from drowning.

Eating a banana and drinking a bottle of Grapette underwater was a different story. To eat, I had to take a breath of air, then take a small bite of banana, because I had to chew and swallow before taking the next breath of air. Drinking was a little harder: I took a deep breath of air, placed my lips around the mouth of the bottle, then I dropped my tongue down creating a small vacuum in my mouth. I turned the bottle bottom's up, poured the soda into my mouth, then swallowed it. During the show the girls pretend to burp after downing a whole bottle of carbonated soda. Half the time they're not acting. Those burps are real!

We mermaids were paid on a unit system: so much for announcing a show, so much for serving as hostess and taking tickets, so much for swimming in a show. Swimming three shows a day was normal. Mermaid trainees stayed in the cottages on the grounds, receiving free rent and free meals at the Patio Restaurant. After completing training they went on the payroll.

My first show was like graduation day. I was so nervous. Peggy told me I'd be even more nervous before my second show but that it would get increasingly easier after that. I remember removing my face mask during fish-feeding the announcer told the people in the audience the mermaids couldn't see them without it. So when I needed a breath of air, I lay the air hose across my cheek and dragged it toward my mouth as if I were blind! I did some silly things at seventeen.

After completing training I swam two to three half-hour shows a day. It took six months to a year to for me to become truly at ease underwater. My breath-holding ability increased gradually. After all, I was perform-ing every day. But along with becoming relaxed comes getting cold. The normal body temperature is 98.6 degrees. The water is 74 degrees. That's 25 degrees' difference. Water is far denser than air, so after half an hour I was COLD!

Even though I was swimming shows, I didn't consider myself a real mermaid until the day I could do the deep dive—no novice performer was ever allowed to do it. You had to be entirely comfortable underwater before even attempting it. At the end of a show, the mermaid chosen to do this dangerous maneuver would position herself over the deepest part of the spring. This is where the boil, one hundred thousand gallons of water a minute, surges up from the subterranean river and strikes the surface. The force is so strong it forms a powerful current and creates a small dome of water in the center of the spring.

When my day came to perform the grand finale, I swam over to the boil and then dramatically "dived," forcing my way down through the water, kicking powerfully until I was out of sight of the audience. About eighty feet down, there is an iron bar wedged between the two sides of the crev-ice, a bar that is still there today. Some girls wrapped their legs around the bar, but I preferred to put my back against the cliff wall and push my feet against a huge boulder. This allowed me to feel secure so I could breathe deeply to relax and prepare myself for the ascent.

My partner in the air chamber above gave two tugs on my air hose. The tugs meant it was time for the air hose to be pulled away. I could take one last breath. I returned the signal with one sharp pull. "I'm ready, take it away." As my partner reeled in the hose, I gazed upward, watching it ascend, spewing bubbles, before it disappeared from my sight and snaked up over the cliff back into the dome air chamber. I watched the air bubbles until they reached the surface. When they were gone it was time to drift upward. I swam out of the strong current, or it would have pushed me to the surface too quickly. I started a series of very slow back dolphins, then stopped and performed an arabesque. These moves were not choreographed; they all depended on my breath-holding ability at the moment. As I rose into view of the audience, my partner (and safety person) swam out of the dome and offered me the air hose. The audience applauded and I took a bow. At that moment, I became a true Weeki Wachee mermaid.

In 1960, the attraction was purchased by some people who had big money and big ideas. Florida Inland Theaters (owned by American Broadcasting Company) built a huge glassed-in theater to replace the 100-seat capacity wooden bench theater.

ABC also placed underwater speakers in the spring so we could hear the music and narration for the shows. Now, for the first time, we could synchronize our movements to music. ABC hired show producers and costume and prop designers. Weeki Wachee became one of the top attractions in the State of Florida. Mermaid wannabees flocked to us from all over the United States and a few from foreign countries. We were on top of the world.

Every day, the publicity department thought up ideas for pictures above and below the water. The subjects included holidays, newsworthy events, picnics, tea parties, barbeques, even Miss Rag Weed Week. How kitschy can you get? We had a staff of three photographers. To prepare to pose for pictures we had to wash our hair. Sounds silly doesn't it? Really clean hair flows much better than oily hair. The photographer in the theater would count down: "three, two, one." We'd grab a breath of air, then someone would pull our hose out of the way, or we'd simply turn off the valve on the hose and drop it. Sometimes we just held onto it. Other times, we'd swim to the surface for air, then swim down again and pose. We'd toss our heads quickly back so our hair floated out of our faces, then brush our hands across our faces to wipe the clinging bubbles away. We'd form the pose, suck in our stomachs, and "SMILE, BABY, SMILE," hoping a fish didn't swim in front of our faces. The photographers seemed to like the redundant phrase, "One more time." They depended on sunlight, so on an overcast day we'd spend a lot of time waiting for that beautiful cloud to slowly move away while we shivered. I don't know if any pictures were rejected because of our goose bumps!

People have asked me, "What's it like to live underwater?" You are weightless, suspended without wires—zero gravity—and yet you can move about with very little effort. It is like drifting in a dream or floating in the clouds except the clouds are made of air bubbles, dancing their way to the surface. The bubbles look like white cotton candy, and they're having their own little race. The larger bubbles always win. When a rainstorm comes, the wind dashes about, rippling and pushing the surface water this way and that. You can see the energy, but you can't feel it. You are apart from it. When the rain begins to fall, hundreds, no thousands, of stars form, twinkling overhead, as the drops strike the surface of the water. It is so beautiful. Oh, for gills! Sometimes, especially in the summer, there is lightning along with the rain showers. Mermaids fear lightning, along with the alligators, poisonous snakes, eels, and aggressive soft-shelled turtles. Lightning can travel a long distance through water; it can strike downriver and shoot up to the spring. You'd be very aware of it if you had contact with any kind of metal: costume parts, metal zippers, safety pins, the air hose's brass fittings. Heaven forbid your body should come in contact with the ground. Touching the ground with rubber flippers, though, would exempt you from feeling shock.

My first experience with lightning was when I was standing barefoot on the wooden floorboards in the air chamber looking through the glass window. I was watching B. J. Steiner perform ballet just in front of me. My turn was coming up. B. J. had exhaled a little too much air and was sinking toward the ledge right before me. She lowered her hands to push off the bottom. At that exact second the lightning struck. I saw the flash. Her body crumpled with a jolt. She pulled herself into the air chamber and shouted, "Let's get the hell out of here!" Luckily, I never felt a thing. Today the mermaids are called out of the water when there is even a threat of a thunderstorm.

Through the years I have heard some funny comments from guests. One of the funniest came from someone who seemed to forget she was looking through water and exclaimed "I didn't know turtles could fly!" Then another time two mermaids were swimming away from the audience on the surface after the show. Their flippers moved up and down as they swam. A little old lady said, "Oh, how sweet, they're still waving goodbye!" I had to scratch my head when I heard someone say, "You know, there's at least three good breaths inside that face mask." But most amazing were the multitudes of people who flatly refused to believe the show was real! The water is that clear. People made up ways we could do the show without really being underwater that were much more difficult than the way we actually did it: the theater windows are aquariums containing fish; the mermaids are suspended by wires; there are large fans blowing their hair. Then there were the other misconceptions. A large number of people thought that we breathed pure oxygen. Below thirty feet oxygen becomes lethal. We'd all be dead! We are breathing compressed air, folks.

I spent thirty-seven years at Weeki Wachee, thirteen or so as a mermaid, then seven years as show producer and choreographer. I learned a lot from our previous show makers: Gloria Hamilton and Jack and Marilyn Nagle. When I first took over as producer and choreographer, we were changing the show every year, alternating between a fairy tale and a musical revue. I especially enjoyed writing shows like *Mermaids on the Moon*. The underwater landscape at Weeki Wachee reminded me of the surface of the moon, and our weightlessness lent itself to visions of outer space. Staging *Peter Pan* was a natural as well. We could actually fly!

At that time we didn't realize those were Weeki Wachee's best years. The big mouse scurried into Central Florida and our attendance dwindled. We stopped changing the show every year to save the cost of new props. But costumes still needed replacing about every six months. Fabric doesn't like being wet all the time. Then I stopped choreographing and was transferred to the bird department where I became a manager. That included handling birds of prey, macaws and cockatoos, as well rehabilitating wild birds. I went from being a mermaid to becoming a falconer. I helped rehabilitate and release two bald eagles using falconry techniques. Now, there's a thrill.

It's been twenty-one years since I left Weeki Wachee. Now, I realize, I never really left. So many memories keep flooding back. So many friends. My daughter, Tasula (Sue) Murray, was once a mermaid. We swam shows together. I get together with a group of retired mermaids several times a year, and I am thrilled when the former mermaids ask me to help in their productions. This group of "formers" swims shows one weekend a month on a volunteer basis, thanks to the generosity of the Florida State Parks system. I must also add that the present-day Weeki Wachee mermaids are not only spectacular, they are phenomenal! Go take a look!

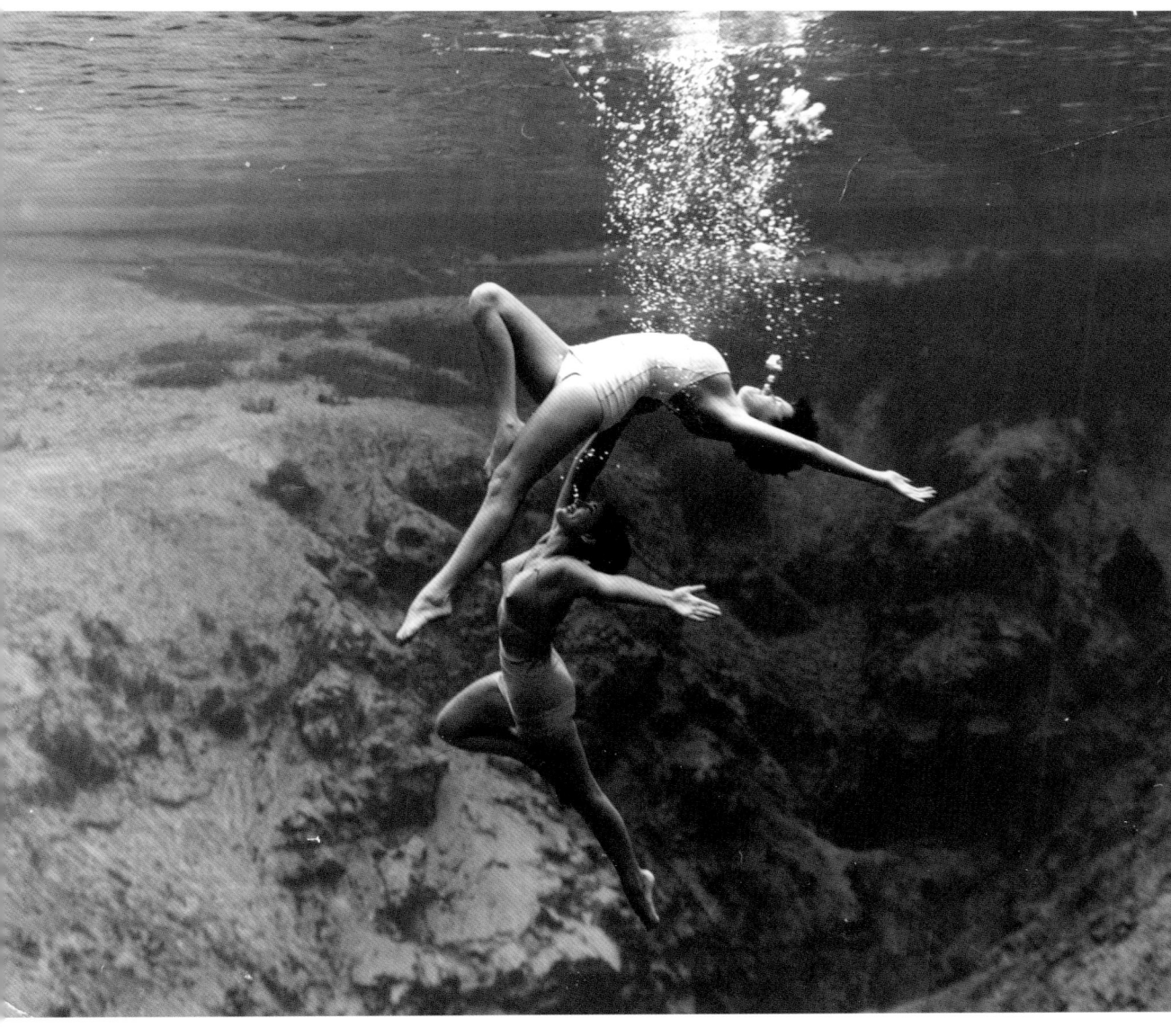

Nancy Tribble Benda (*bottom*) and Sis Meyers met
Newt Perry at Wakulla Springs when they were teenagers. He trained them to perform underwater then
invited them to help train more mermaids when he
opened Weeki Wachee in 1946. Here, Nancy and Sis
perform Weeki Wachee's trademark pose, the adagio.
Photo by Ted Lagerberg. By permission of Nancy
Tribble Benda.

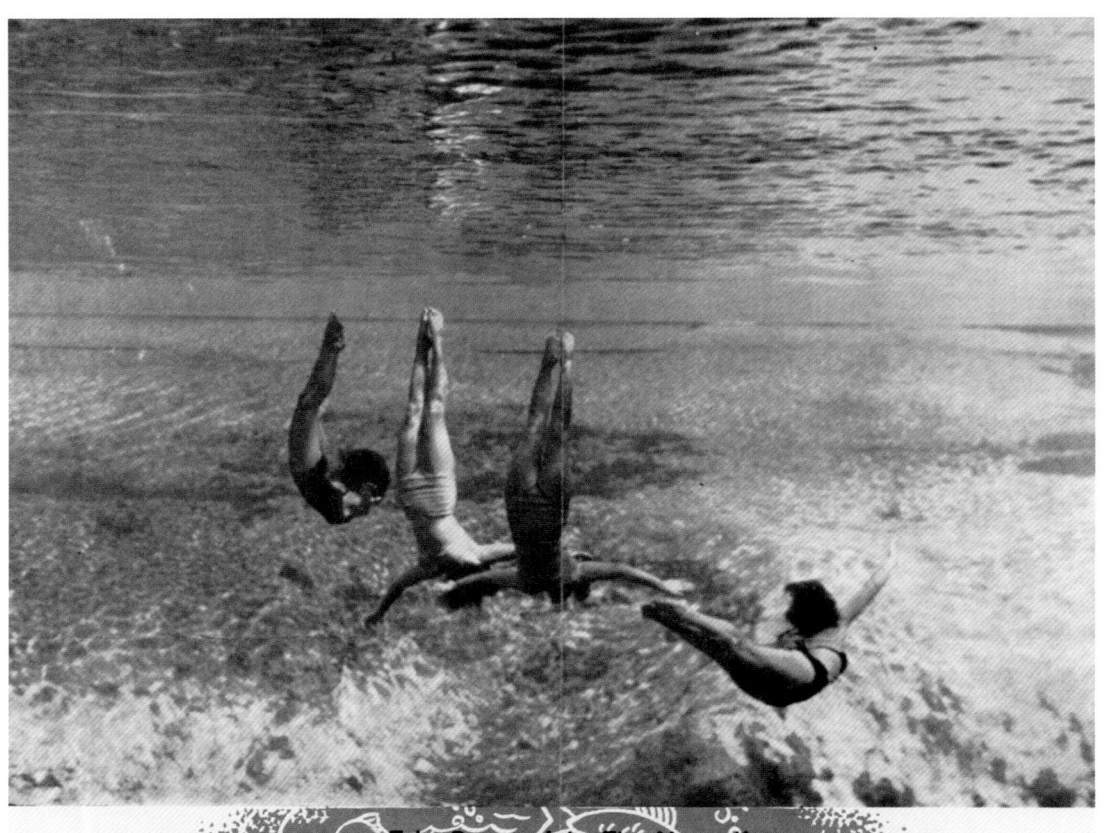

Take Pictures Like This Yourself
of the
UNDERWATER BABE'S BALLET
Seen from the World's ONLY
UNDERWATER THEATRE

One hundred persons can view these dramatic underwater ballet shows at the same time! You are actually SITTING BELOW THE SURFACE OF THE WATER . . . seeing the amazing swimming . . . the deep diving by experts . . . the constantly changing panorama of marine life in the breath-taking depths of the deepest and clearest spring in the world . . . so beautiful . . . so thrilling!

Photos by Modern Photographers
New Port Richey, Florida

Weeki Wachee's first brochure gave top billing to "The Mountain Underwater." Inside the brochure, though, was this enticing image of the mermaids performing the "Underwater Babe's Ballet," 1947. Photo by Ted Lagerberg. By permission of Mary Darlington Fletcher.

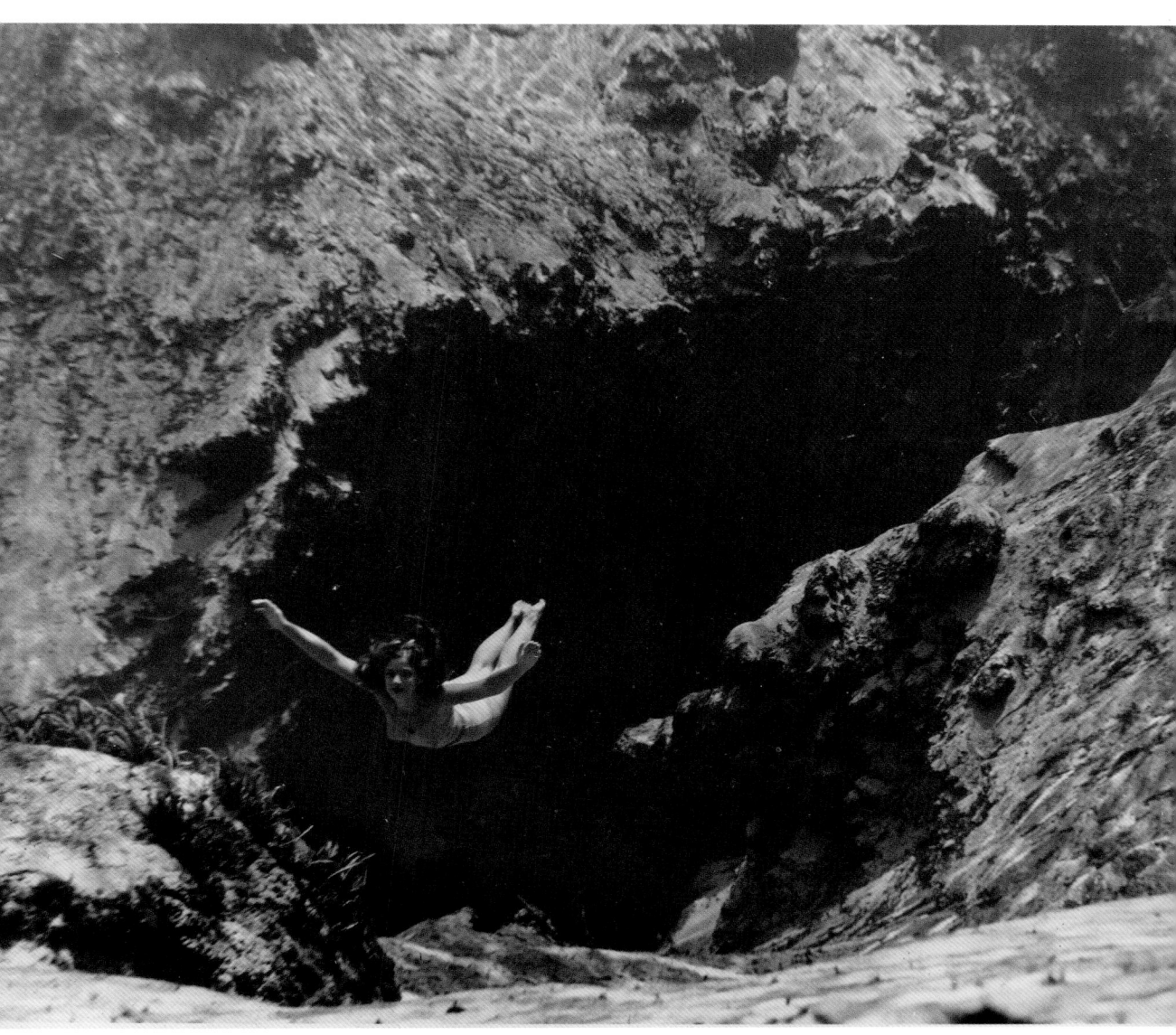

Before Weeki Wachee opened in 1947, Nancy
Tribble Benda posed for some promotional photographs. Here she appears to be flying over the
Mountain Underwater, as Weeki Wachee was first
billed, 1947. Photo by Ted Lagerberg. By permission
of Nancy Tribble Benda.

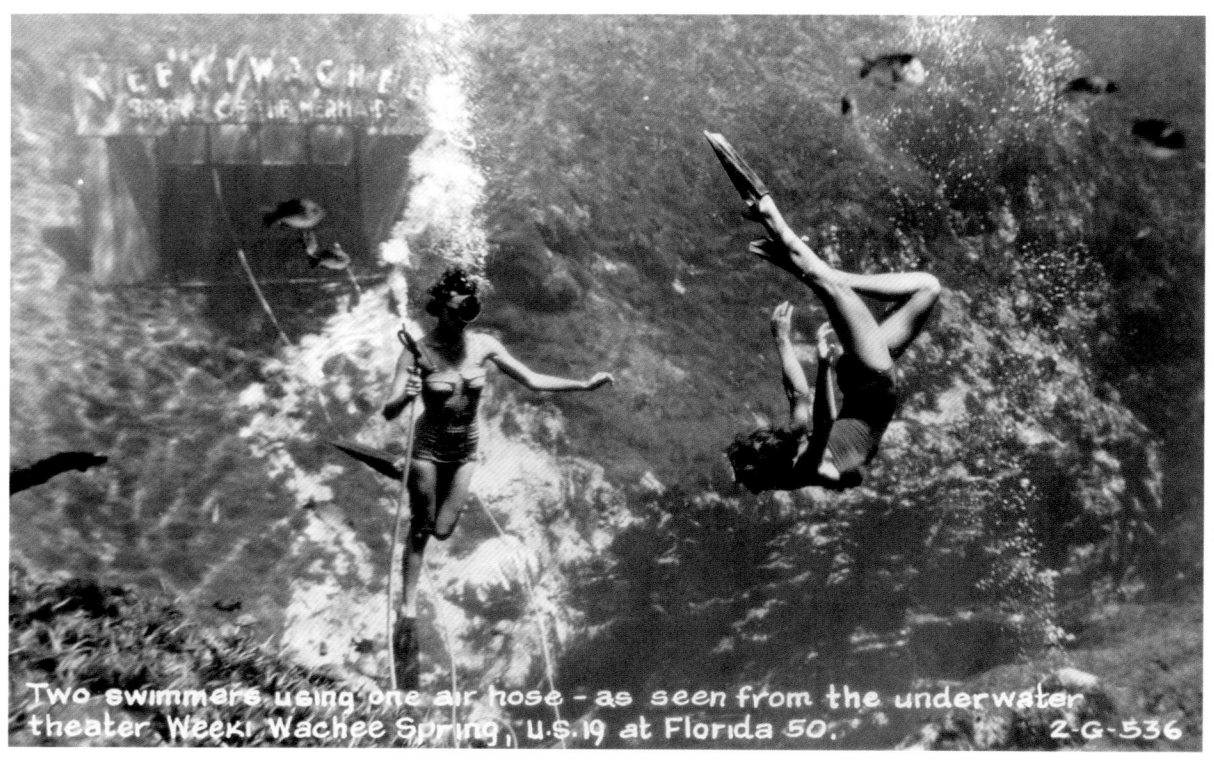

Two swimmers using one air hose – as seen from the underwater theater Weeki Wachee Spring, U.S. 19 at Florida 50.

2-G-536

The performers at Weeki Wachee used air hoses developed by Newt Perry, ca. 1947. By permission of Ginger Stanley Hallowell.

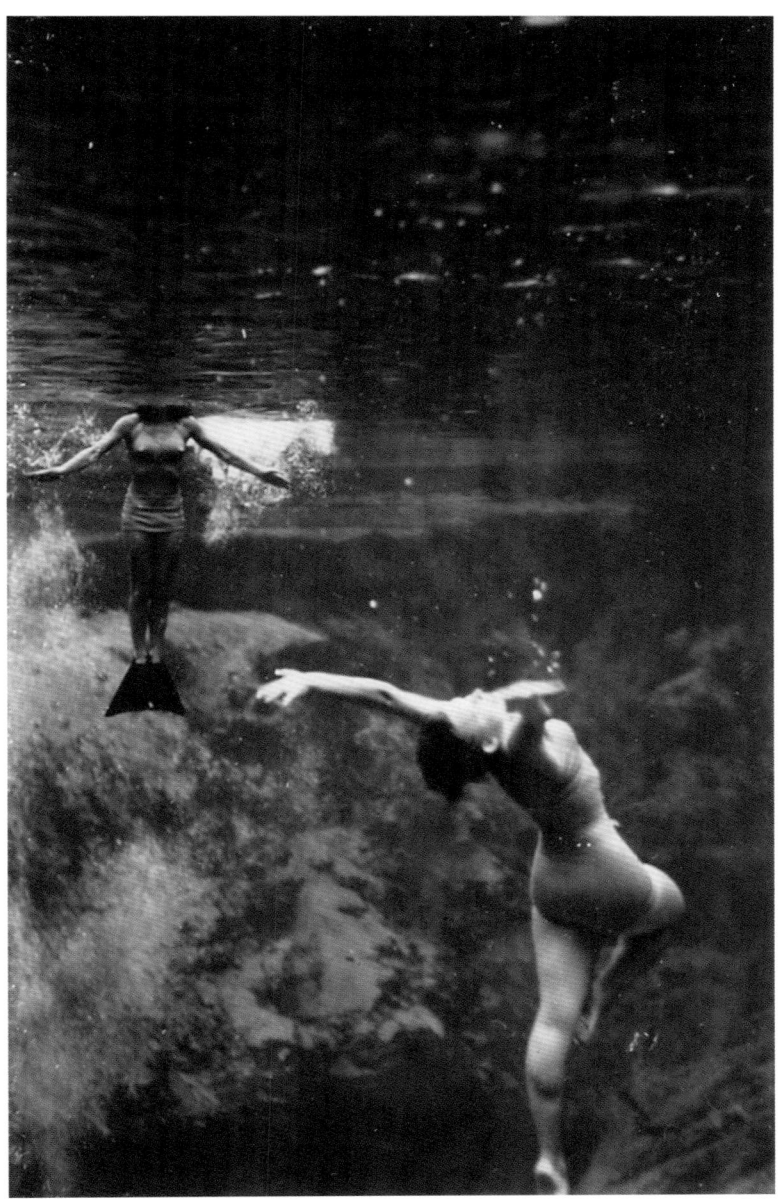

The first Weeki Wachee mermaids did not wear tails or any other costumes. They simply performed ballet in the spring to the sound of silence as no music was piped into the theater, 1947. By permission of Dianne Wyatt MacDonald.

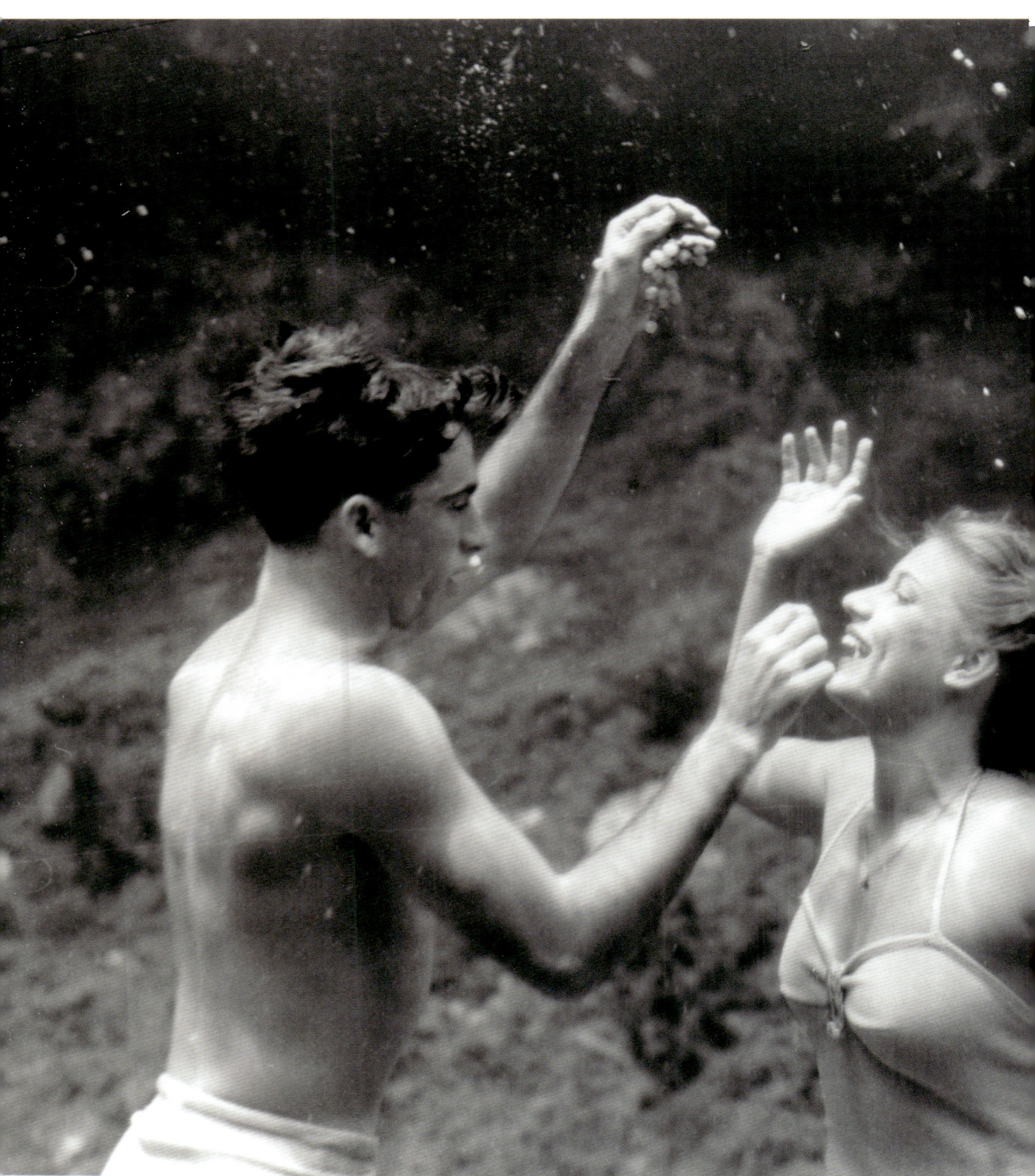

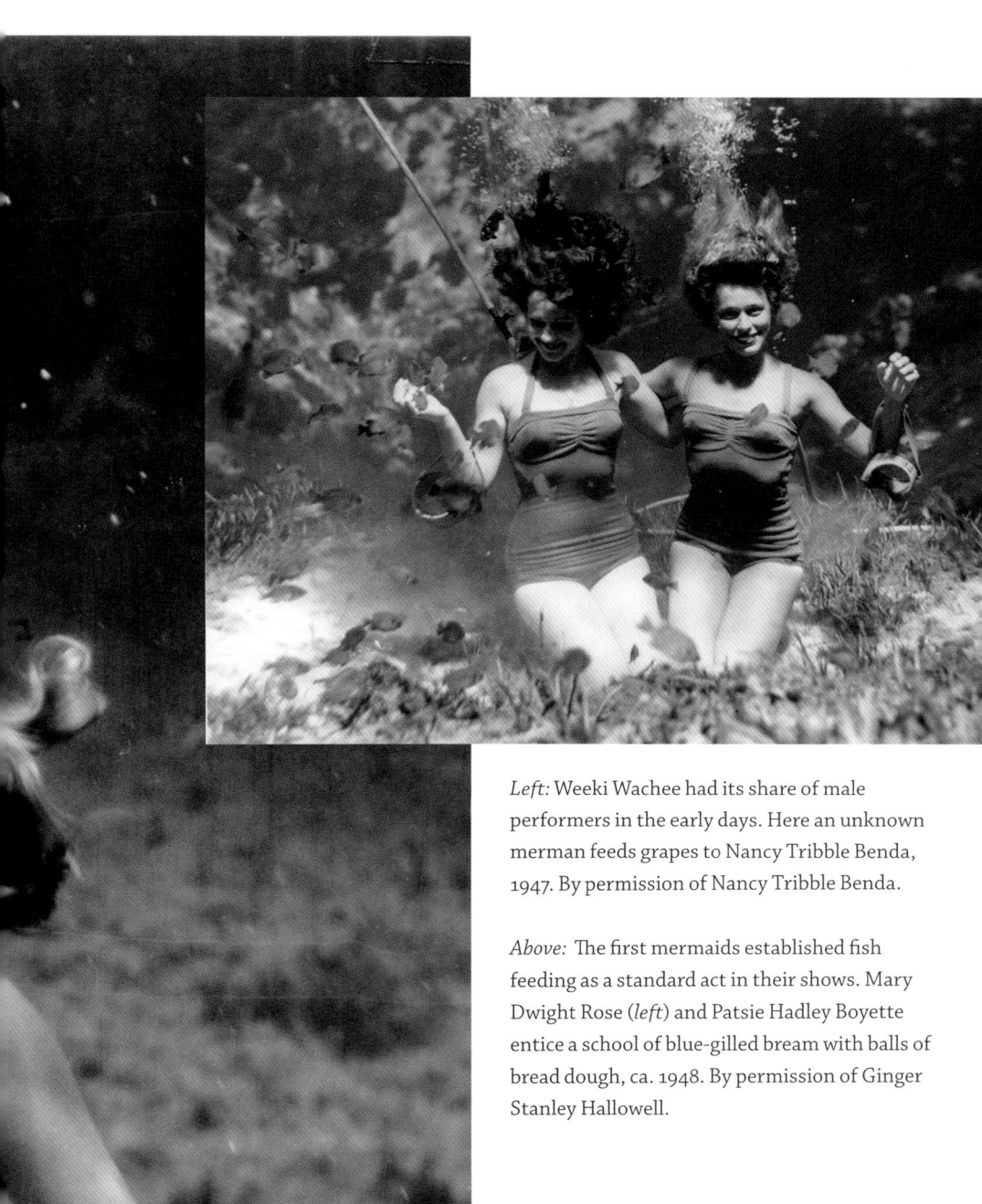

Left: Weeki Wachee had its share of male performers in the early days. Here an unknown merman feeds grapes to Nancy Tribble Benda, 1947. By permission of Nancy Tribble Benda.

Above: The first mermaids established fish feeding as a standard act in their shows. Mary Dwight Rose (*left*) and Patsie Hadley Boyette entice a school of blue-gilled bream with balls of bread dough, ca. 1948. By permission of Ginger Stanley Hallowell.

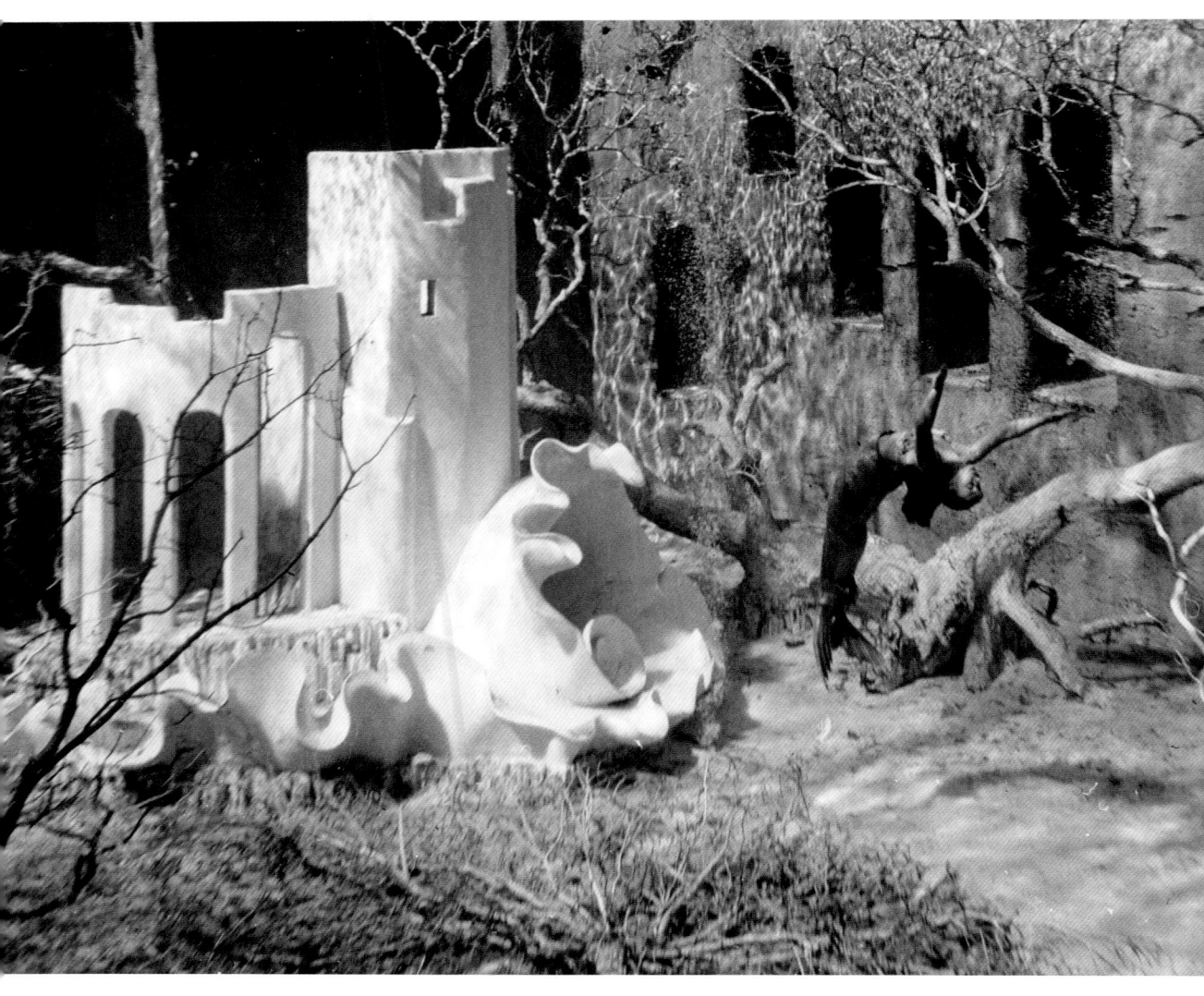

Shortly after Weeki Wachee opened, MGM studios began filming *Mr. Peabody and the Mermaid* at the spring. Star Ann Blyth tries out her tail in front of the castle on the underwater set, 1948. By permission of Nancy Tribble Benda.

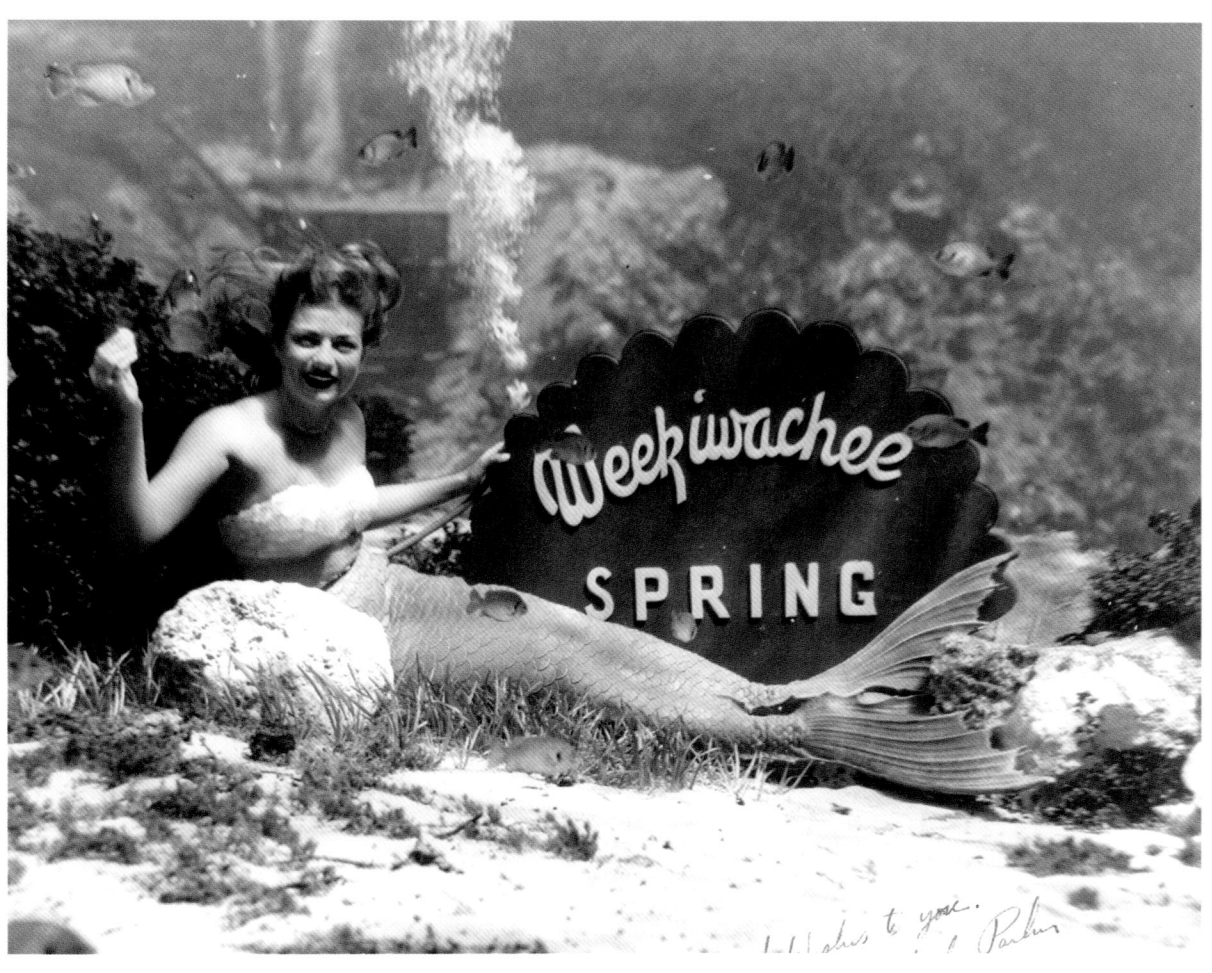

Nancy Tribble Benda wears the Mr. Peabody tail she was fitted for in Hollywood,
1948. In the beginning, Weekiwachee
was one word, but Newt Perry decided to
split it into two words so it could fit on
signs more easily. By permission of Nancy
Tribble Benda.

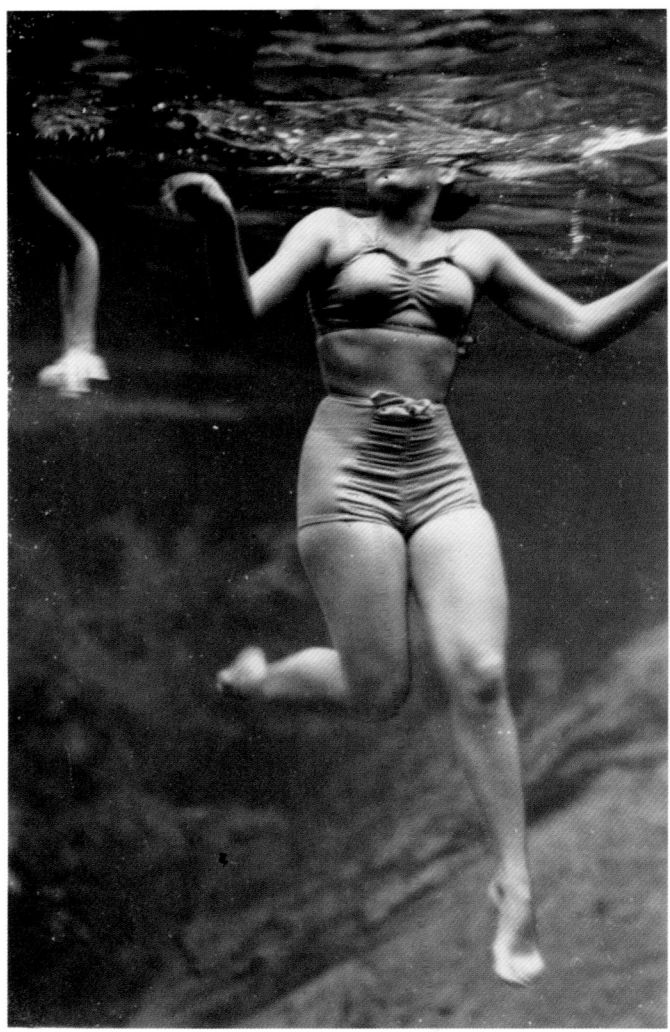

The Aqua Belles didn't use the air hoses Newt Perry invented. Instead, they swam to the surface for gulps of air, and dove down into the spring to continue performing. Patsie Hadley Boyette takes a breather, 1947. By permission of Dianne Wyatt MacDonald.

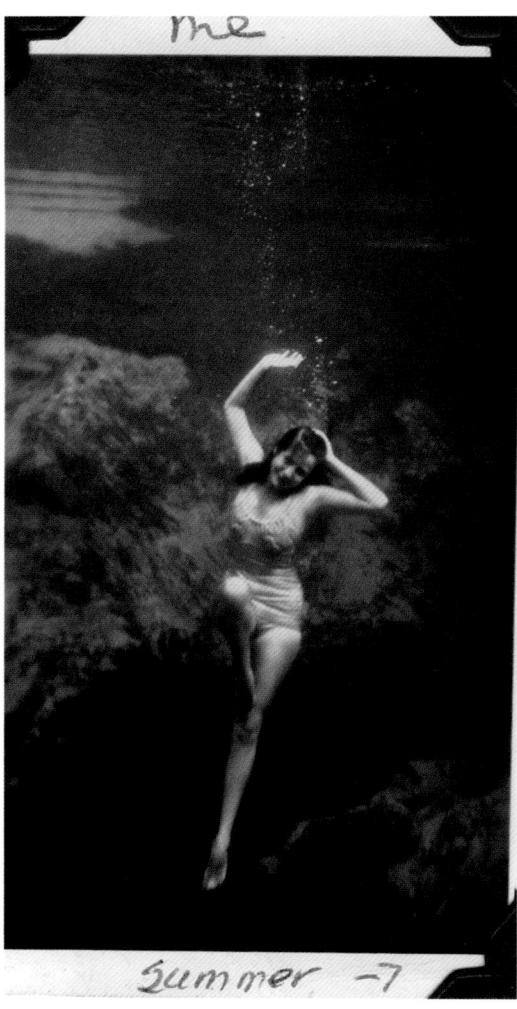

Newt Perry traveled over to St. Petersburg to engage the Aqua Belles to come over to Weeki Wachee to perform. In this photo from her scrapbook, Dianne Wyatt MacDonald offers the photographer a shy smile, 1947. By permission of Dianne Wyatt MacDonald.

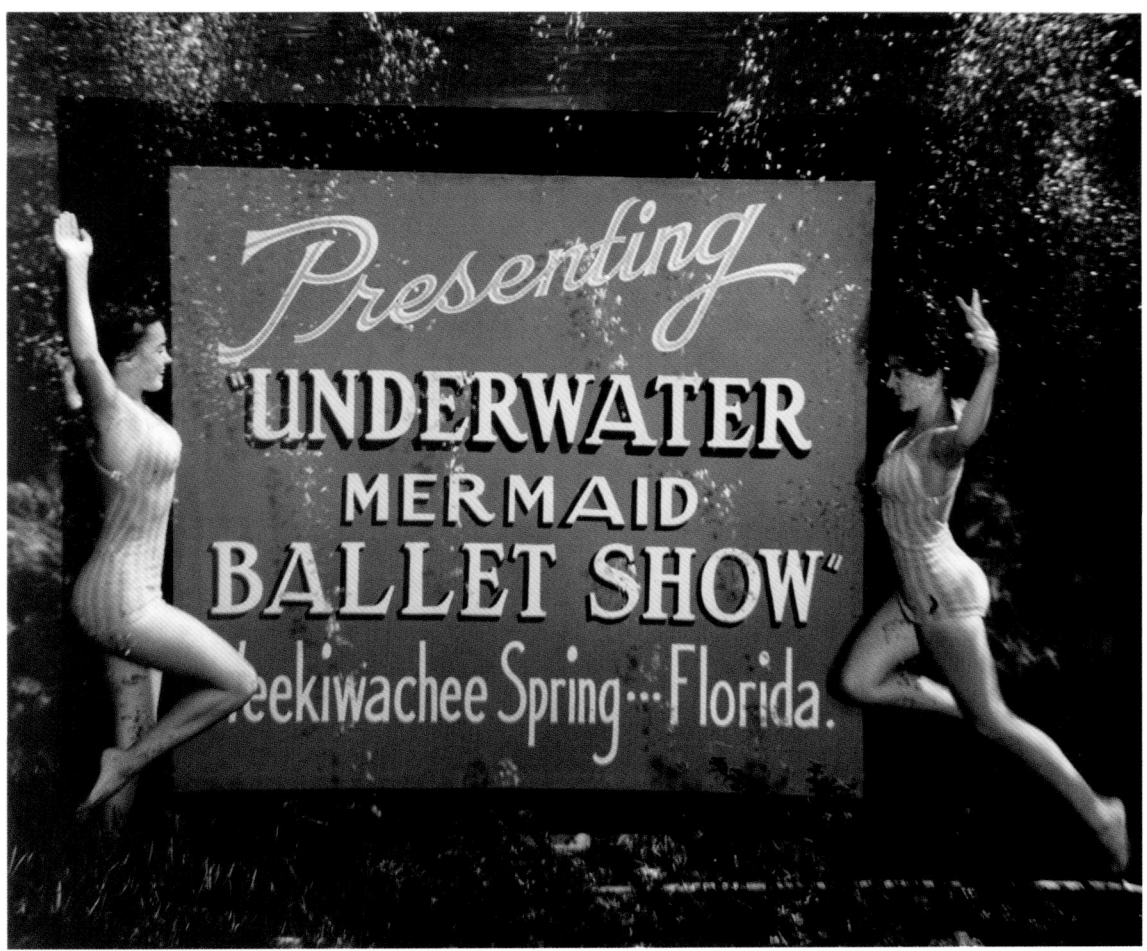

Mary Dwight Rose (*left*) and Fran
Dwight Gioe pose with the underwater billboard advertising the mermaid
show, ca. 1948. By permission of
Ginger Stanley Hallowell.

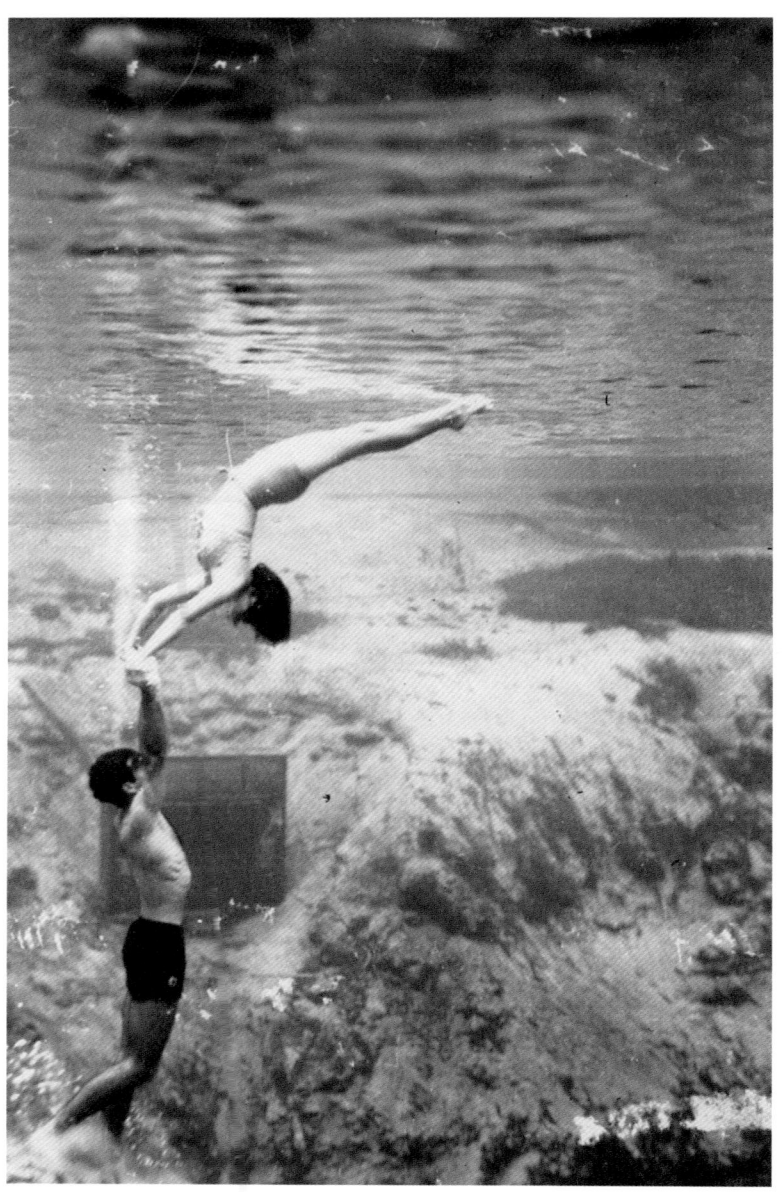

Bill Amick was one of the first male performers at Weeki Wachee. Here he performs ballet with Dianne Wyatt MacDonald. The airlock is in the background, 1947 By permission of Dianne Wyatt MacDonald

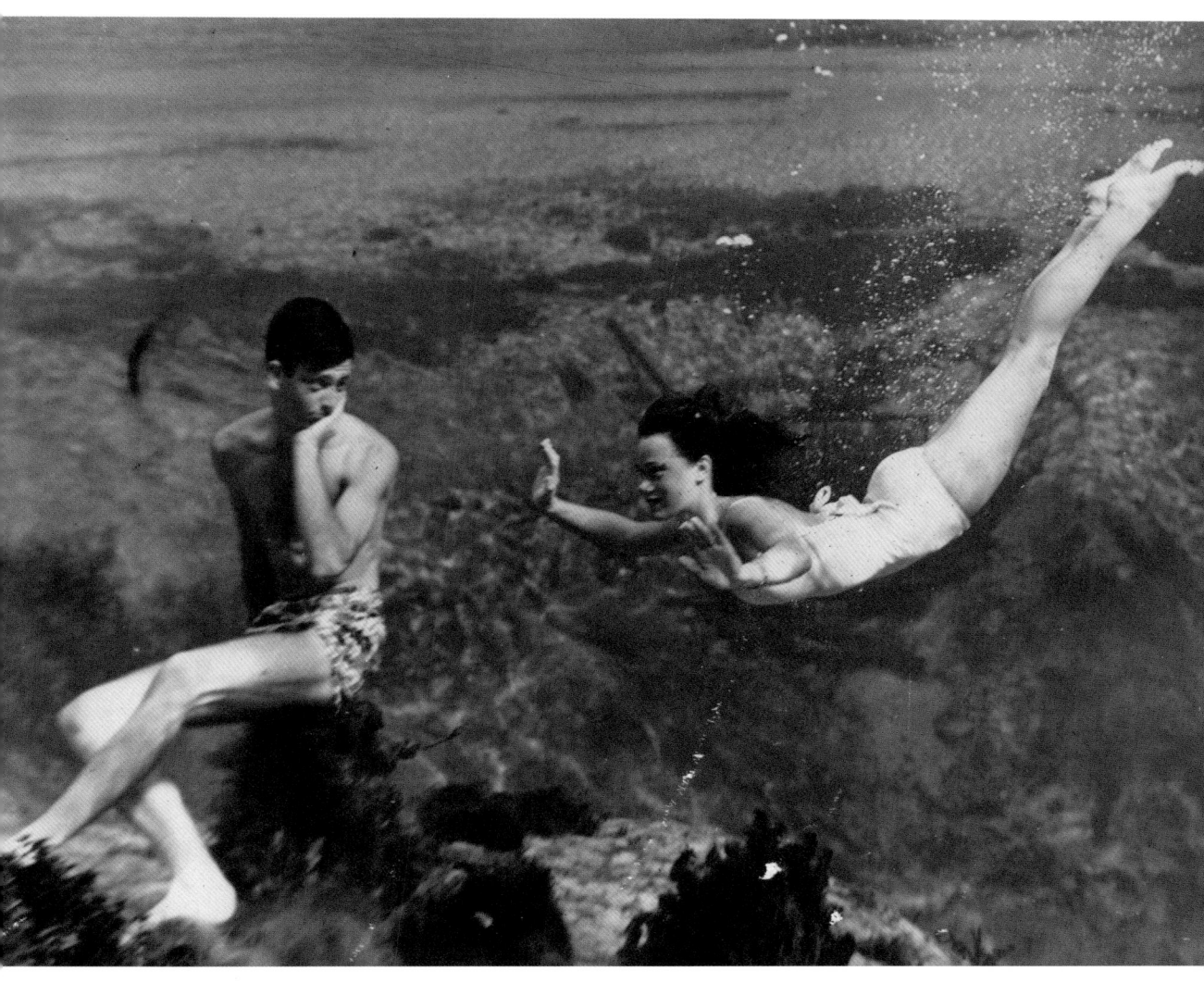

Mary Darlington Fletcher seems to catch
Ned Stevens by surprise in this late 1940s
photograph. By permission of Mary
Darlington Fletcher.

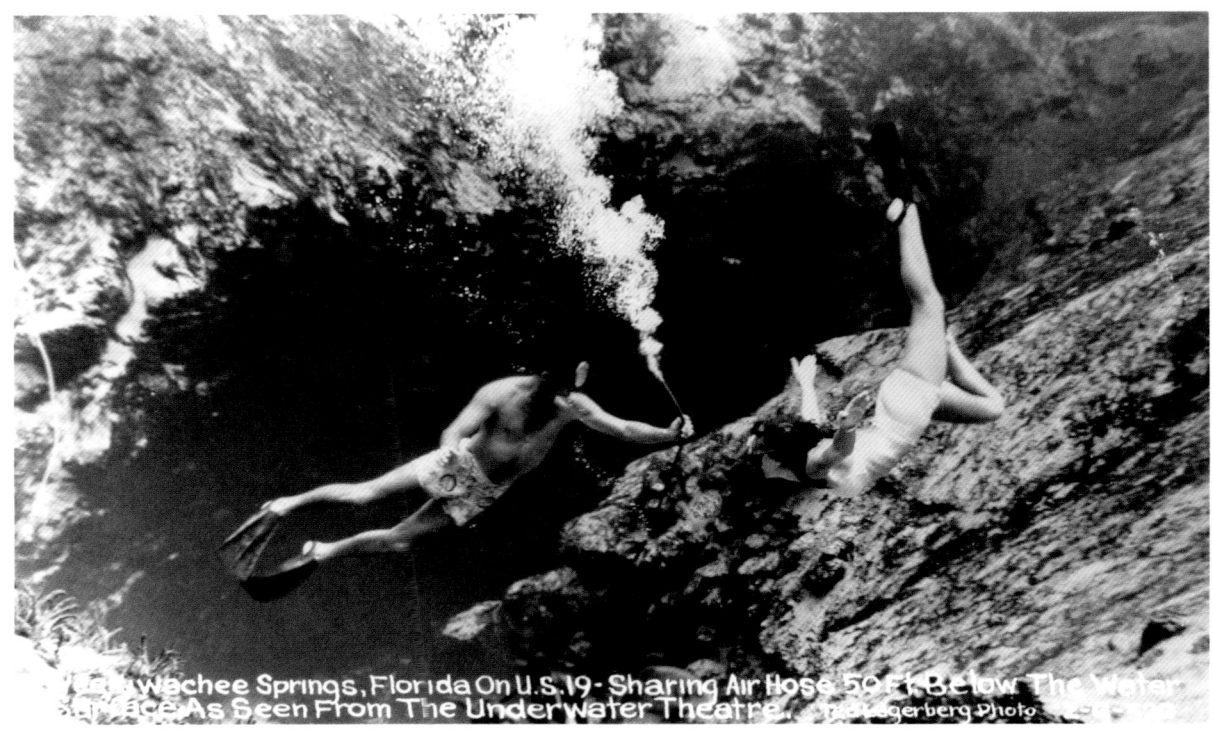

Weeki Wachee Springs, Florida On U.S. 19 - Sharing Air Hose 50 Ft. Below The Water Surface As Seen From The Underwater Theatre.   Ted Lagerberg Photo

Ed Darlington drove his Model A to Weeki Wachee on weekends to perform ballet with his sister Mary Darlington (*right*), 1947. These two are among the "original mermaids and mermen." Photo by Ted Lagerberg. By permission of Mary Darlington Fletcher.

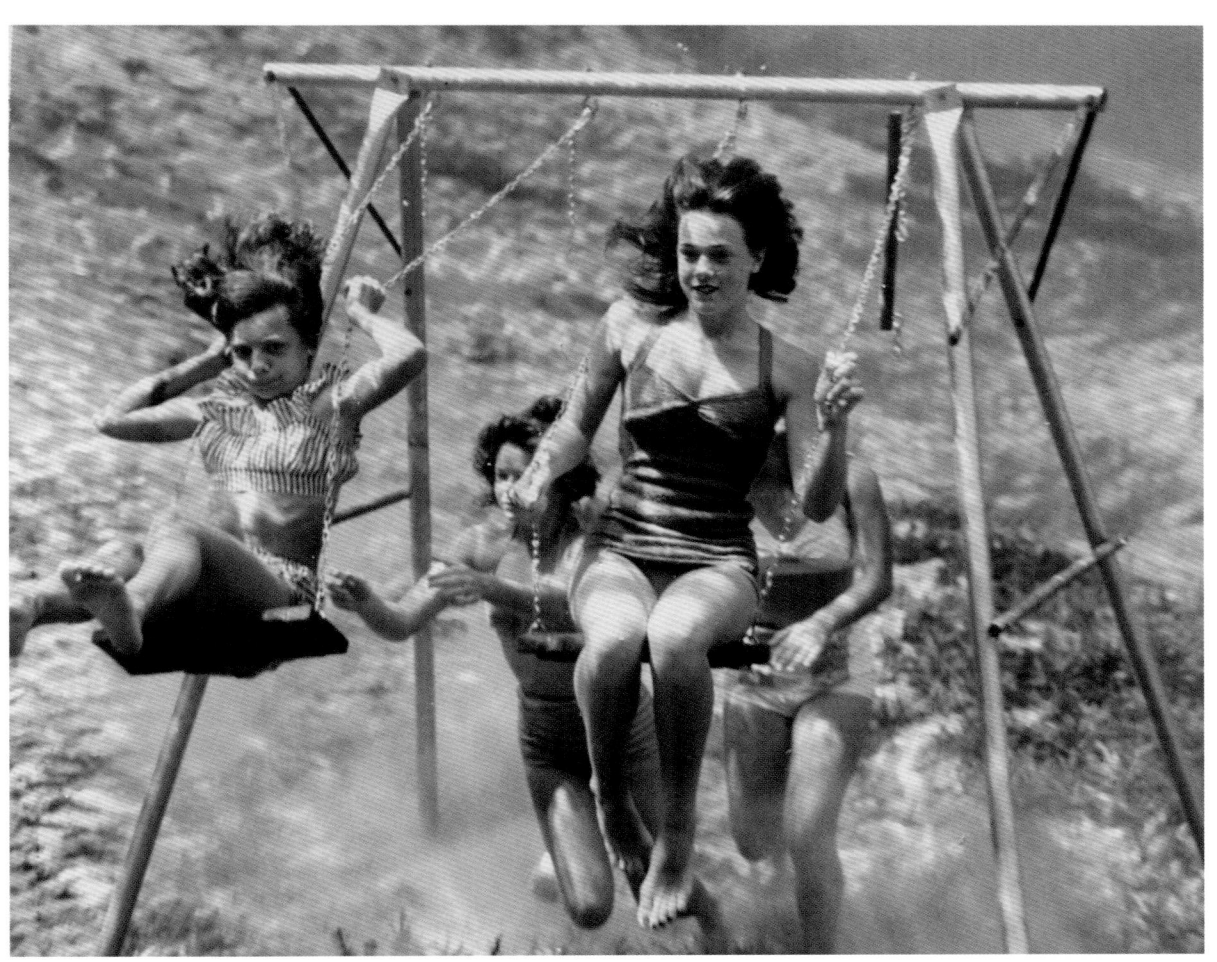

Mary Darlington Fletcher (*forefront*)
hit Weeki Wachee's playground
with some friends for this promotional shot, 1948. Newspaper editors
couldn't believe the photo was made
underwater. By permission of Mary
Darlington Fletcher.

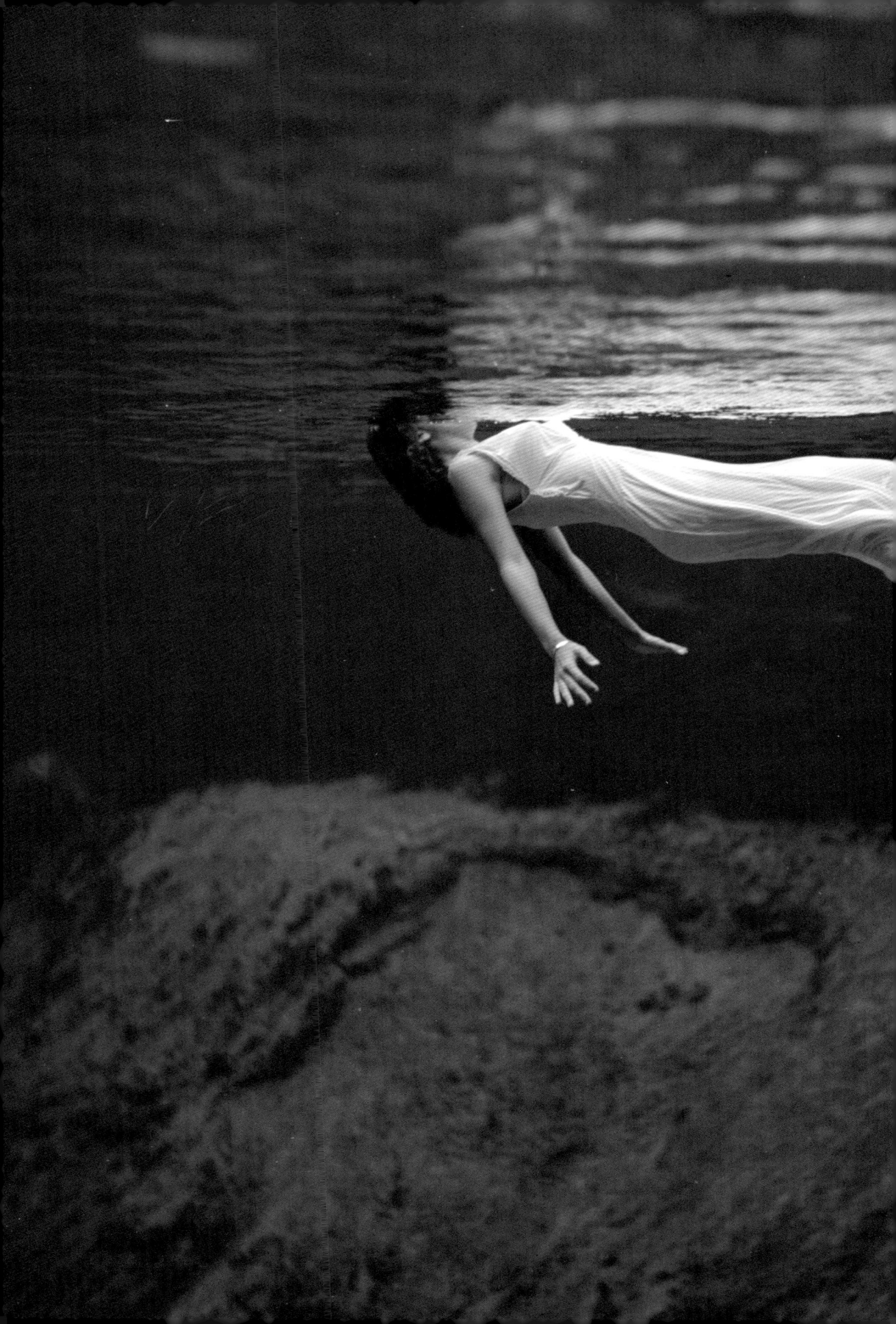

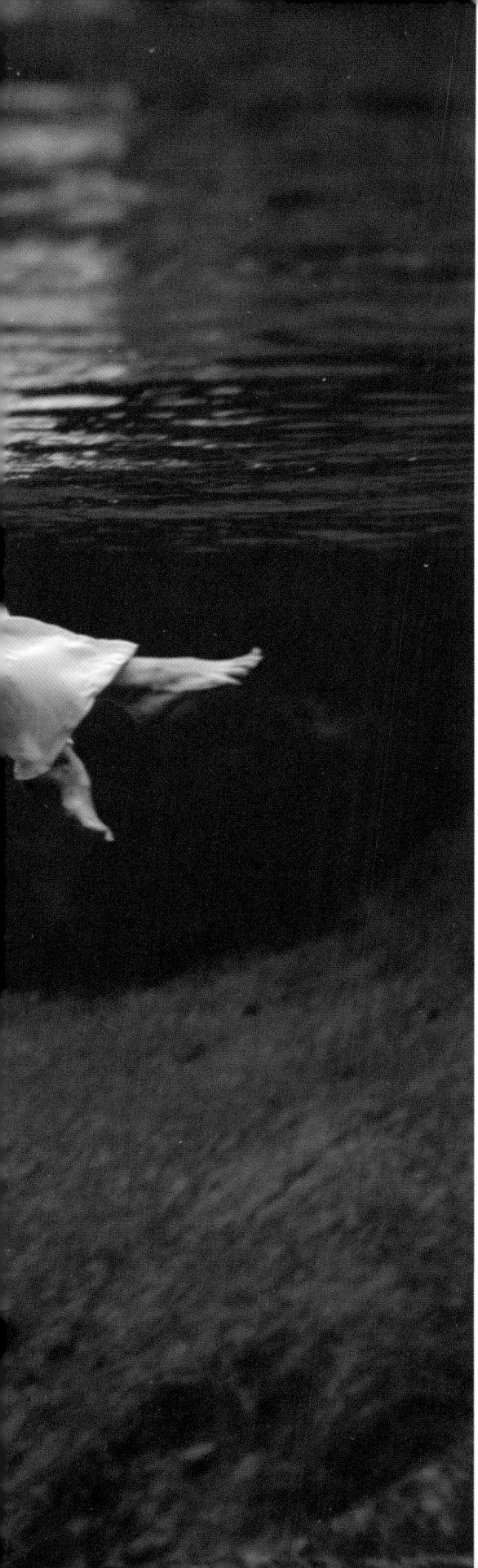

Weeki Wachee caught the eye of
Harper's Bazaar photographer Toni
Frissell, who took this iconic shot for
the magazine in 1947. Courtesy of the
Library of Congress.

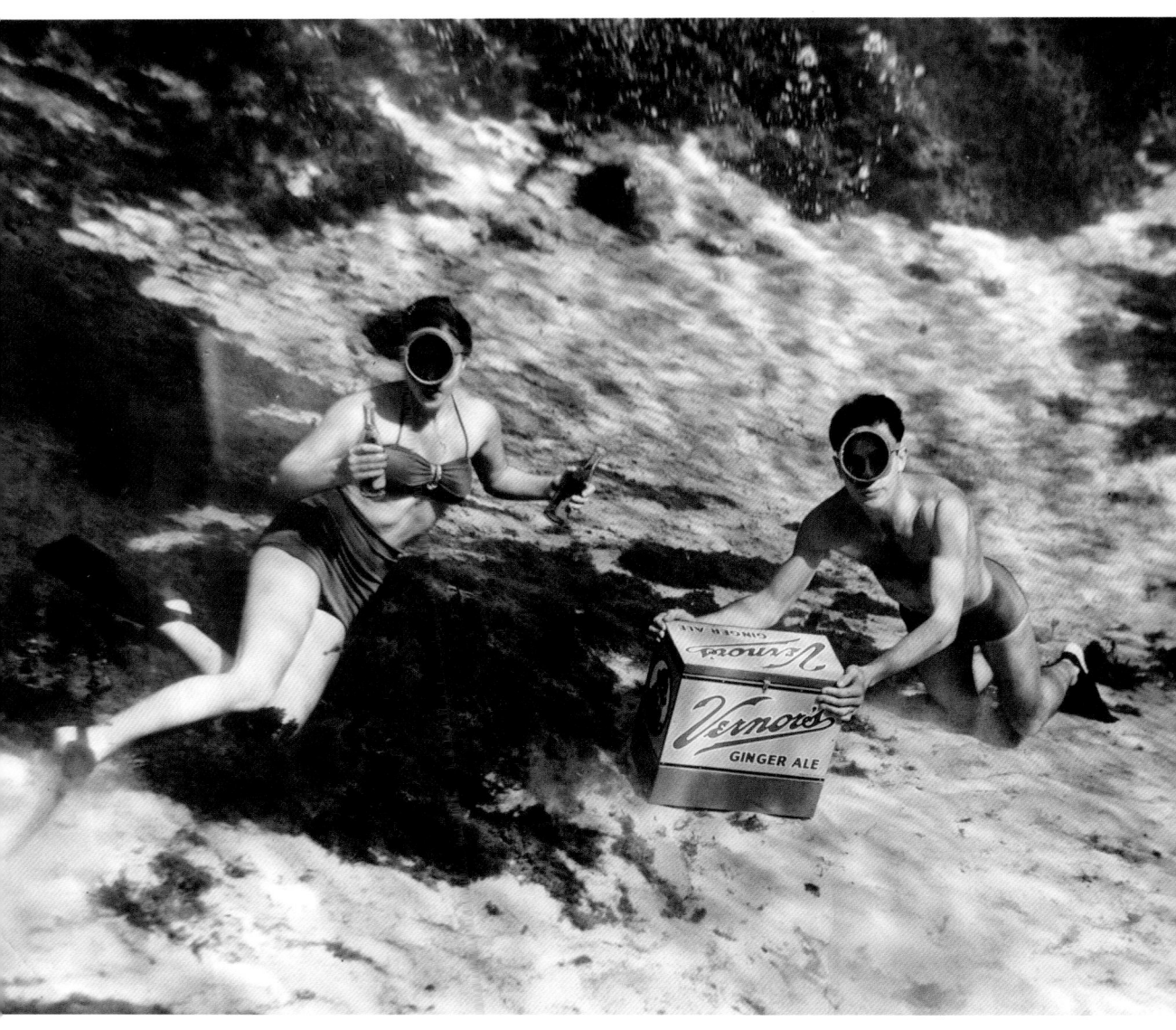

The early mermaids drank everything
underwater it seems, from orange soda
to Grapette to Vernor's Ginger Ale. By
permission of Ginger Stanley Hallowell.

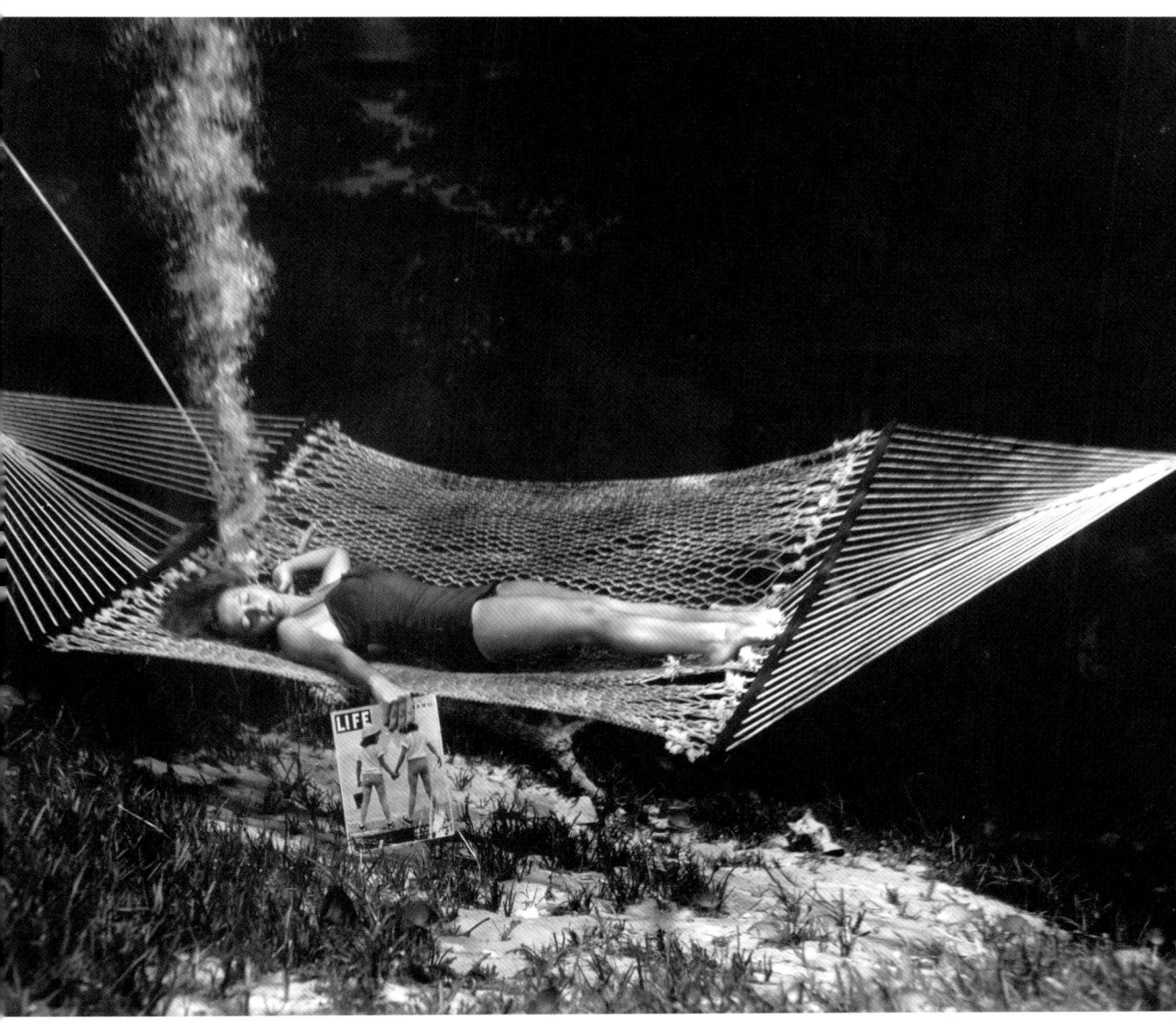

Newt Perry posed his oldest daughter, Eileen
Perry Hogshead, in this hammock with a cello-
phane wrapped copy of *Life Magazine*, hoping
the editors would publish his photo on the
cover, ca. 1950. Unfortunately, they didn't. By
permission of Eileen Perry Hogshead.

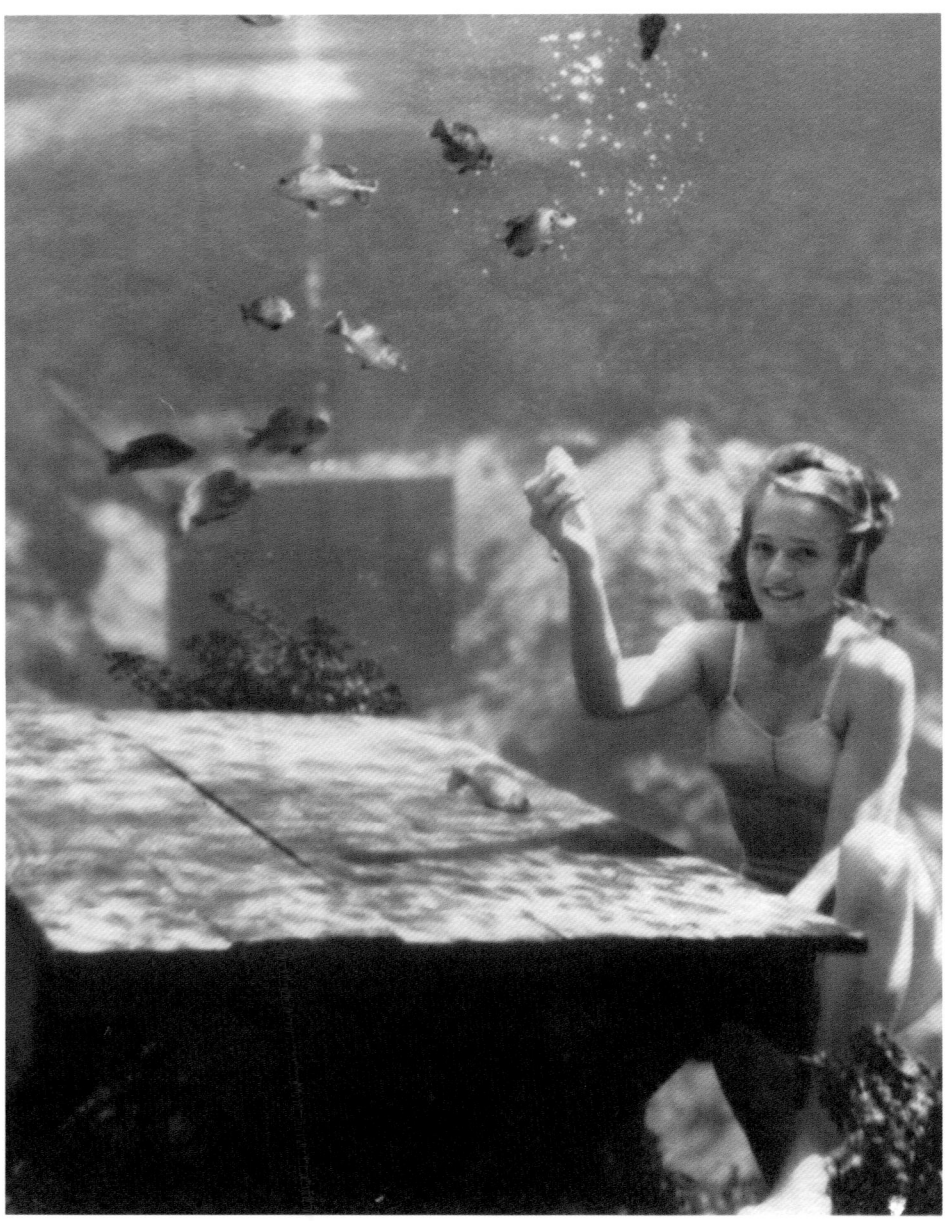

Eileen Perry Hogshead performed at Weeki
Wachee during the summers she spent with
her father. She is thirteen in this photo, 1948.
By permission of Eileen Perry Hogshead.

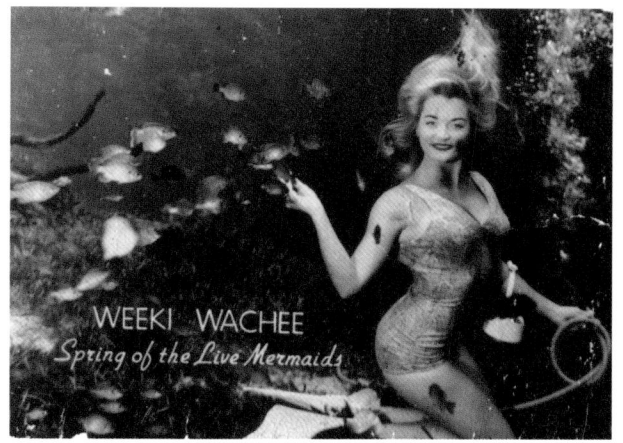

Left: Florence McNabb feeds the fish in this photo postcard. By permission of Bonita Colson.

Below: The very youngest Weeki Wachee mermaid was Eugenia Scofield. Eugenia was nine years old when she made her swimming debut at the spring in 1949. Her friend, Katherine Allen, age 8, was supposed to make her debut as well, but she got sick. By permission of Kevin Griffin.

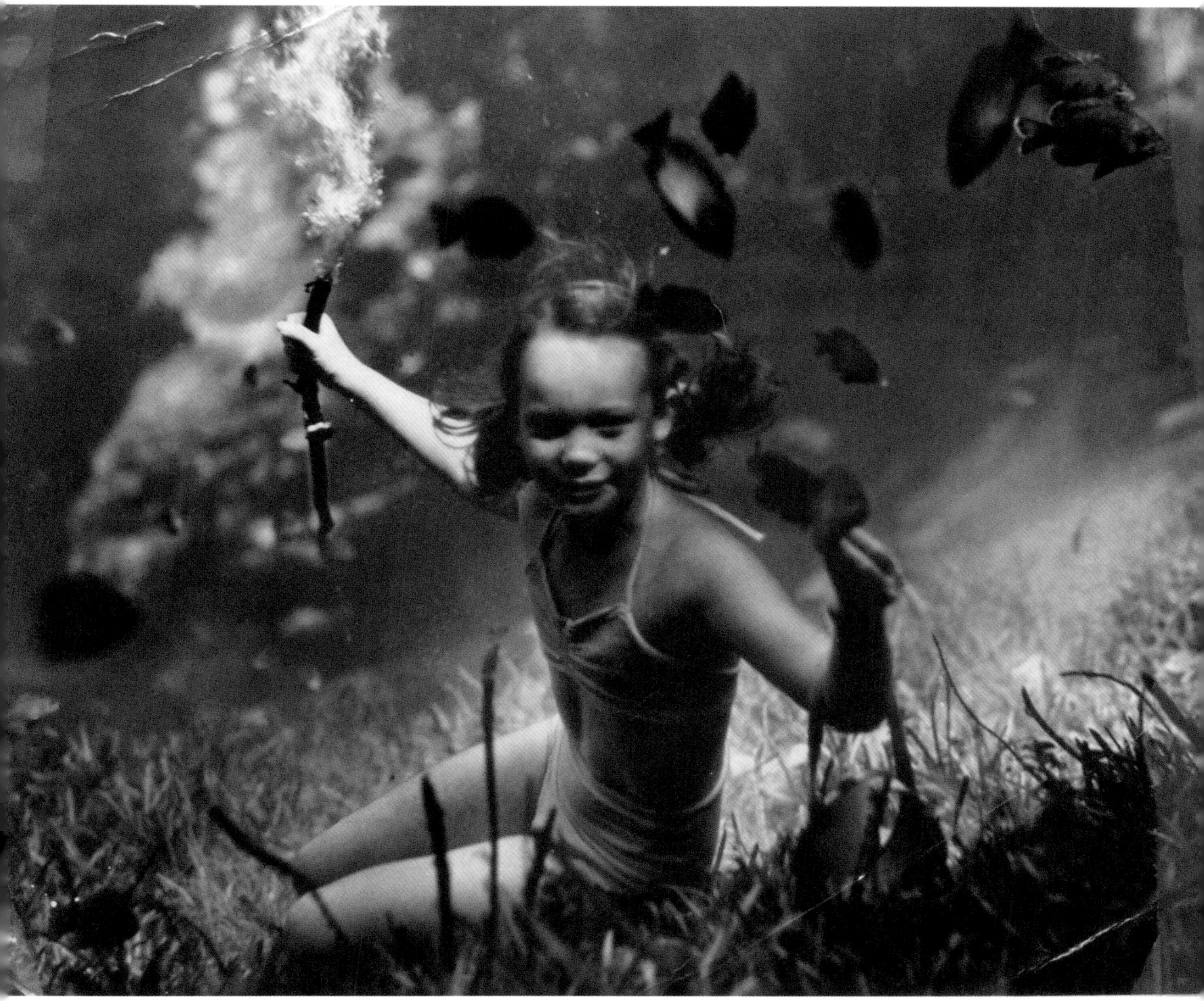

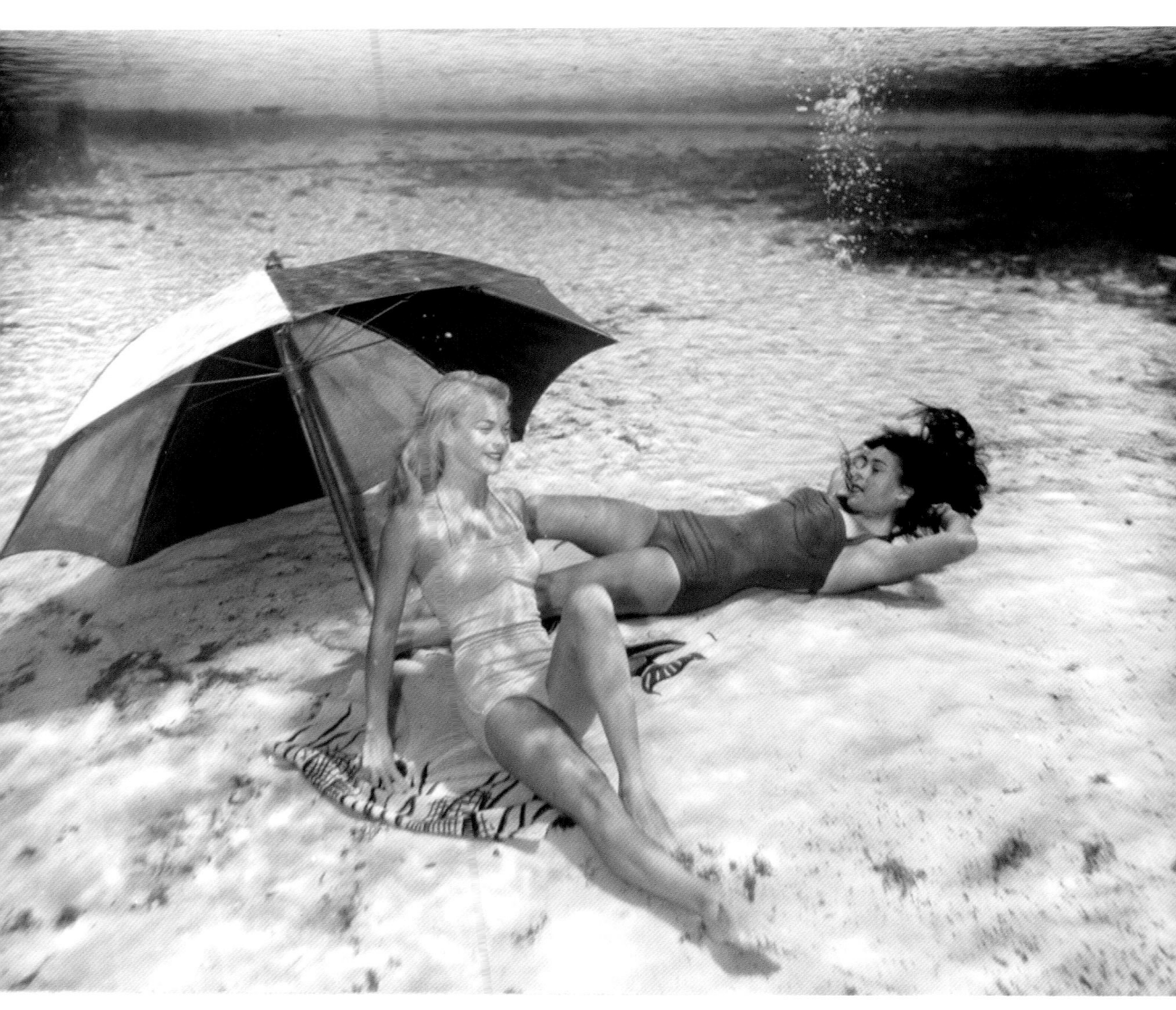

Ginger Stanley Hallowell (*left*) and
Merle Ivey sunbathe underwater at
Weeki Wachee, 1951. By permission of
the Florida State Archives.

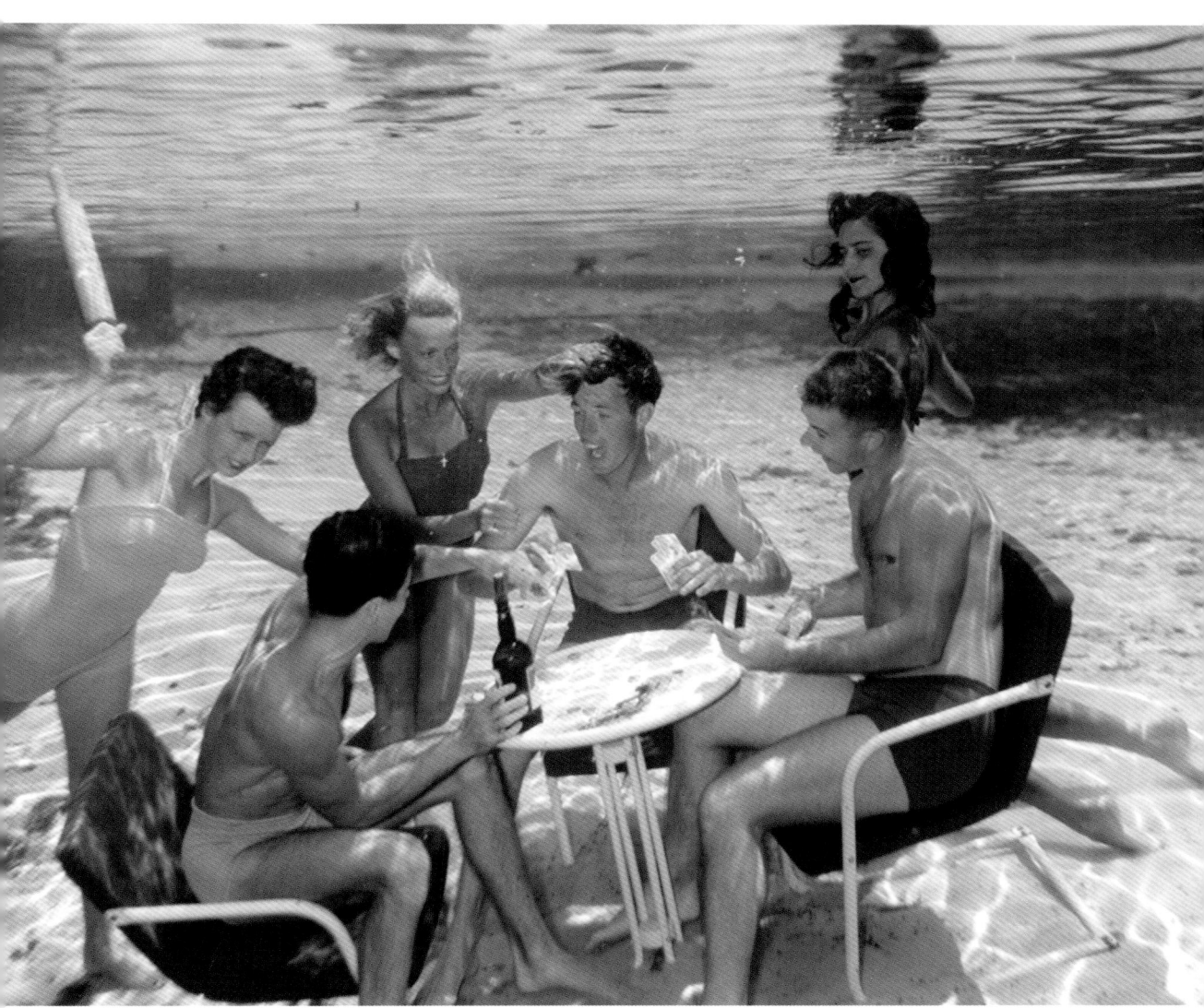

An underwater poker game goes awry: *from left*, Shirley and Dick Woolery, Patsie and Bud Boyette, Rudy and Thelma Hala-buck, 1951. By permission of the Florida State Archives.

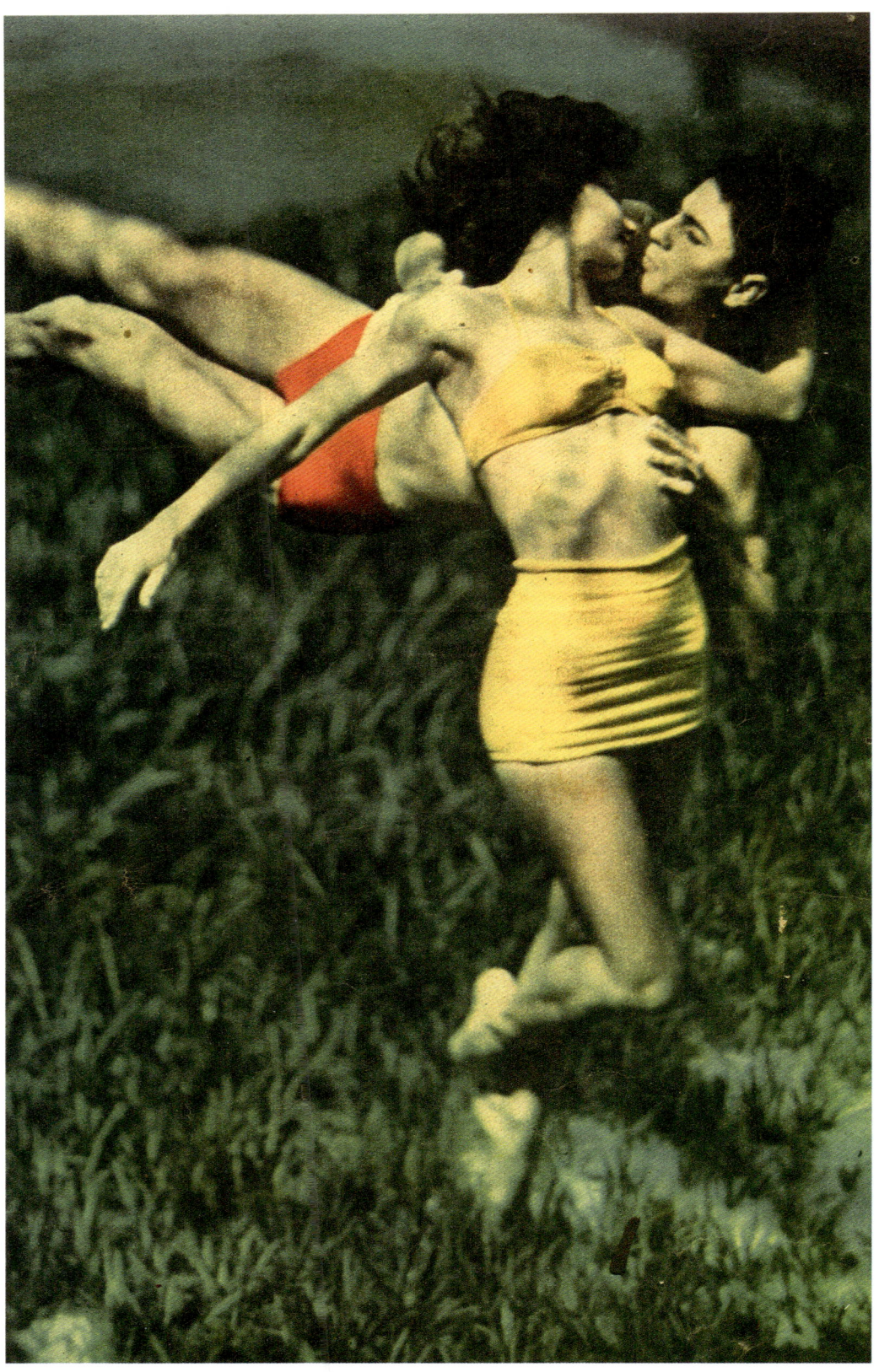

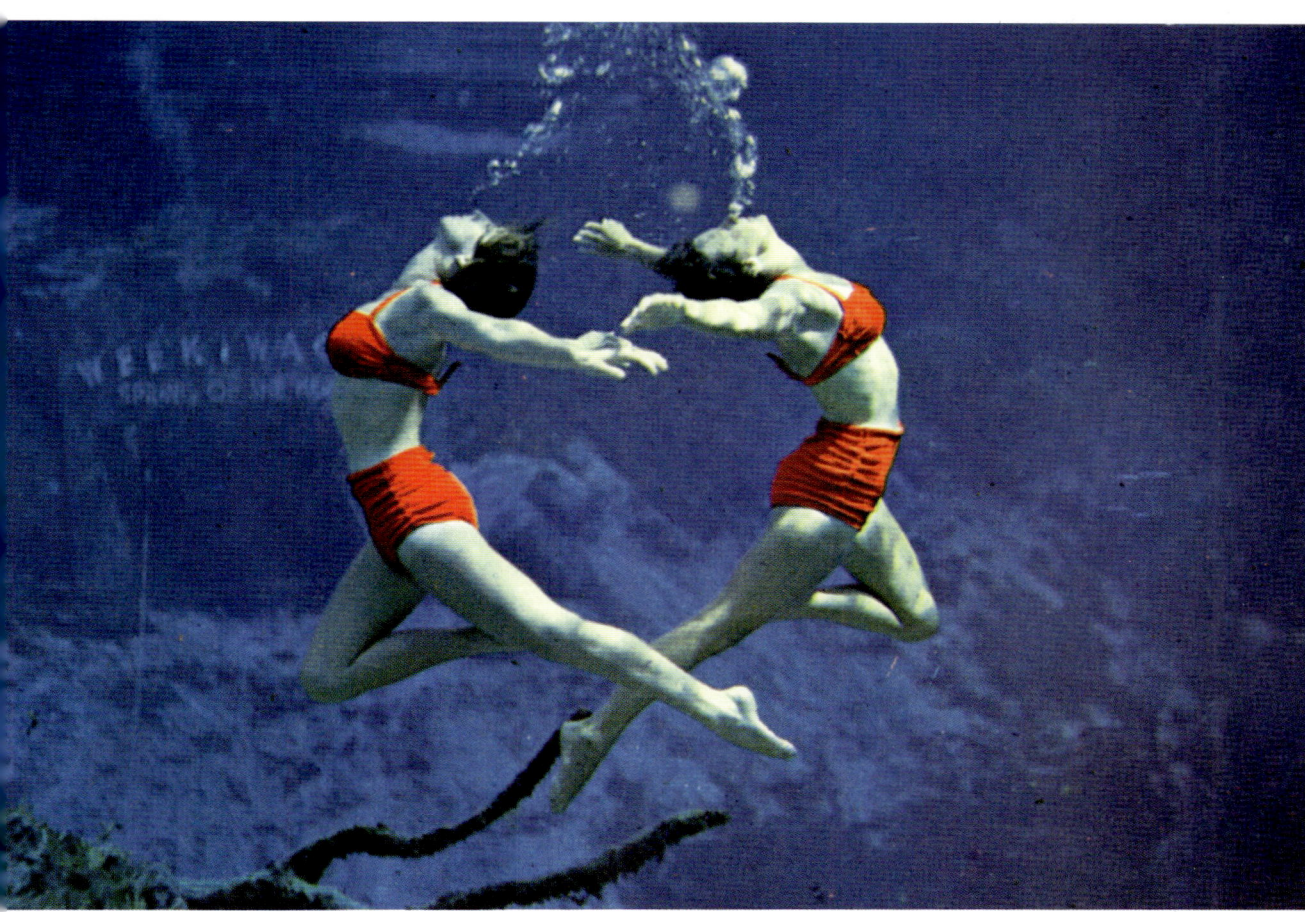

Facing page: Bill Amick and Mary Dwight Rose strike a romantic pose deep in the spring, ca. 1948. By permission of Mary Dwight Rose.

Above: Wearing red swimsuits these mermaids strike a pose creating a blue heart, ca. 1950. By permission of Bonita Colson.

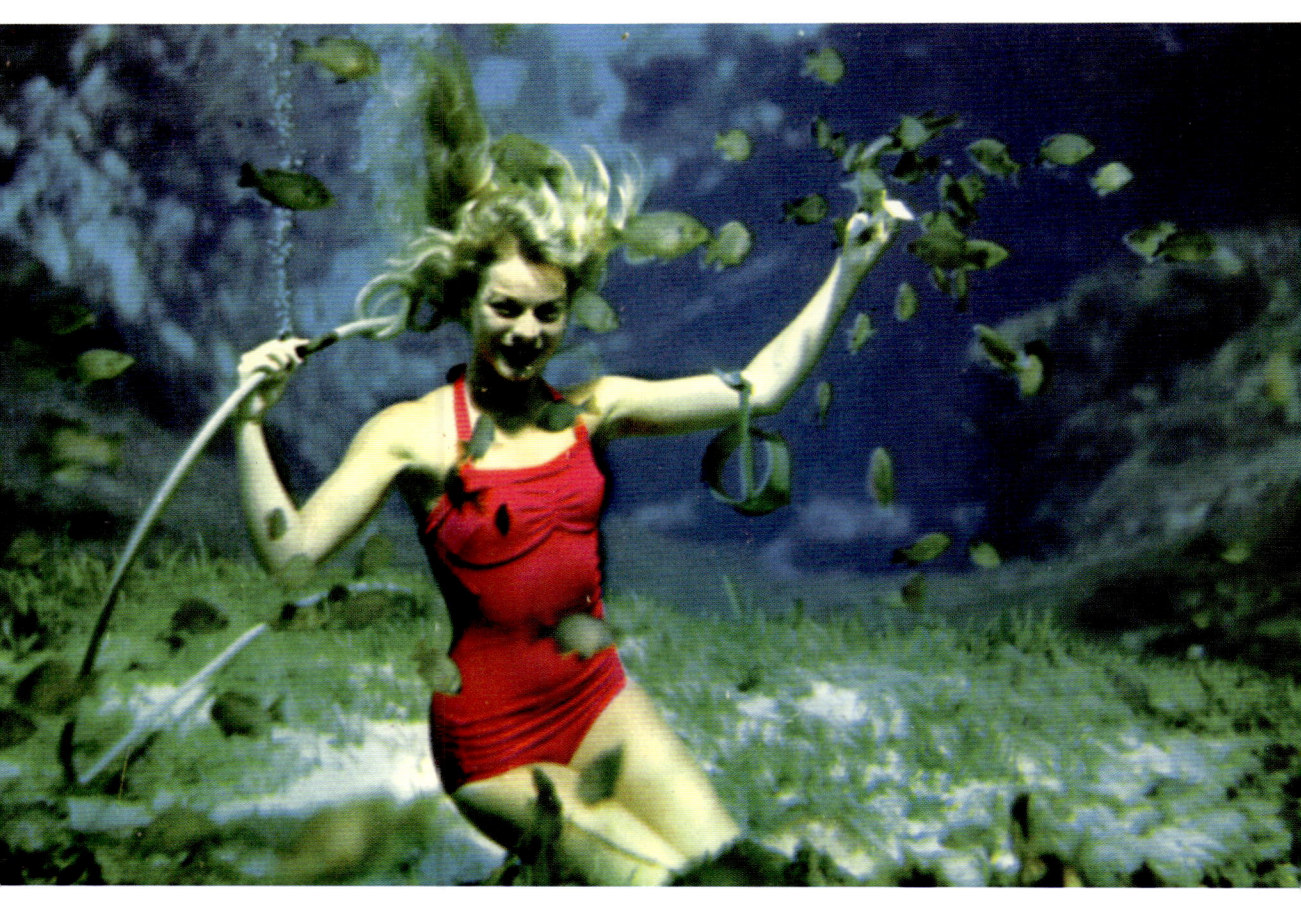

Ginger Stanley Hallowell kept the blue-gilled bream well fed and contented with compacted balls of bread, 1951. The fish became very friendly with the mermaids once they learned of this treat. By permission of Bonita Colson.

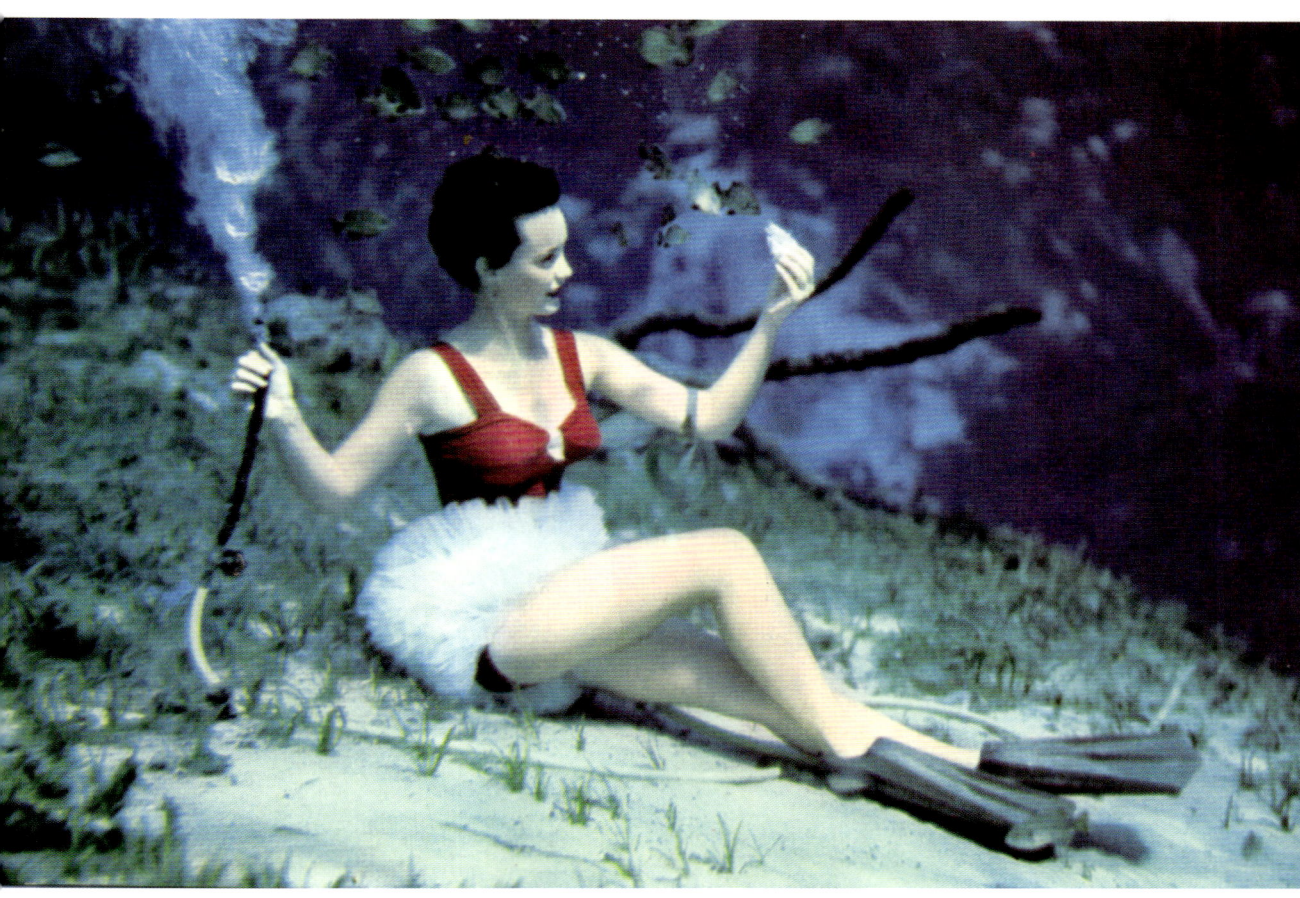

Weeki Wachee's fish never went hungry with the mermaids around. Pat Brett feeds them in this 1953 photo. By permission of Bonita Colson.

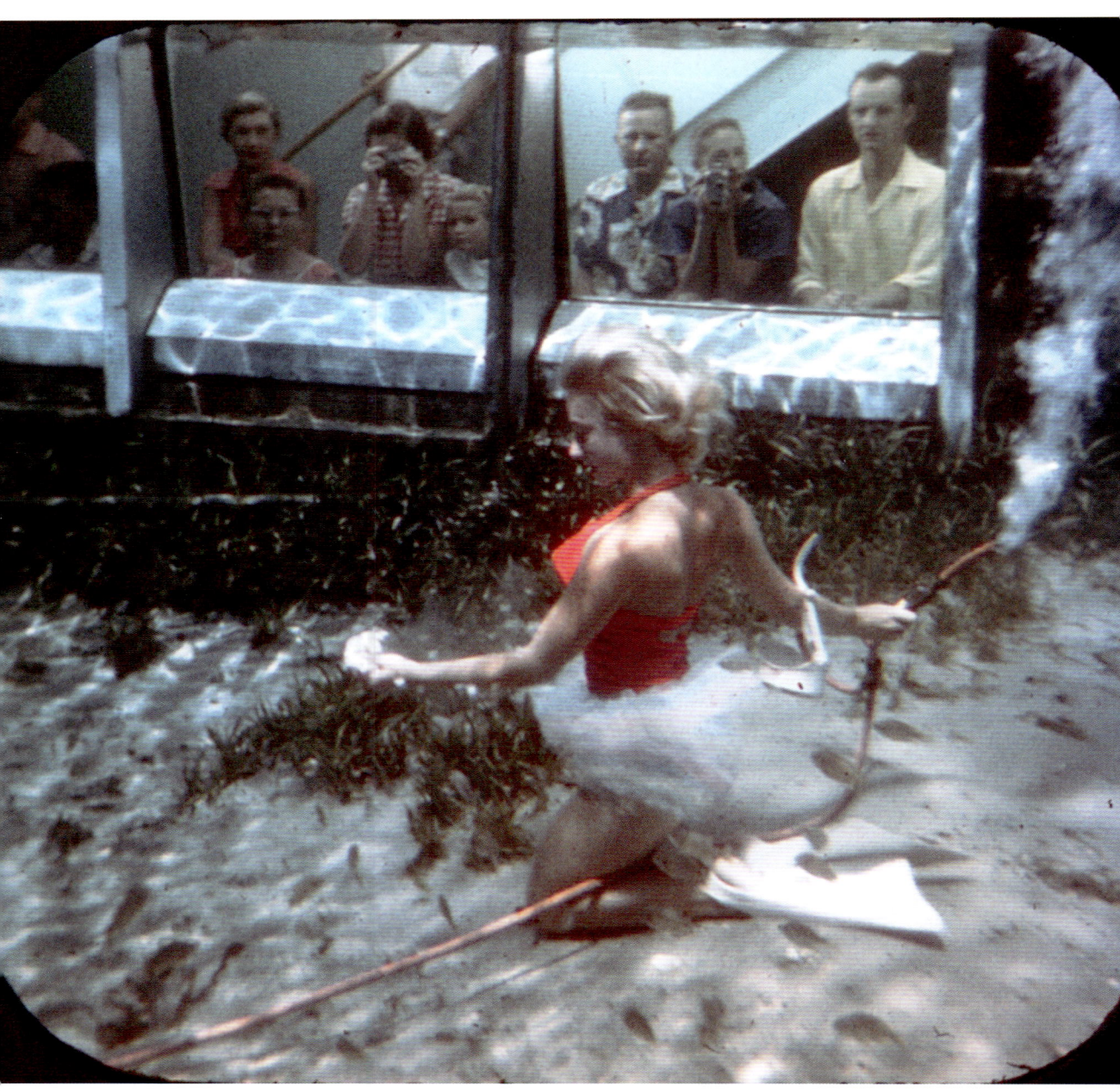

A mermaid prepares to feed the fish as the audience looks on from inside the first theater, ca. 1951. Author's collection.

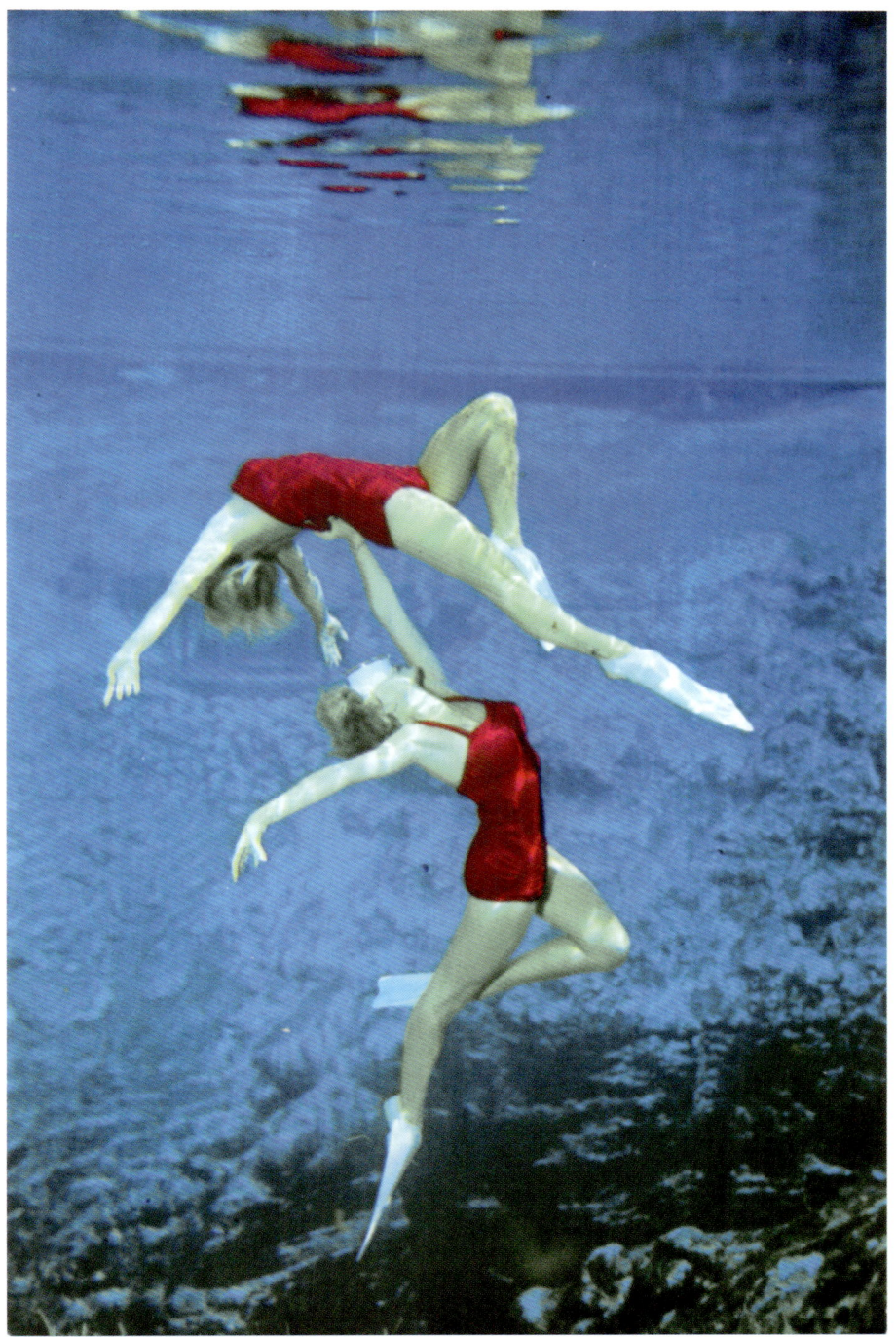

Donna Karosa (*above*) and Patsie Hadley
Boyette perform the adagio pose as they
ride the current of the spring up to the
surface, 1954. Photo by Ted Lagerberg.
By permission of Bonita Colson.

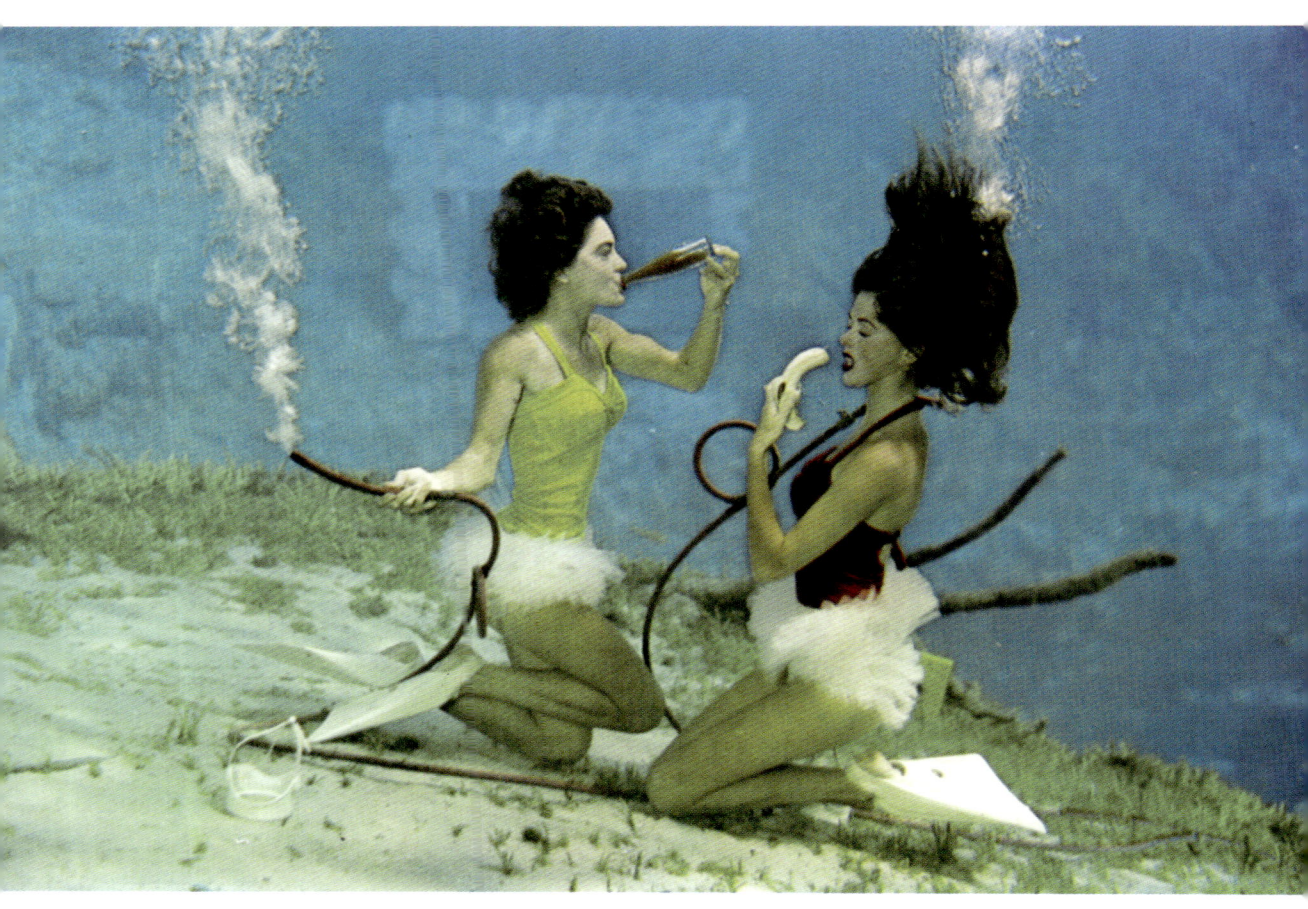

Jeanie Brooks and Sandy Mills eat and
drink underwater in this 1958 photo.
Photo by Ted Lagerberg. By permission
of Vera Huckaby.

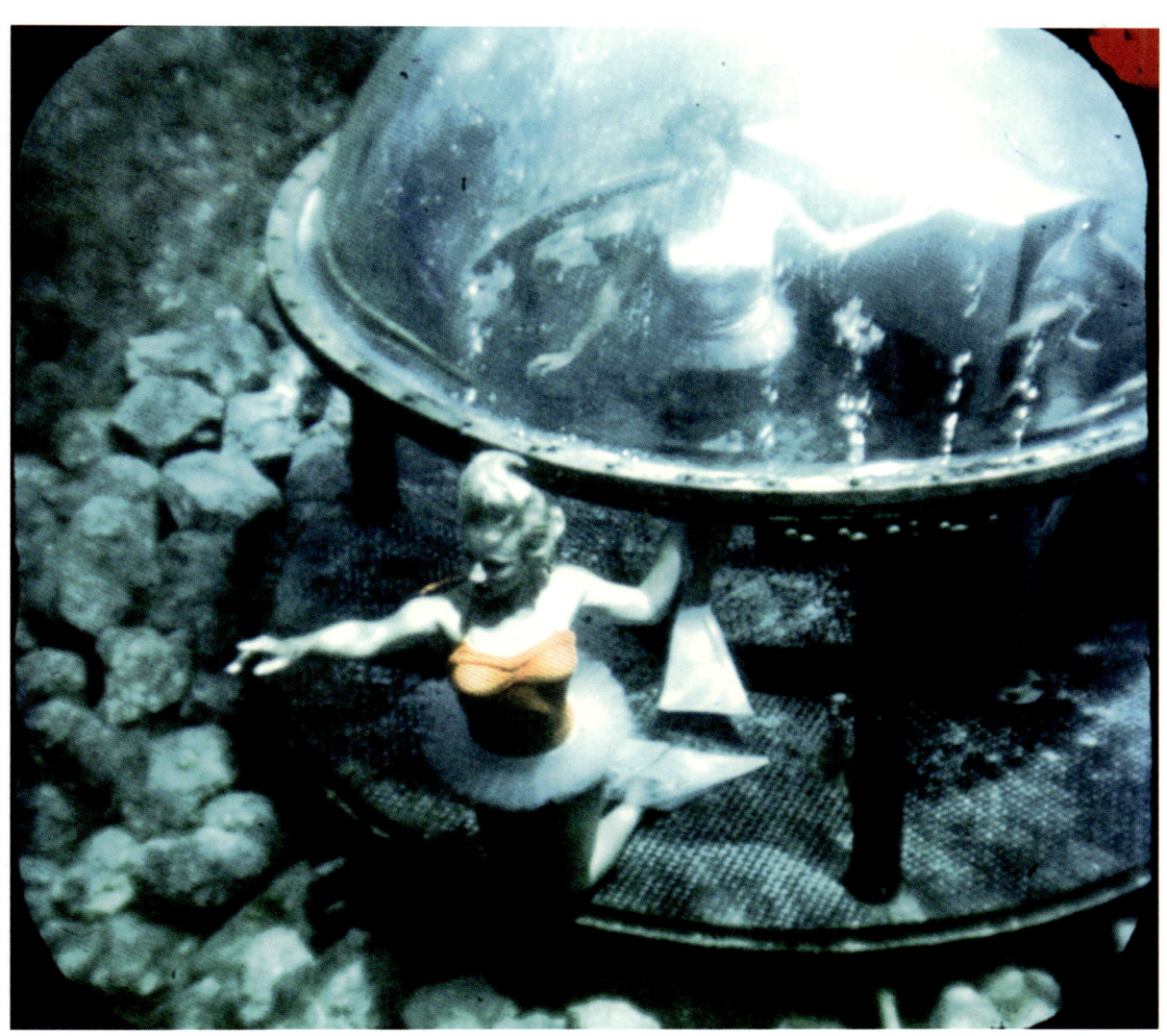

Donna Karosa steps outside the air-lock while another mermaid waits within, 1959. Author's collection.

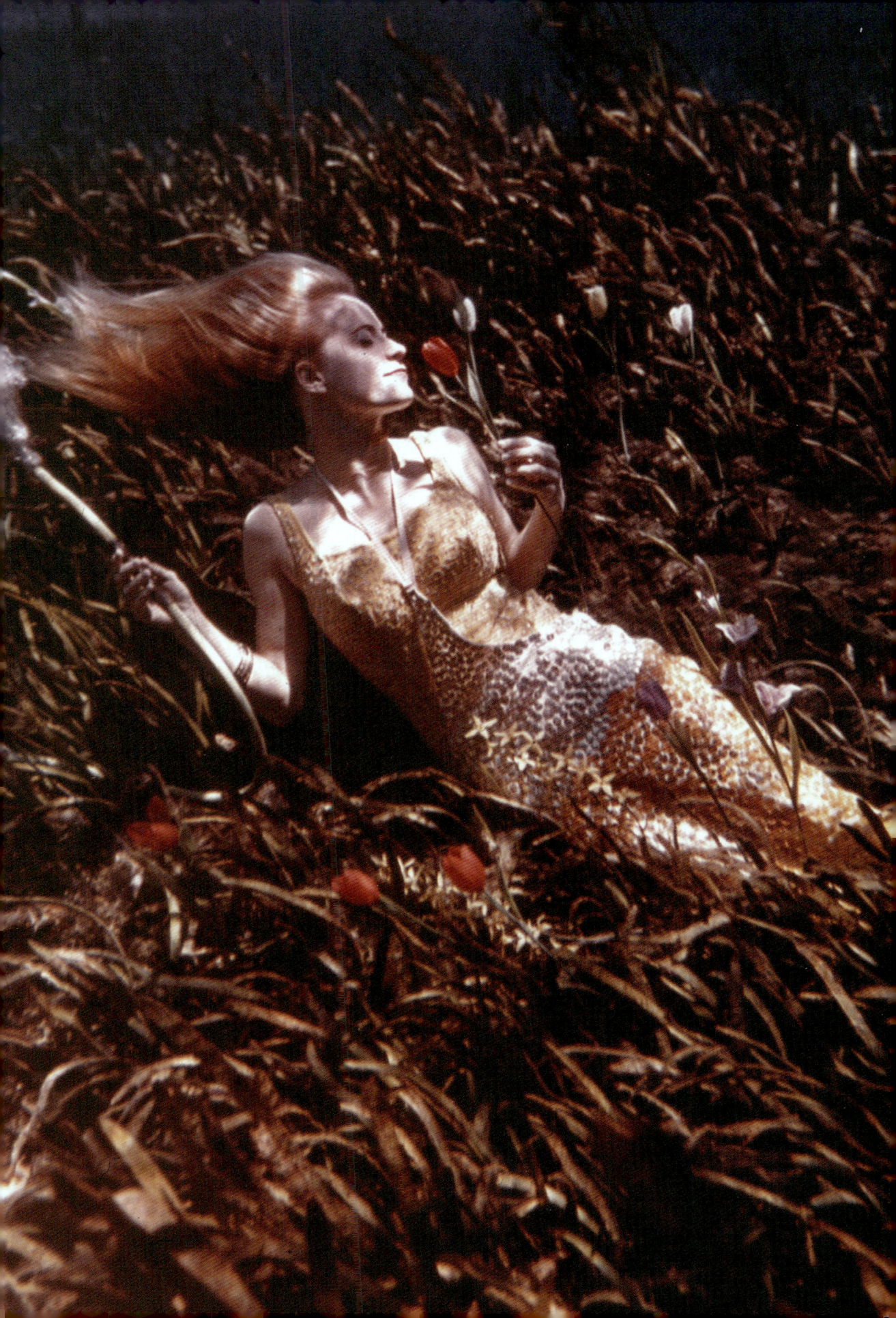

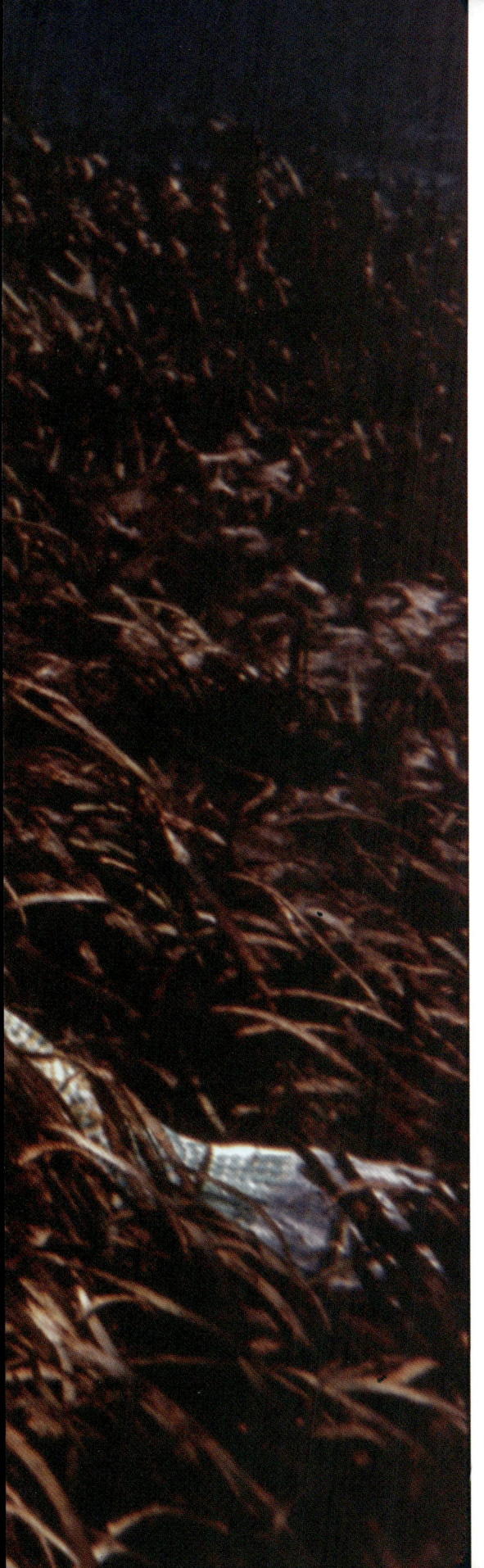

Mermaid costumes first appeared in the shows in 1960. Applying the sequins was labor intensive; each was sewn on one at a time. Terry Hamlet pretends to smell the tulips in a bed of eel grass, which is difficult underwater as no sniffing is allowed, 1962. By permission of Genie Young.

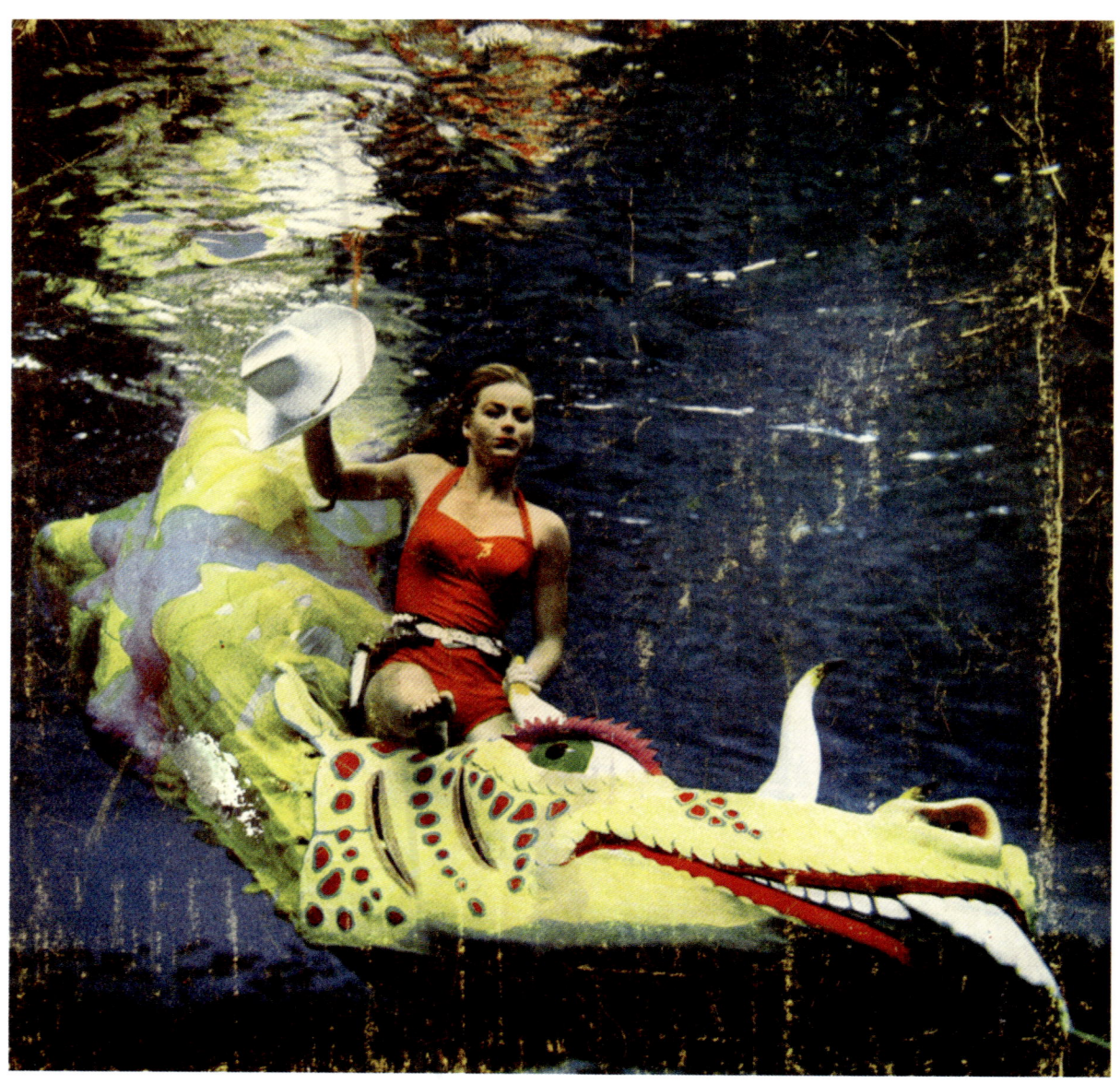

Bonita Colson tames Wiley Willy,
star of the Underwater Circus Show,
in this award-winning photograph,
1962. Photo by Weaver Tripp. By
permission of Bonita Colson.

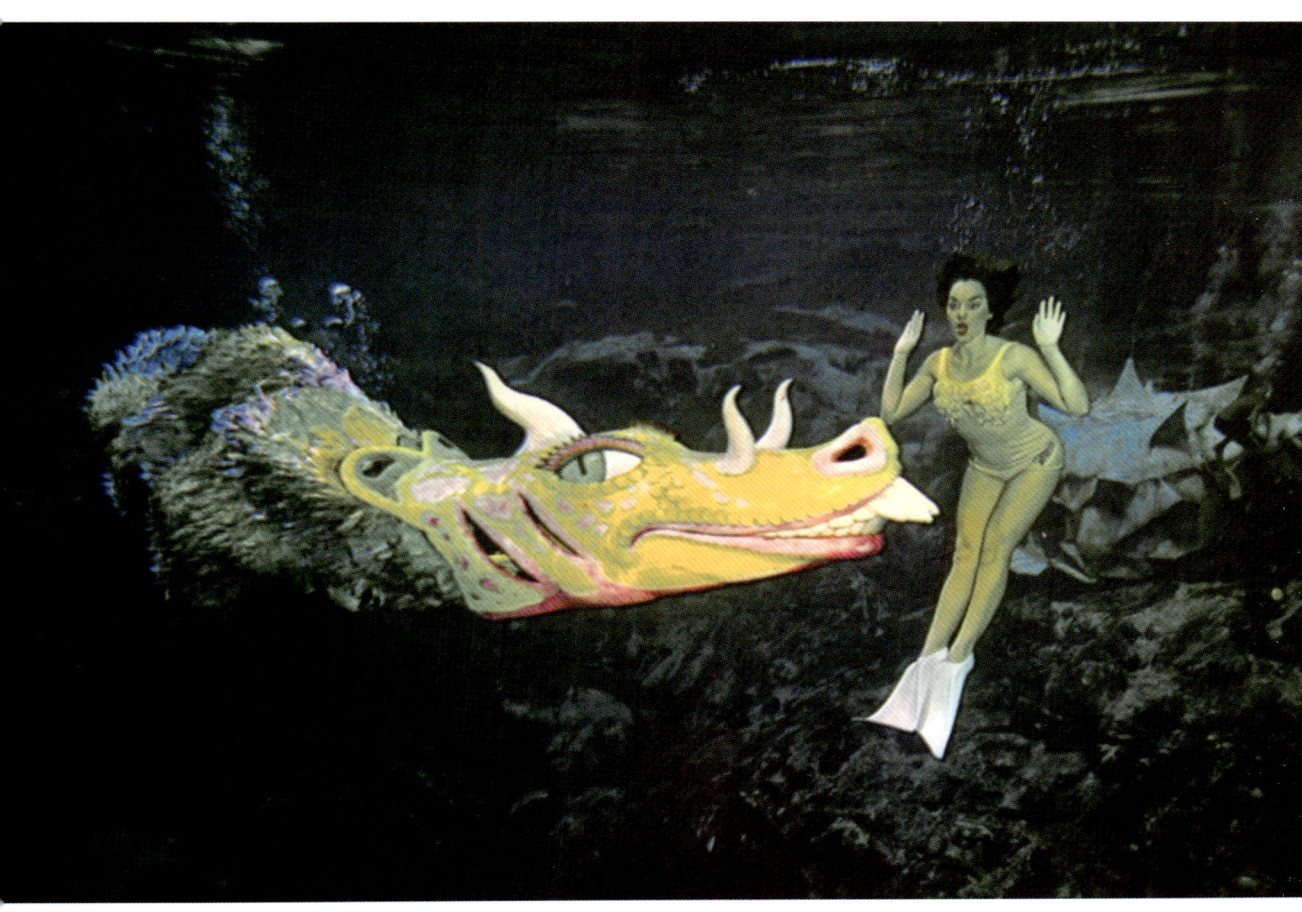

Wiley Willy tries to frighten the
mermaids again, but Linda Sanchez
isn't intimidated, 1962. By permission of Bonita Colson.

Marilyn Reed Allen tries out her new wings and finds it's easy to fly underwater, 1960. Photo by Sparky Schumacher. By permission of Sparky Schumacher.

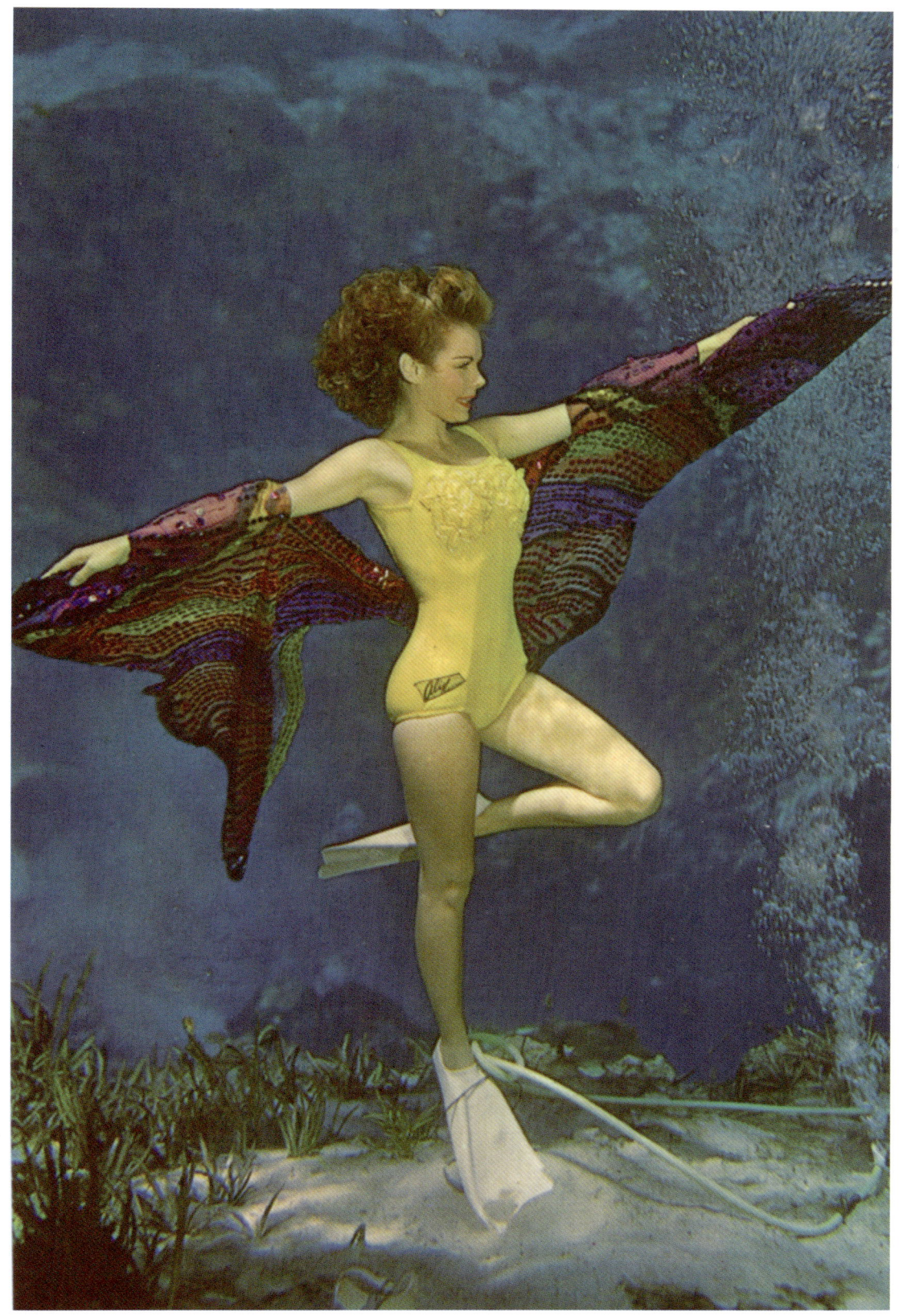

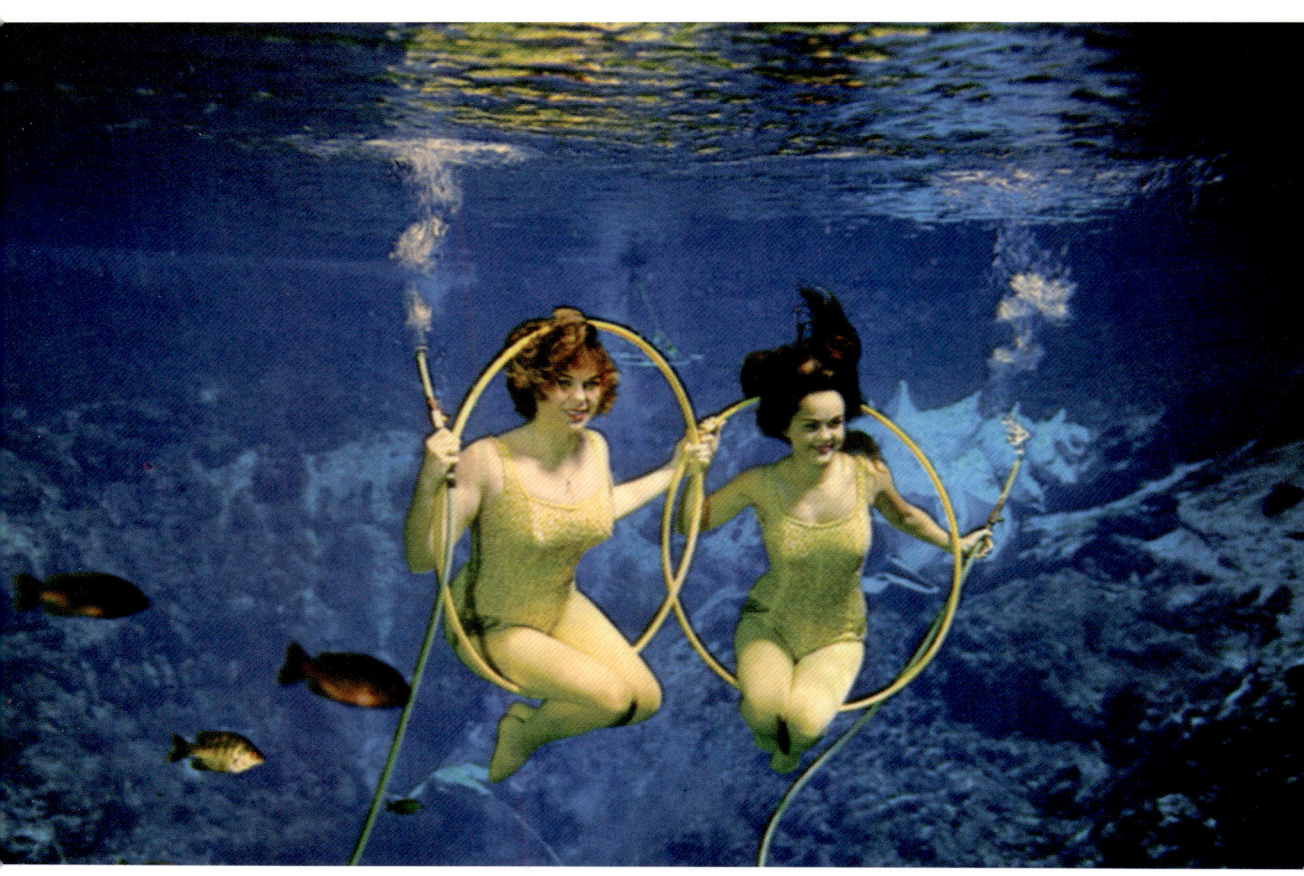

Who would have thought you could use hula hoops underwater? Donna South (*left*) and Shirley Walls perform "Balling the Jack" for the Underwater Circus Show, 1962. Photo by Sparky Schumacher. By permission of Bonita Colson.

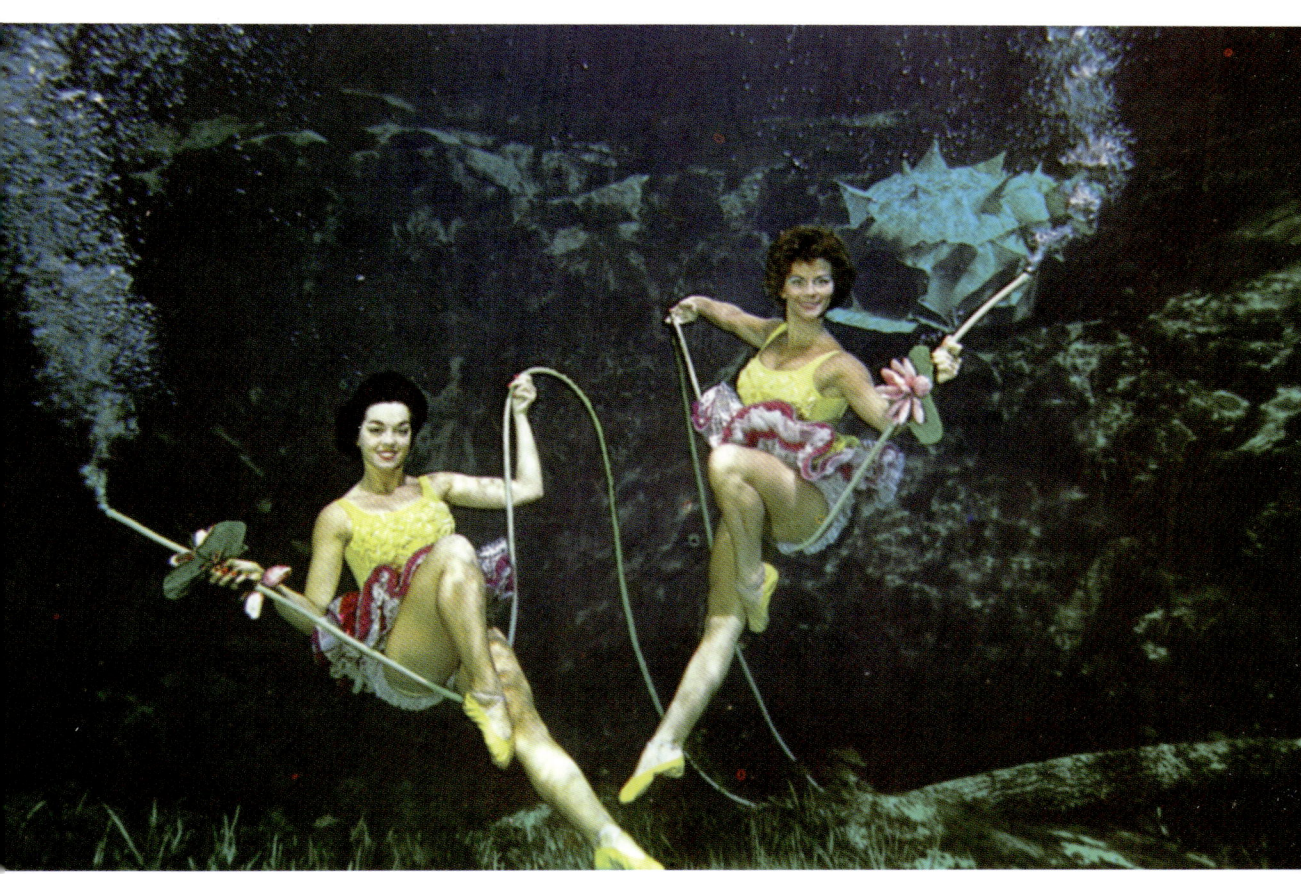

Linda Sanchez (*left*) and Lou Spikes
Ferreira use the air hoses as swings in
this shot from the Underwater Circus
Show, 1962. Photo by Ted Lagerberg.
By permission of Bonita Colson.

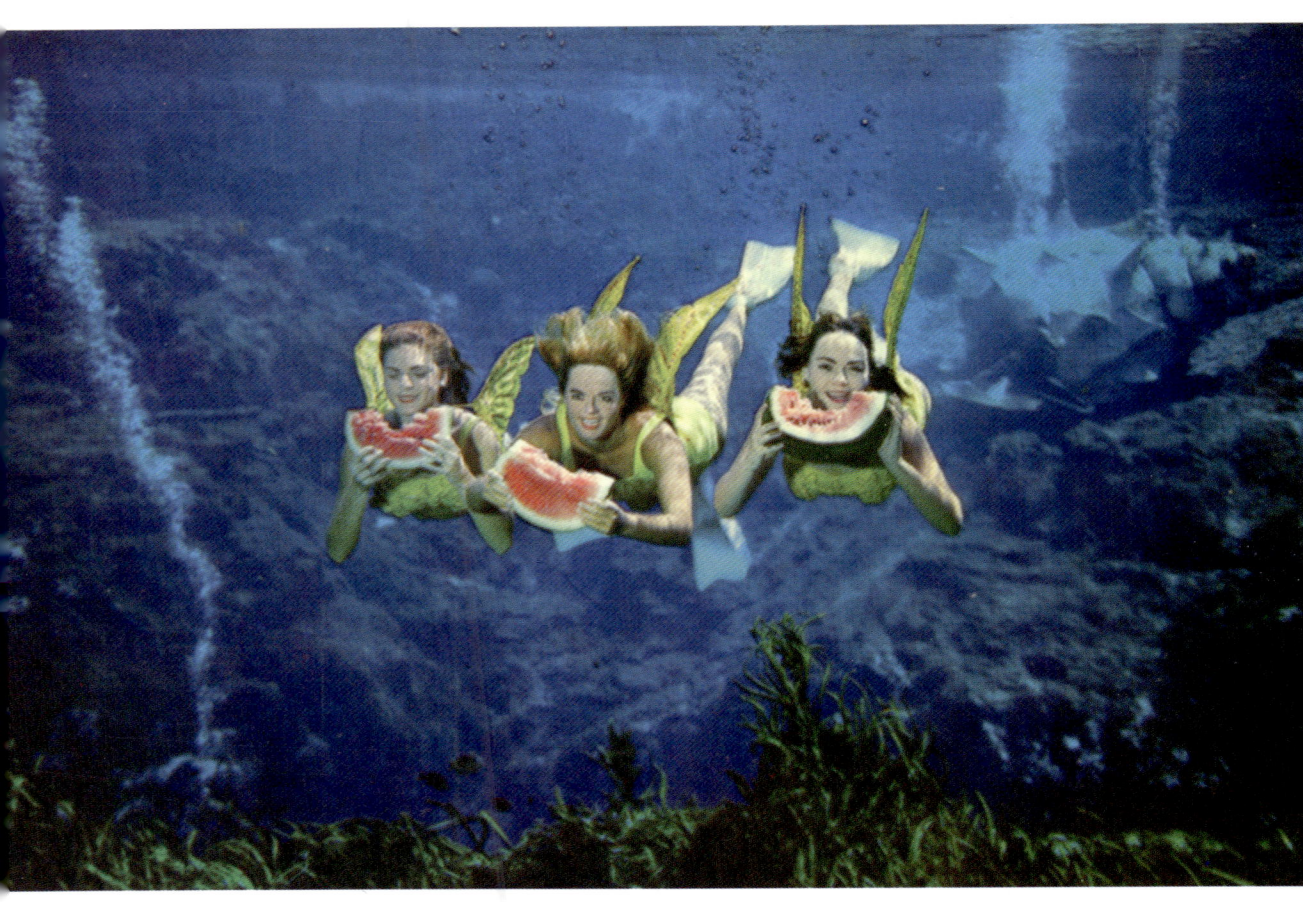

Gail Sherouse (*left*), Kathy Aspenal (*center*), and Jeanette Purdin demonstrate that there is no mess eating watermelon underwater, 1962. Photo by Ted Lagerberg. By permission of Bonita Colson.

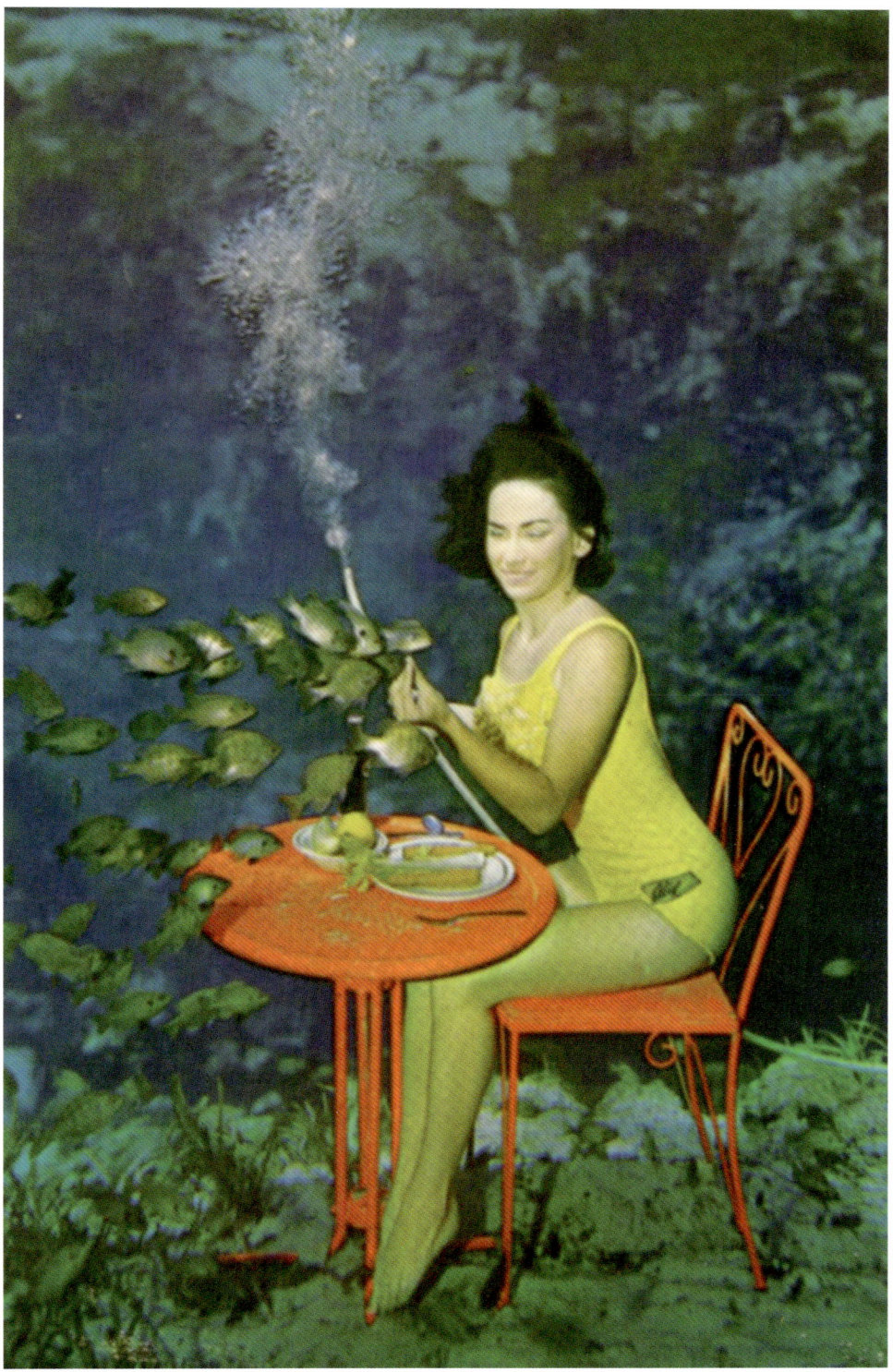

Bonnie Georgiadis takes a break from her
own lunch to feed the fish at this underwater café, 1960. Photo by Ted Lagerberg.
Author's collection.

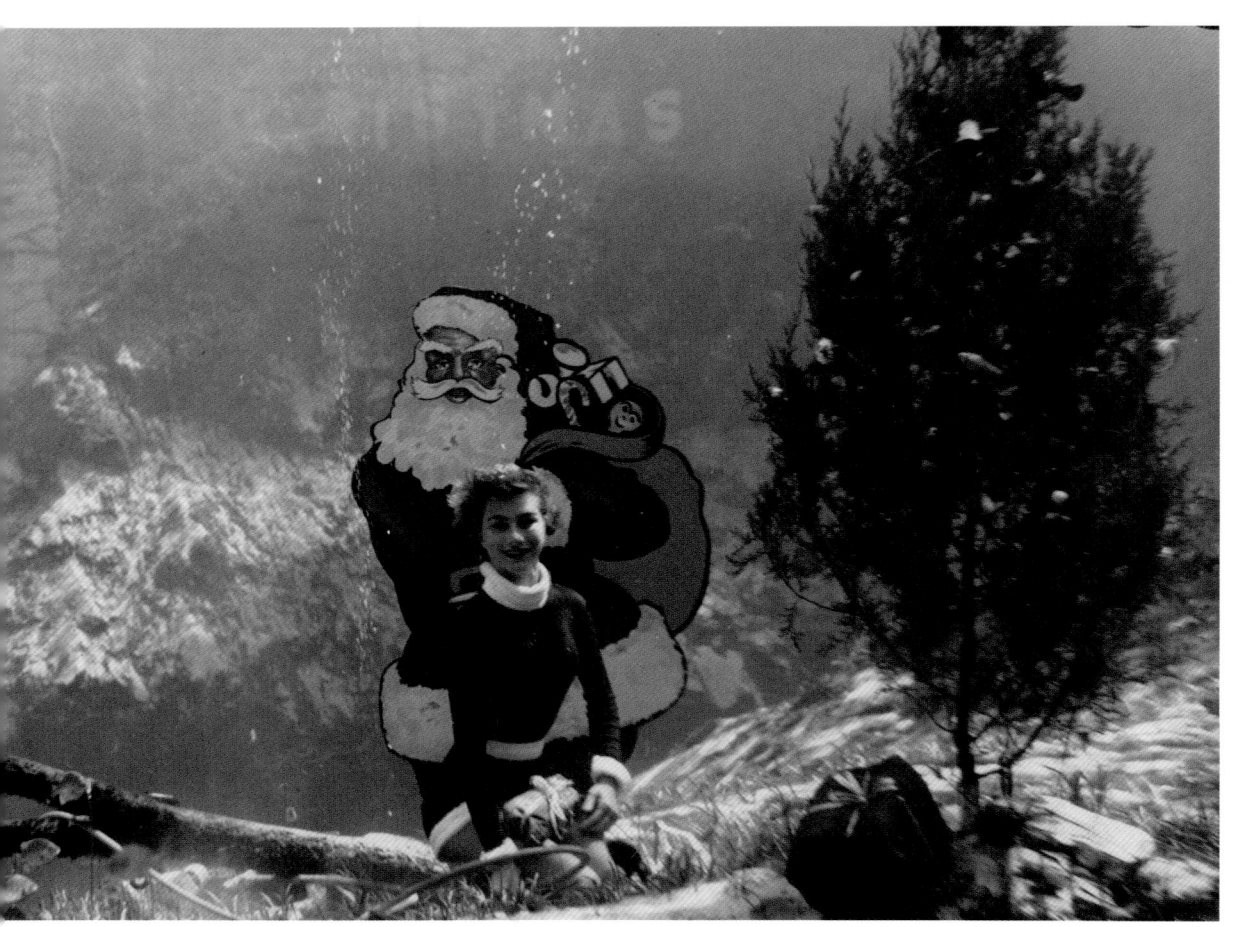

Kay Finney donned a Christmas outfit to pose with a cutout Santa for this photograph. A fish checks out the present she holds in her lap, 1955. By permission of Kay Finney.

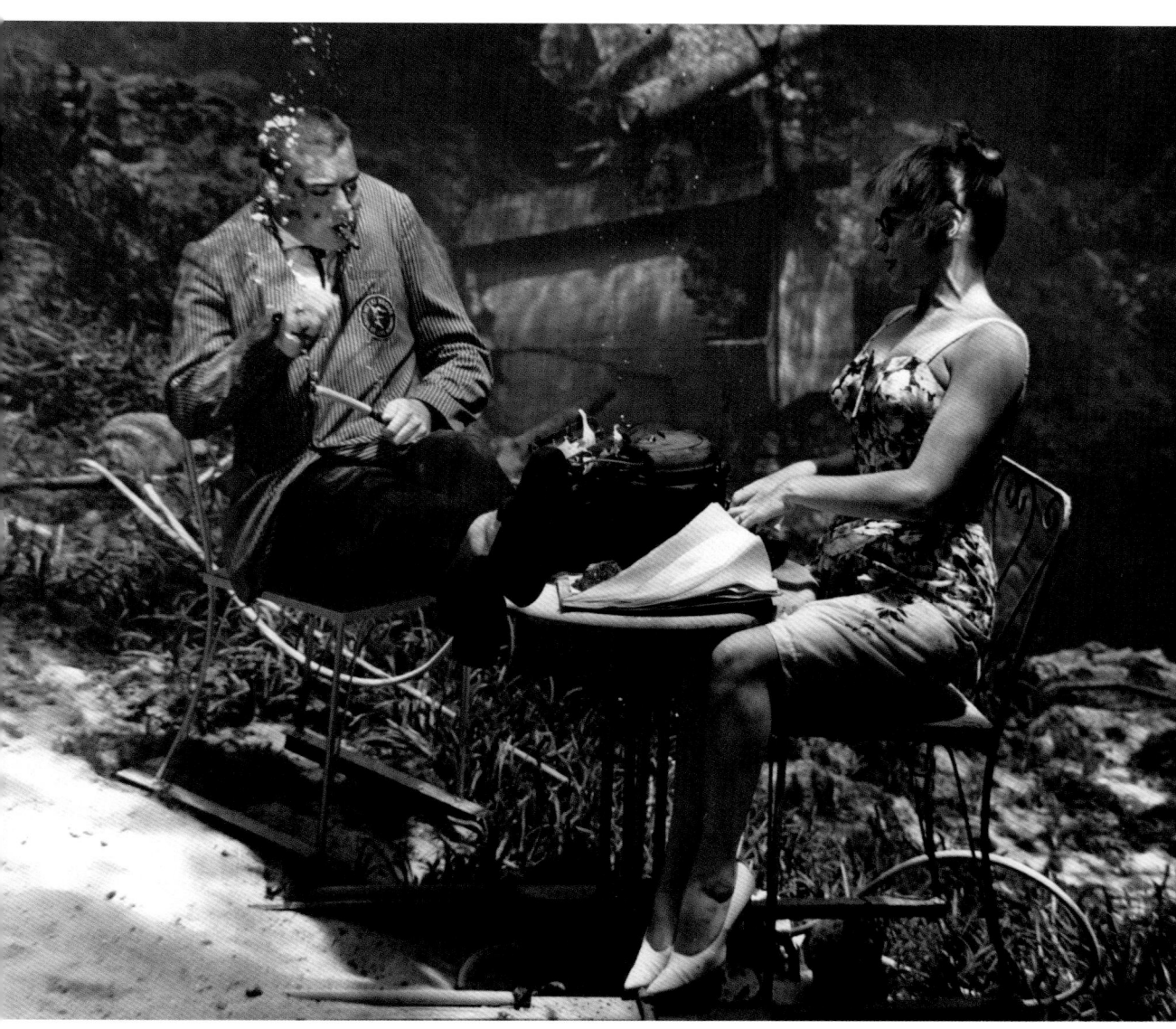

Donna South prepares to take dictation from Bill Huckaby in their underwater office, 1963. By permission of Vera Huckaby.

Diane Fry put on high-heeled pumps and
a black dress for a day out in the spring,
1965. By permission of Vera Huckaby.

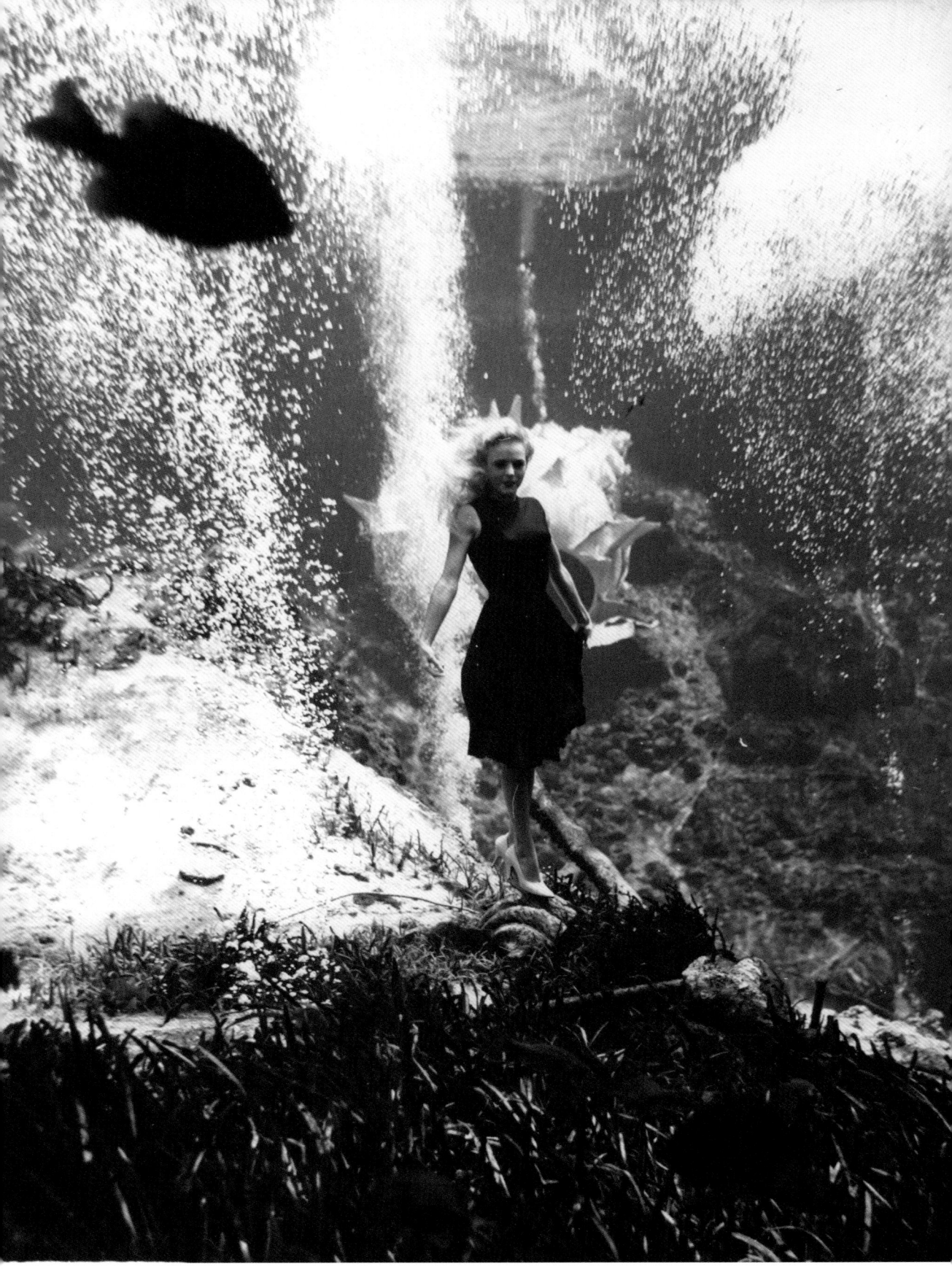

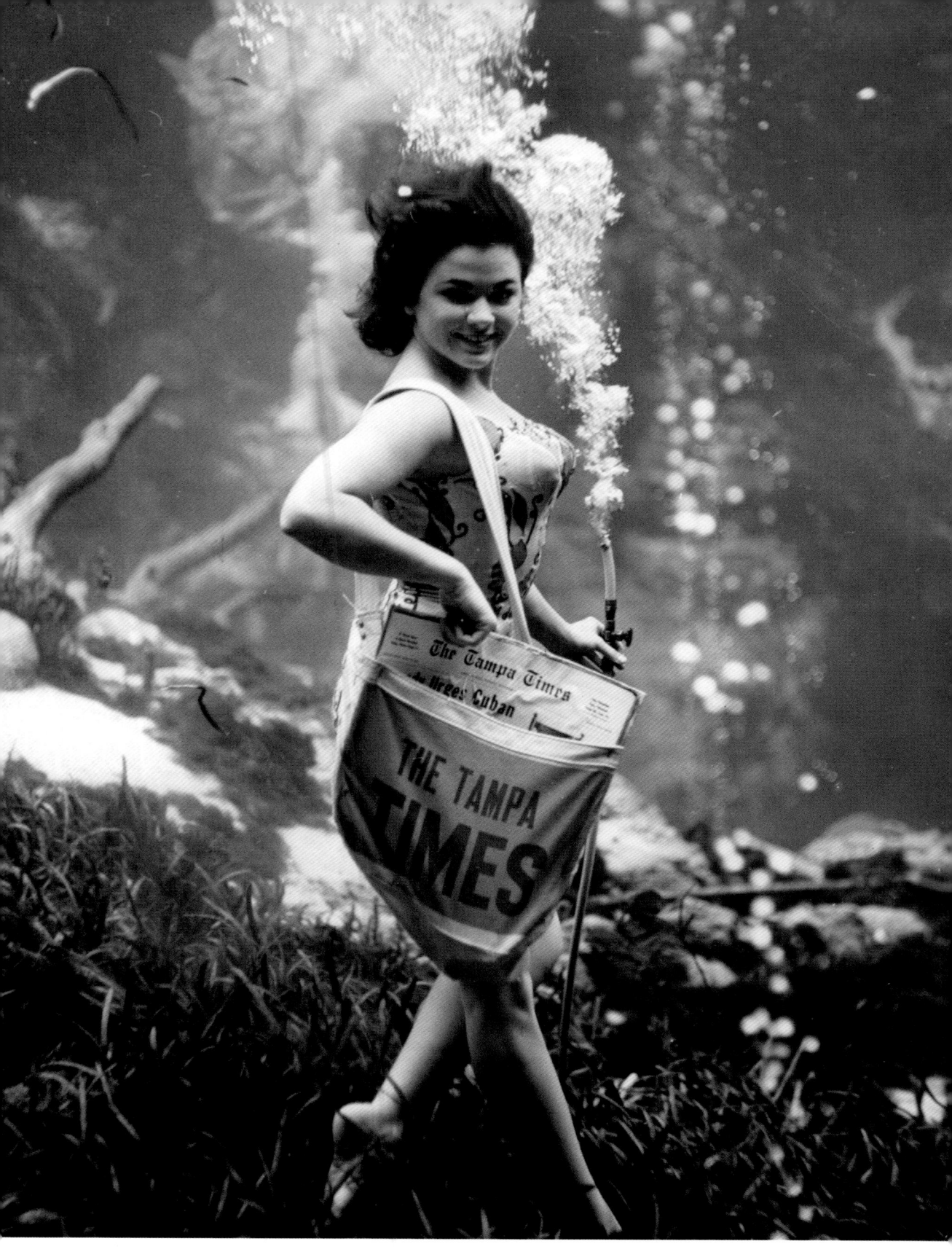

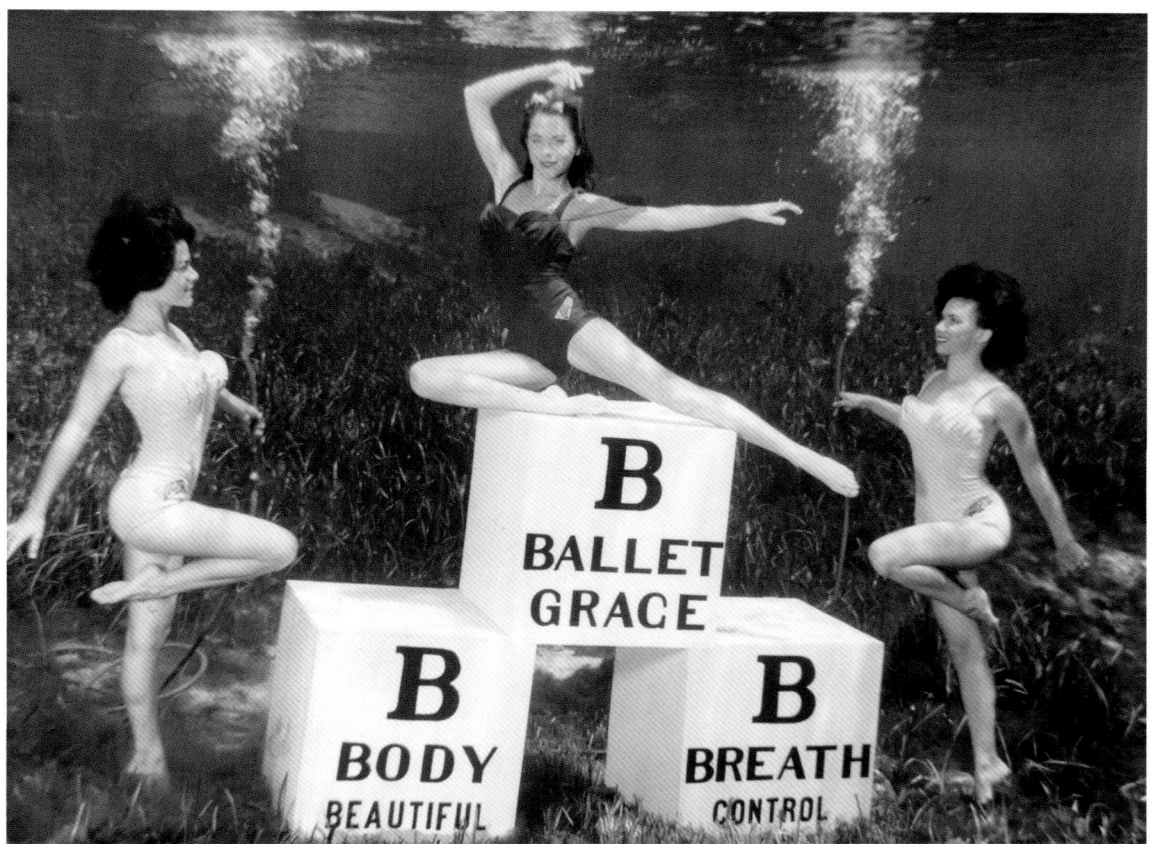

Facing page: Dede Parmer delivers papers
to the mermaids in this 1964 era shot.
By permission of Vera Huckaby.

Above: Vicki Smith (*left*), Mary Sue Clay,
(*center*), and Bonnie Georgiadis demonstrate the 3 Bs of mermaiding in this 1960
photo. By permission of Bonnie Georgiadis.

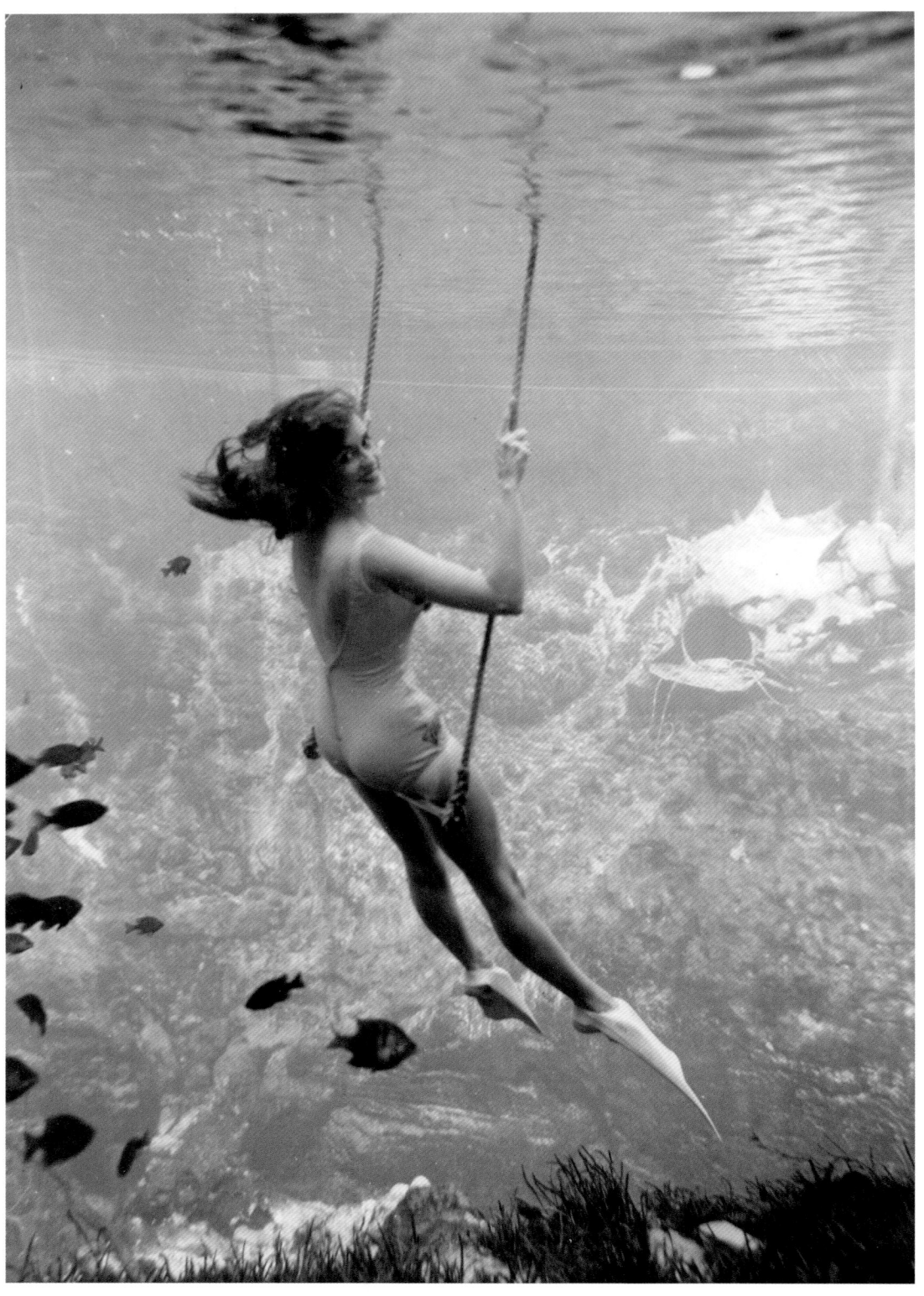

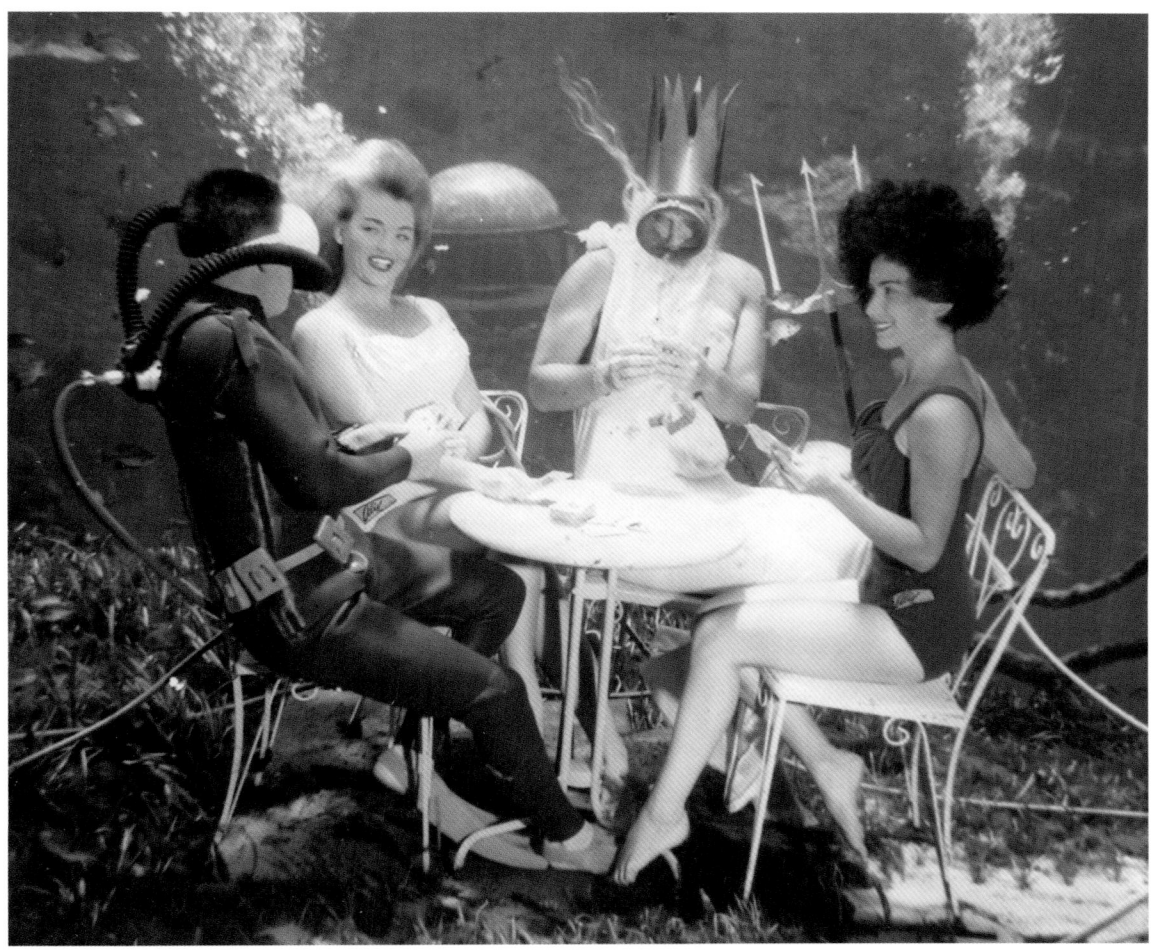

Facing page: Beth Goldsby swings underwater
amid a school of fish, 1960. By permission of
Bonnie Georgiadis.

Above: There are no poker faces here. Florence
McNabb (*left*) and Bonnie Georgiadis hold the
best cards in this game with King Neptune and
a fellow diver. The maintenance staff must have
had a ball building these props, then weighing
everything down, 1958. By permission of Bonnie
Georgiadis.

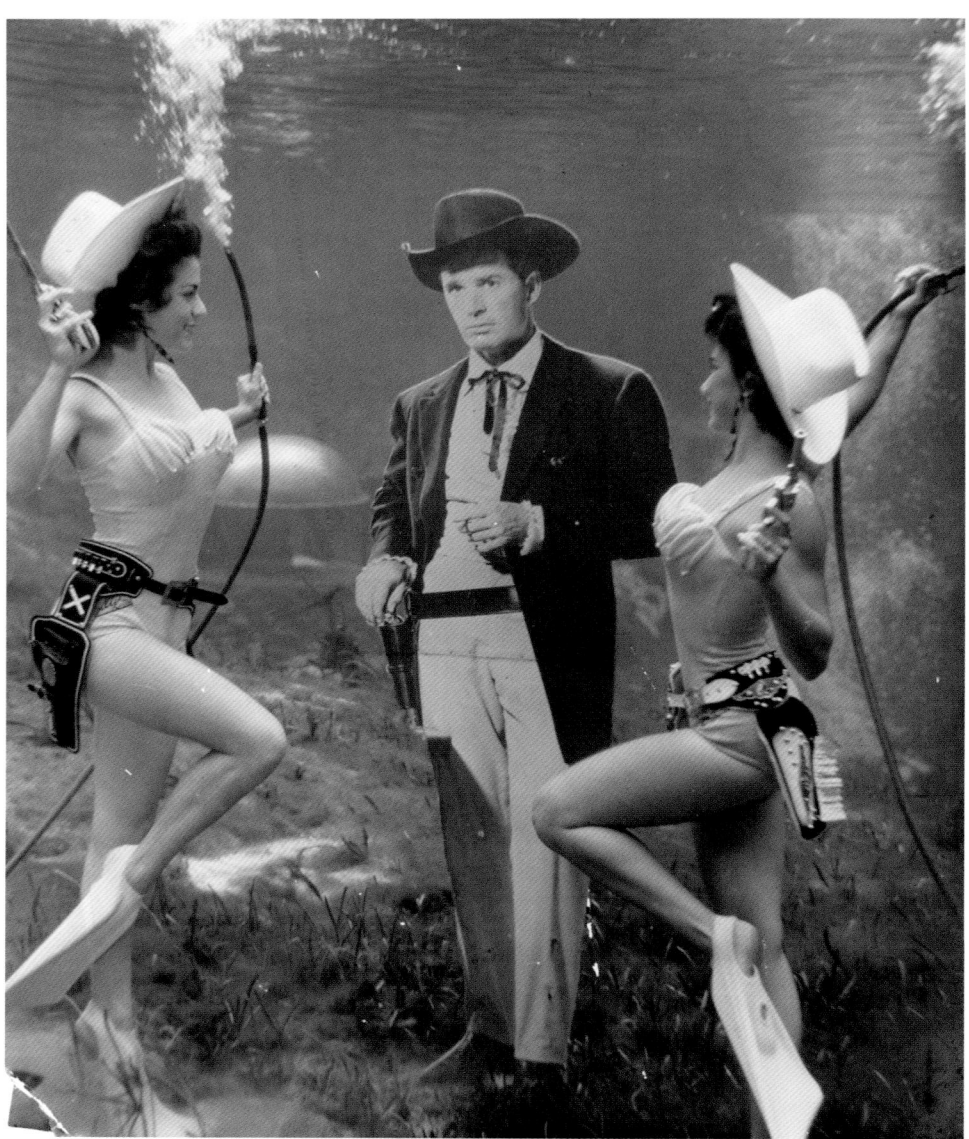

Above: Fastest draw in the South. Vicki
Smith (*left*) and Bonnie Georgiadis outdraw
a cutout of Brett Maverick (James Garner),
1962. By permission of Bonnie Georgiadis.

Facing page: Jean Miller pretends to feed a
mullet wearing a mask and fins—the fish,
that is, not Jean, 1962. Photo by Sparky
Schumacher. By permission of Sparky
Schumacher.

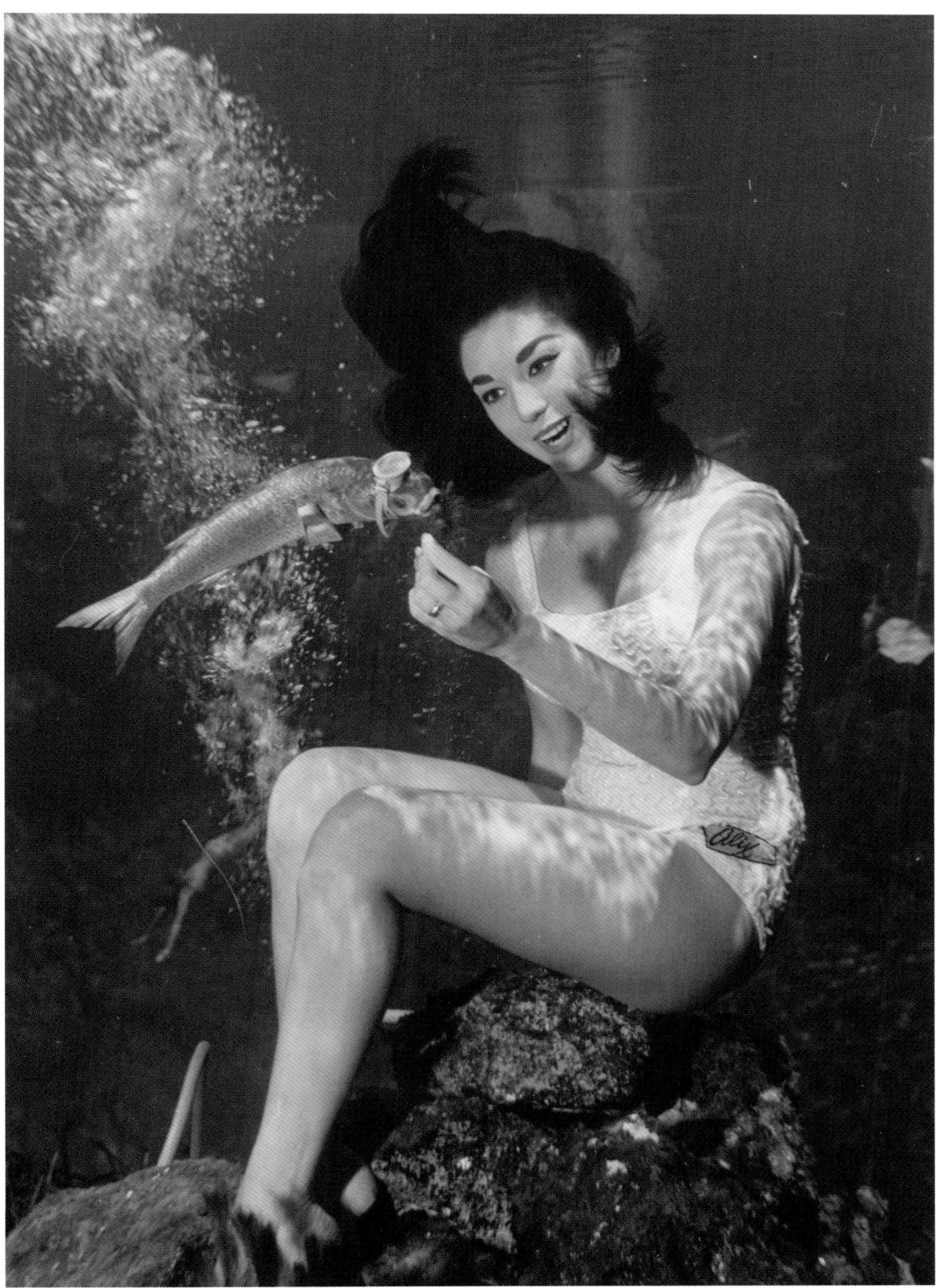

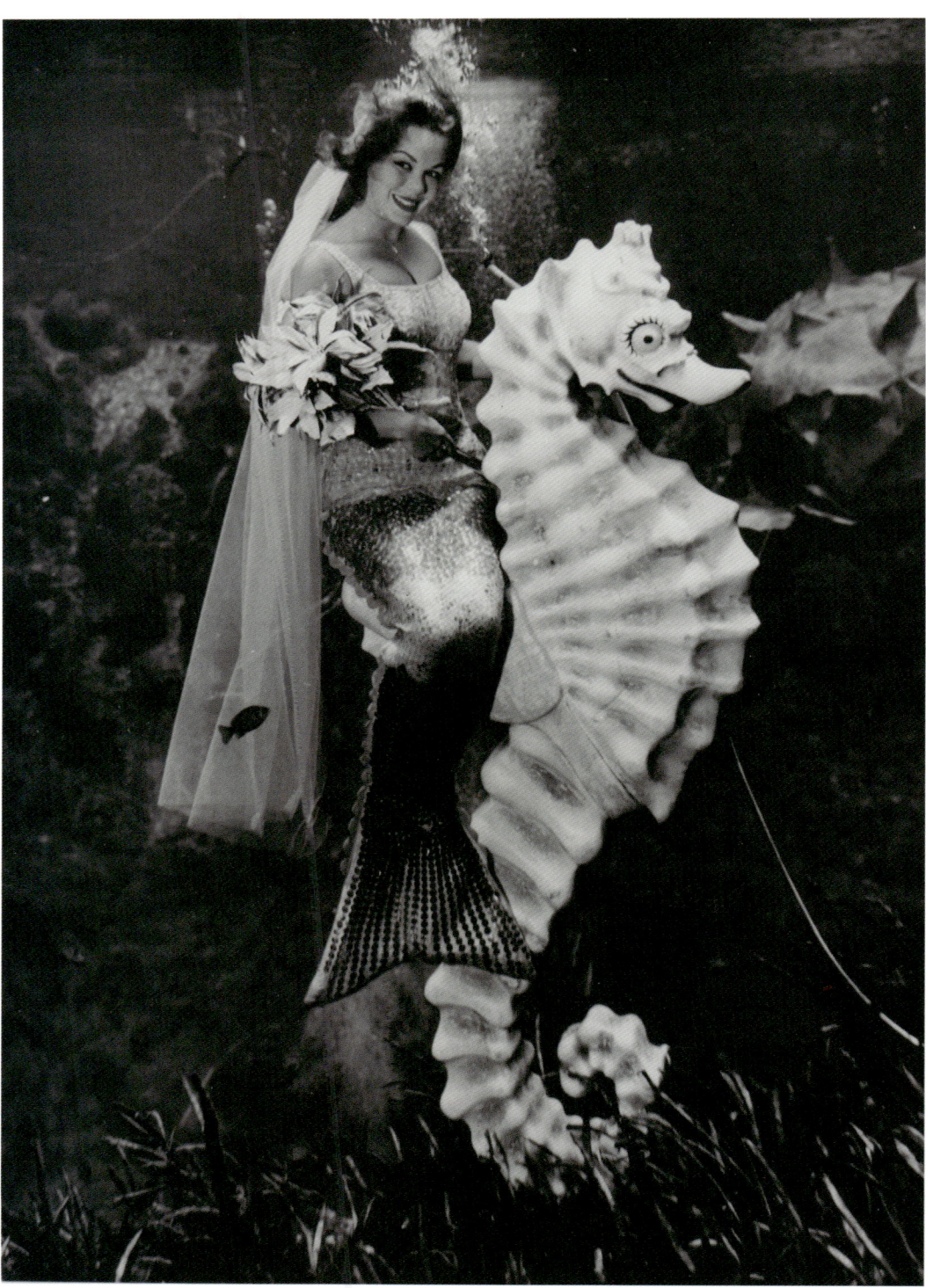

Barbara Owens rides Bubbles the Seahorse
on her way to an imaginary wedding, 1962.
Photo by Sparky Schumacher. By permission of Sparky Schumacher.

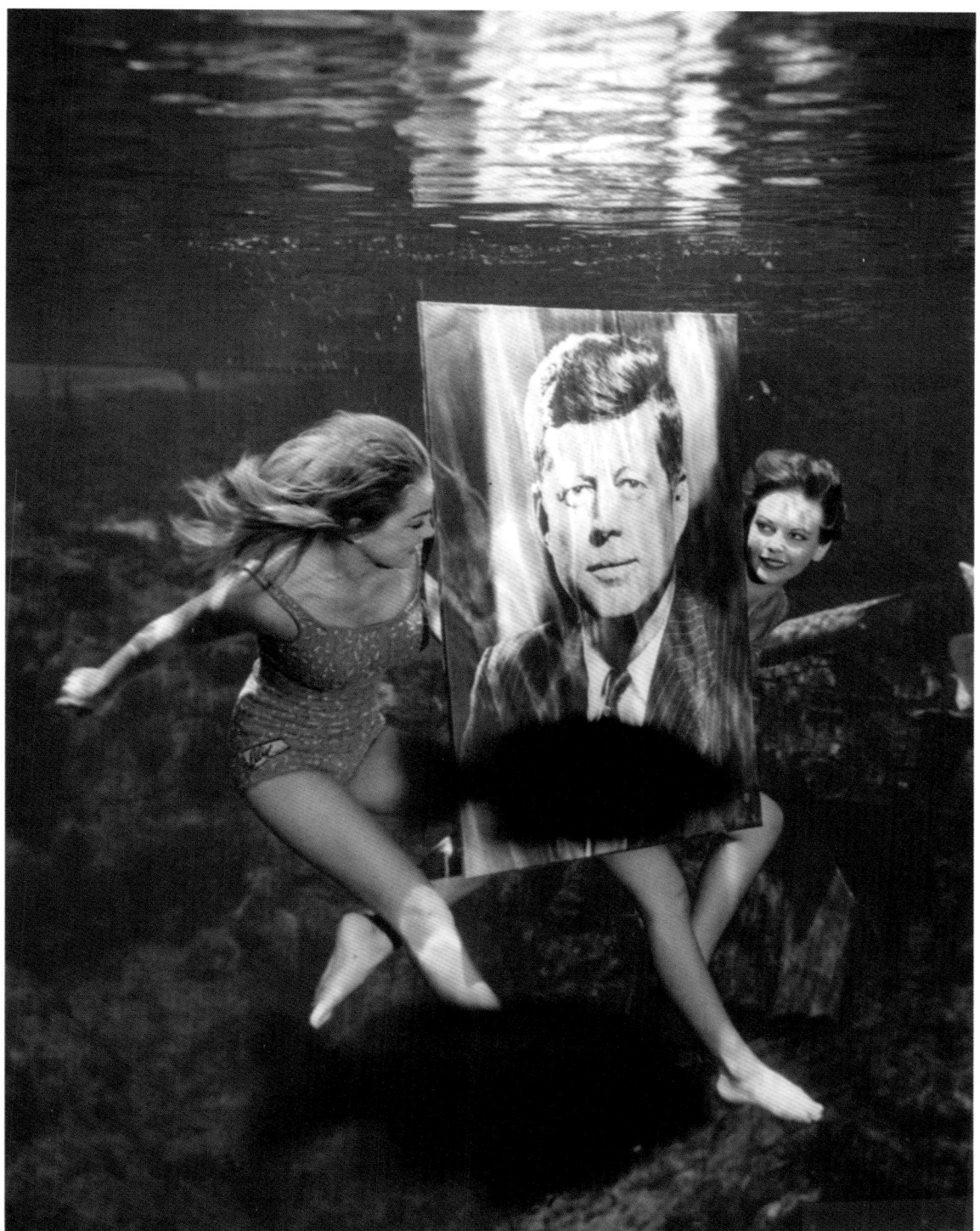

Vera Huckaby (*left*) and Marjorie Hite honor
President John F. Kennedy. Even the fish get
in on the action, 1963. By permission of Vera
Huckaby.

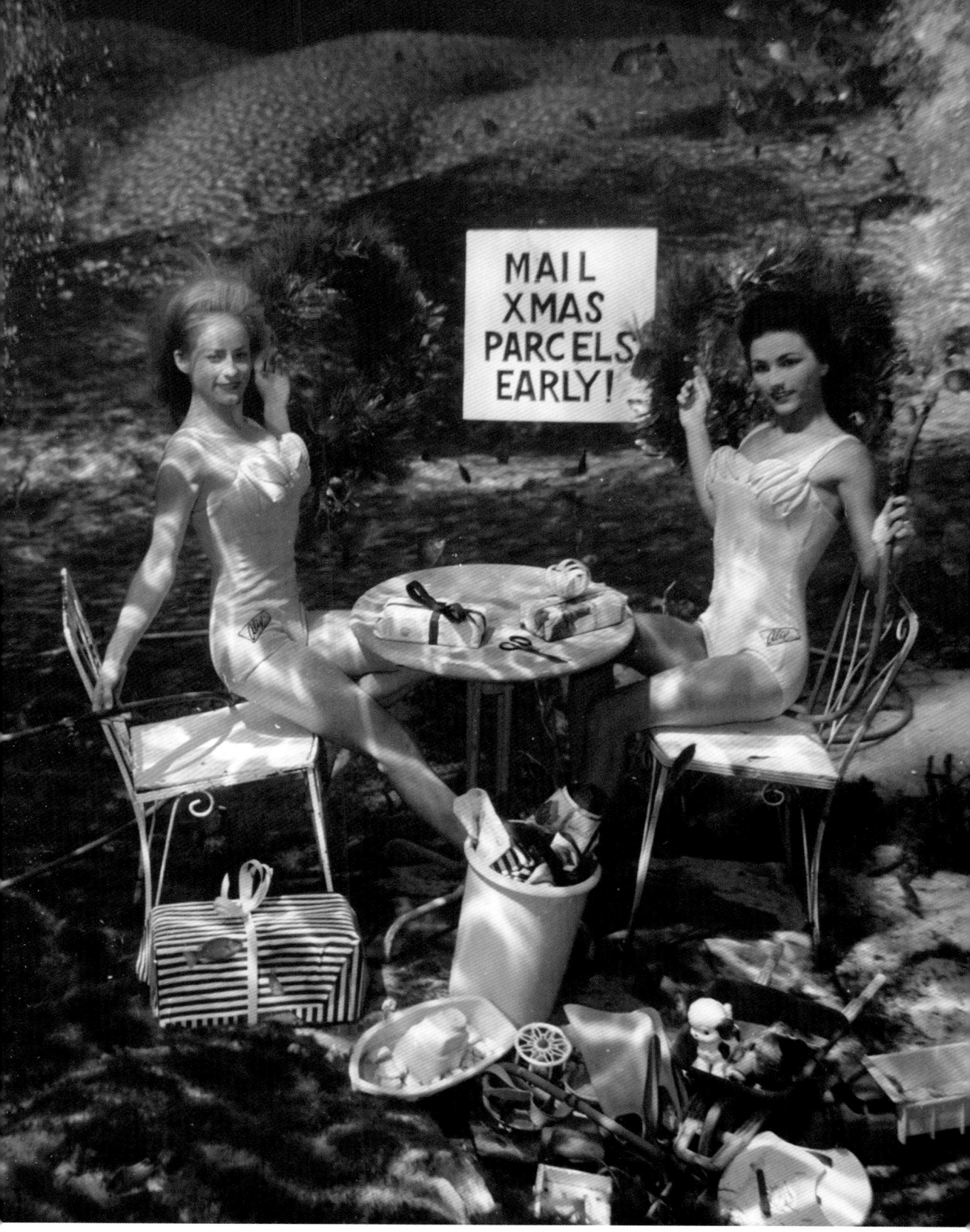

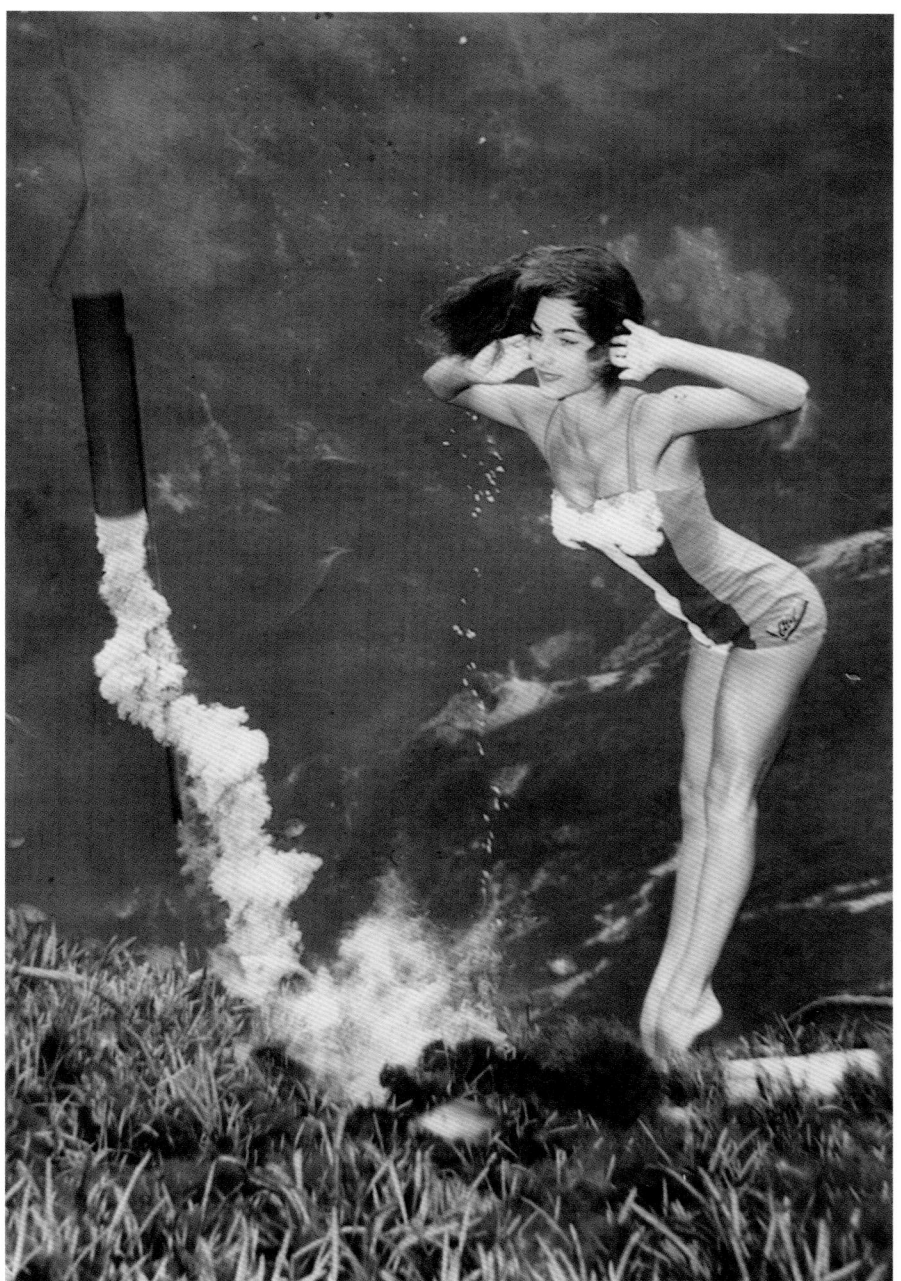

Facing page: In 1962 Weeki Wachee sent out this
Christmas reminder to newspapers across the
country. Terry Hamlet (*left*) and Kay Finney sit before wrapped presents that are suspiciously similar
to bricks. By permission of Kay Finney.

Above: Fireworks underwater? They sure are quiet.
Kay Finney gets wet to celebrate the Fourth of
July, 1954. By permission of Kay Finney.

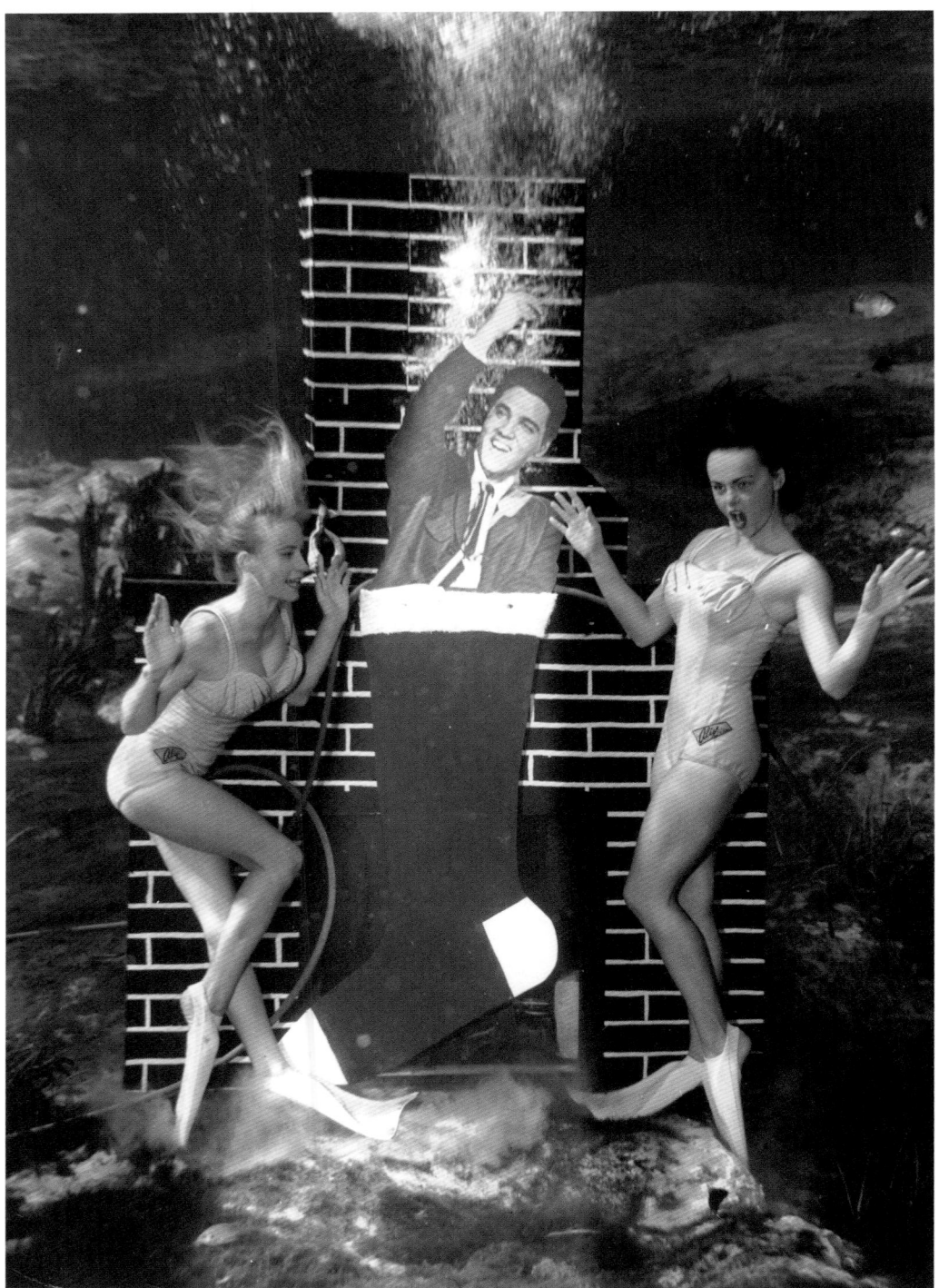

The real Elvis arrived at Weeki Wachee in 1961. Two years later, mermaids Terry Hamlet (*left*) and Sandy Lawhun celebrated Christmas with his cutout to demonstrate that his underwater fan club was still going strong. By permission of Alan Scott.

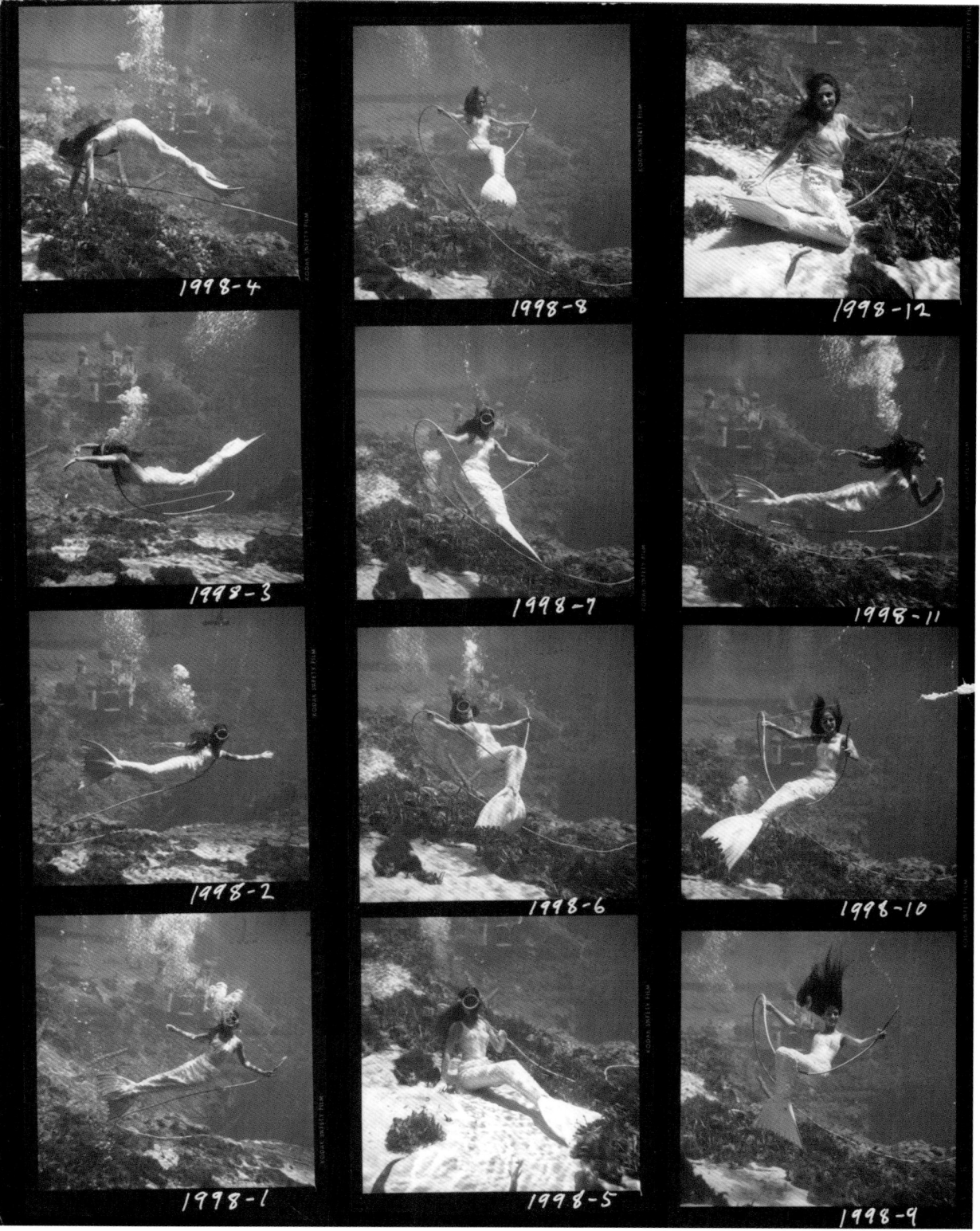

This proof sheet shows some of the poses
Genie Young goes through to get one shot
good enough to send out to the papers,
1964–65. By permission of Genie Young.

Bonnie Georgiadis rides a dolphin in this 1966 public relations photo. Photo by Sparky Schumacher. By permission of Sparky Schumacher.

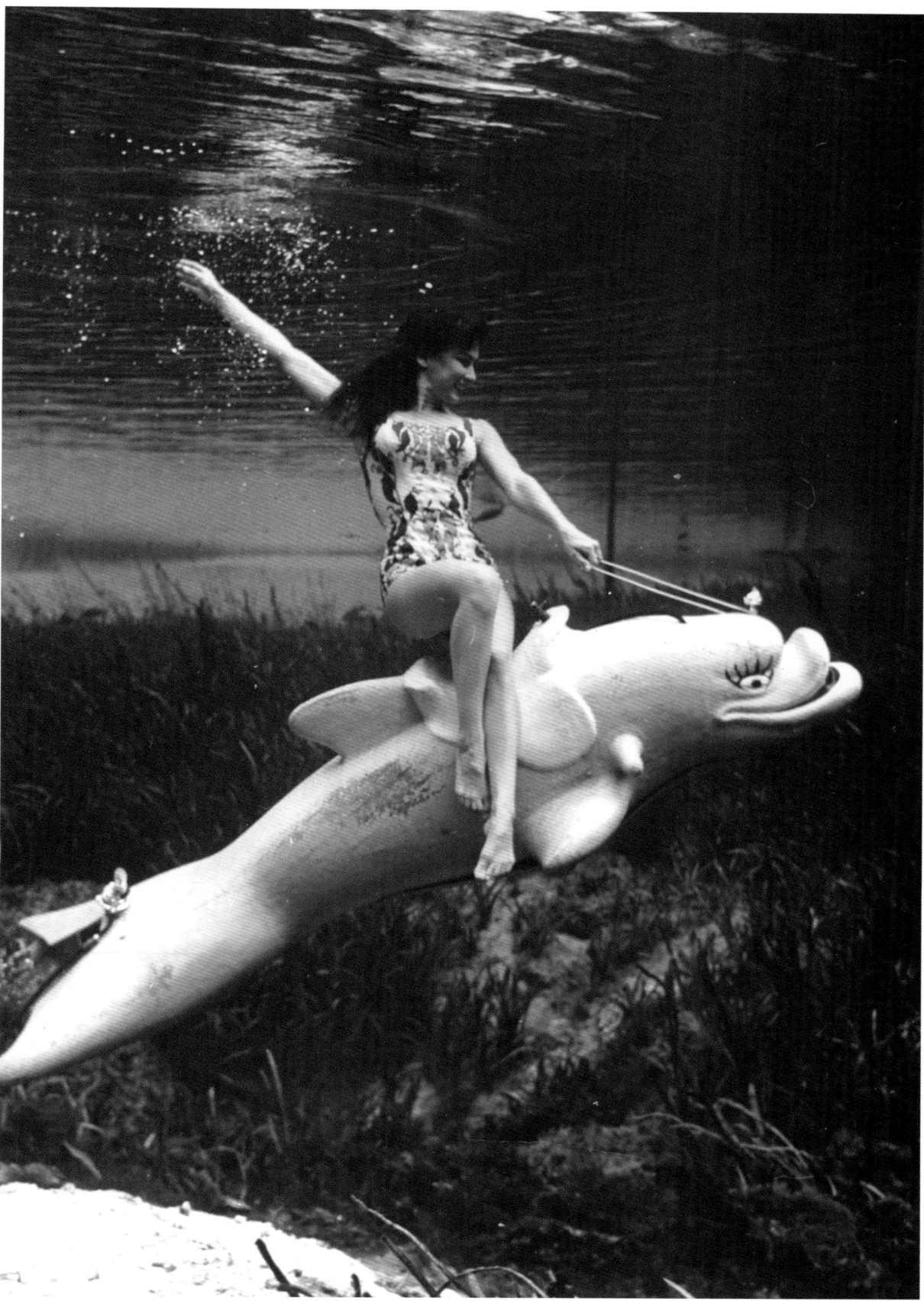

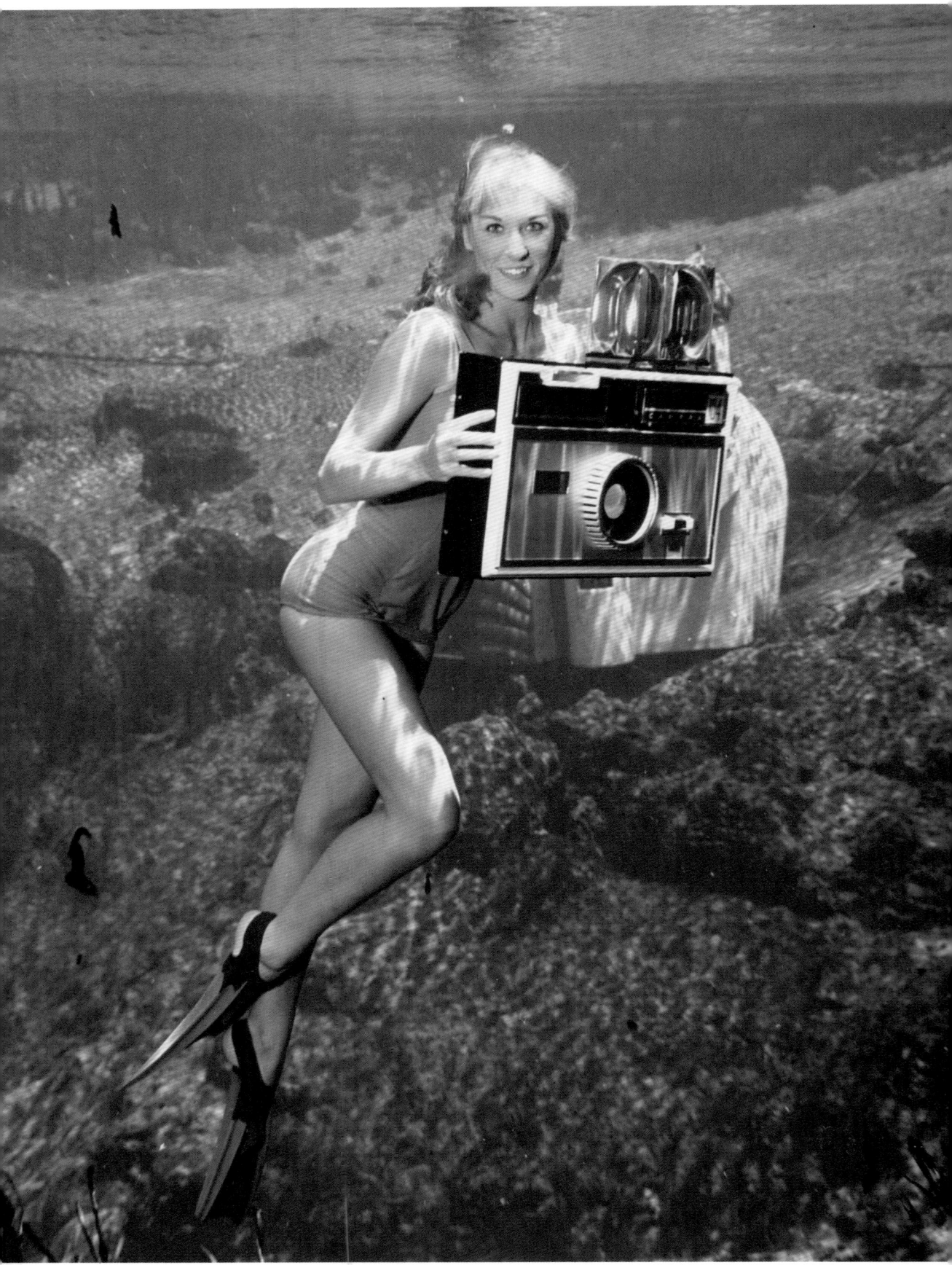

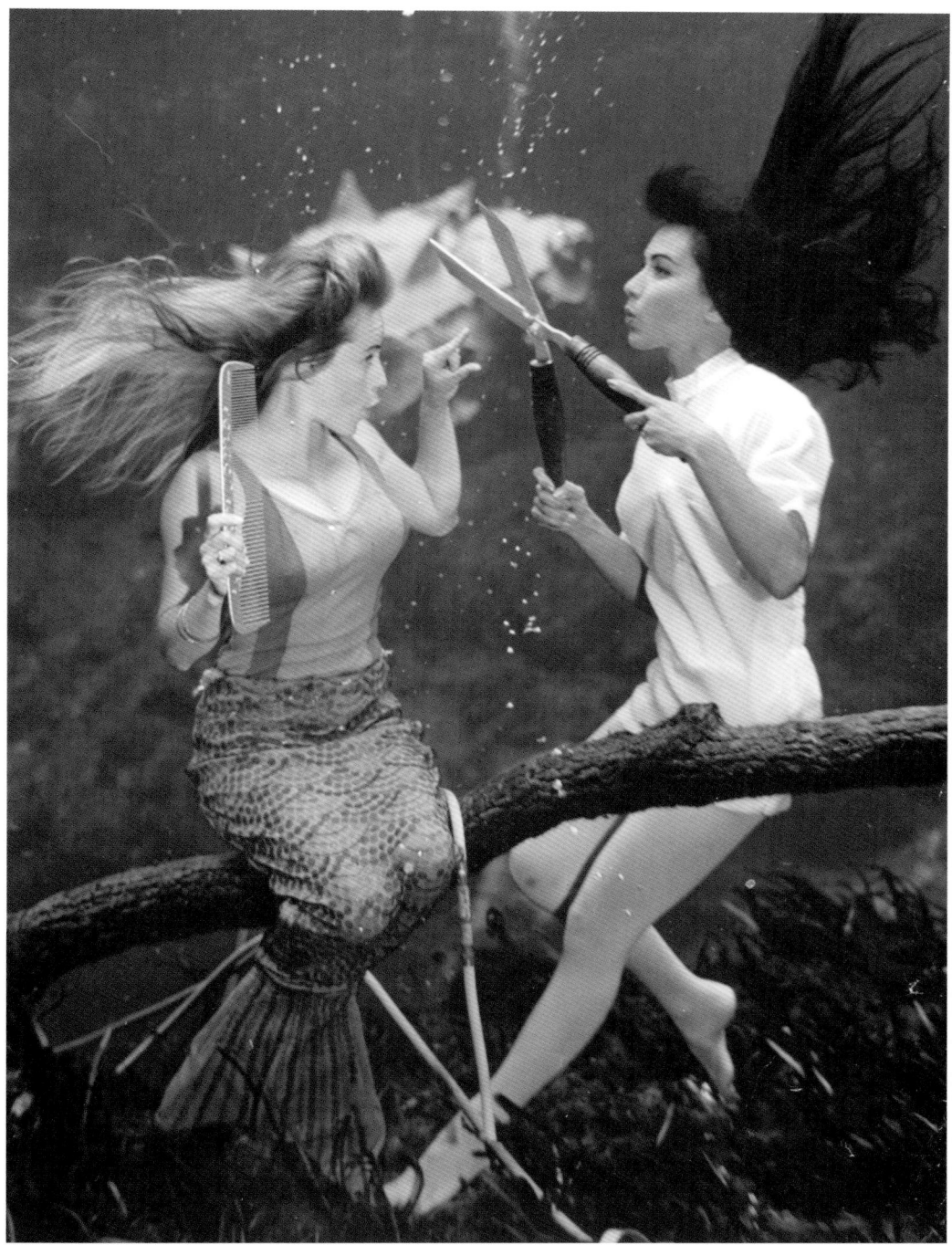

Facing page: Mermaid shutterbug Tracy Williams demon-strates underwater photography at its best with this very wide lens, 1966. By permission of Allen Scott.

Above: Just a little off the top, says Mermaid Terry Hamlet to clipper-wielding Bonnie Georgiadis. Bonnie's husband was a barber, and now she wants to try her hand at cutting hair, 1966. By permission of Bonnie Georgiadis.

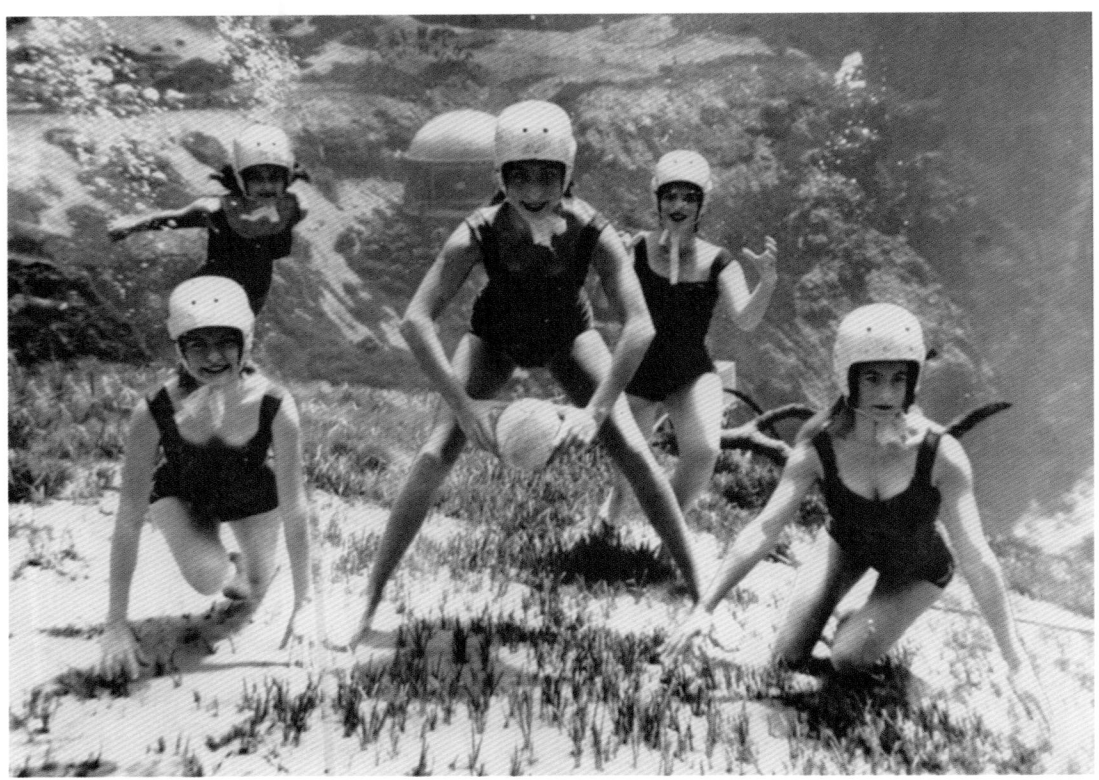

Above: Apparently the mermaids played football in between shows, 1967. By permission of Bonnie Georgiadis.

Facing page: All those bream and only one little bass—and he's not big enough to swallow any of those guys. Bonnie Georgiadis feeds them all, 1967. By permission of Bonnie Georgiadis.

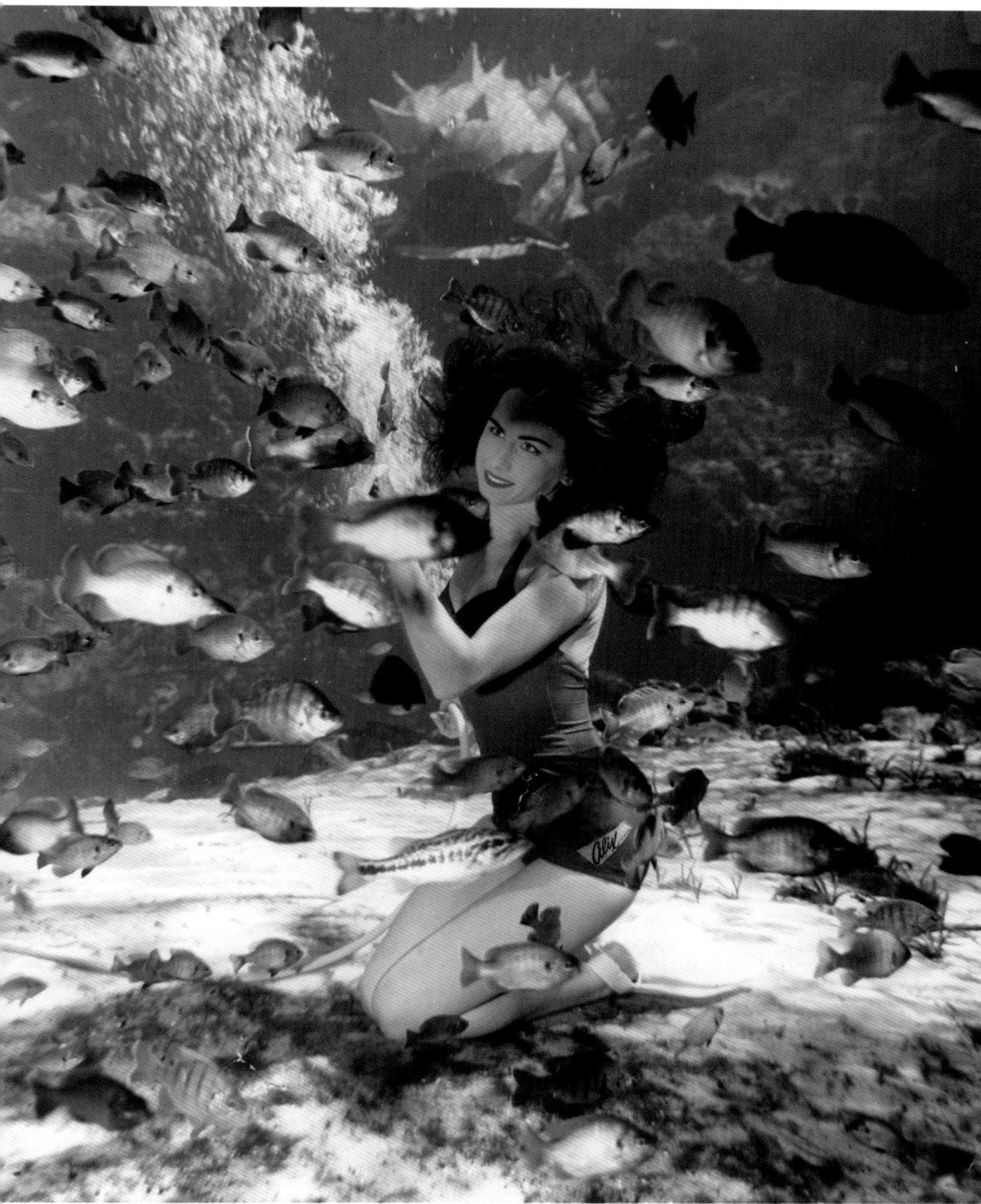

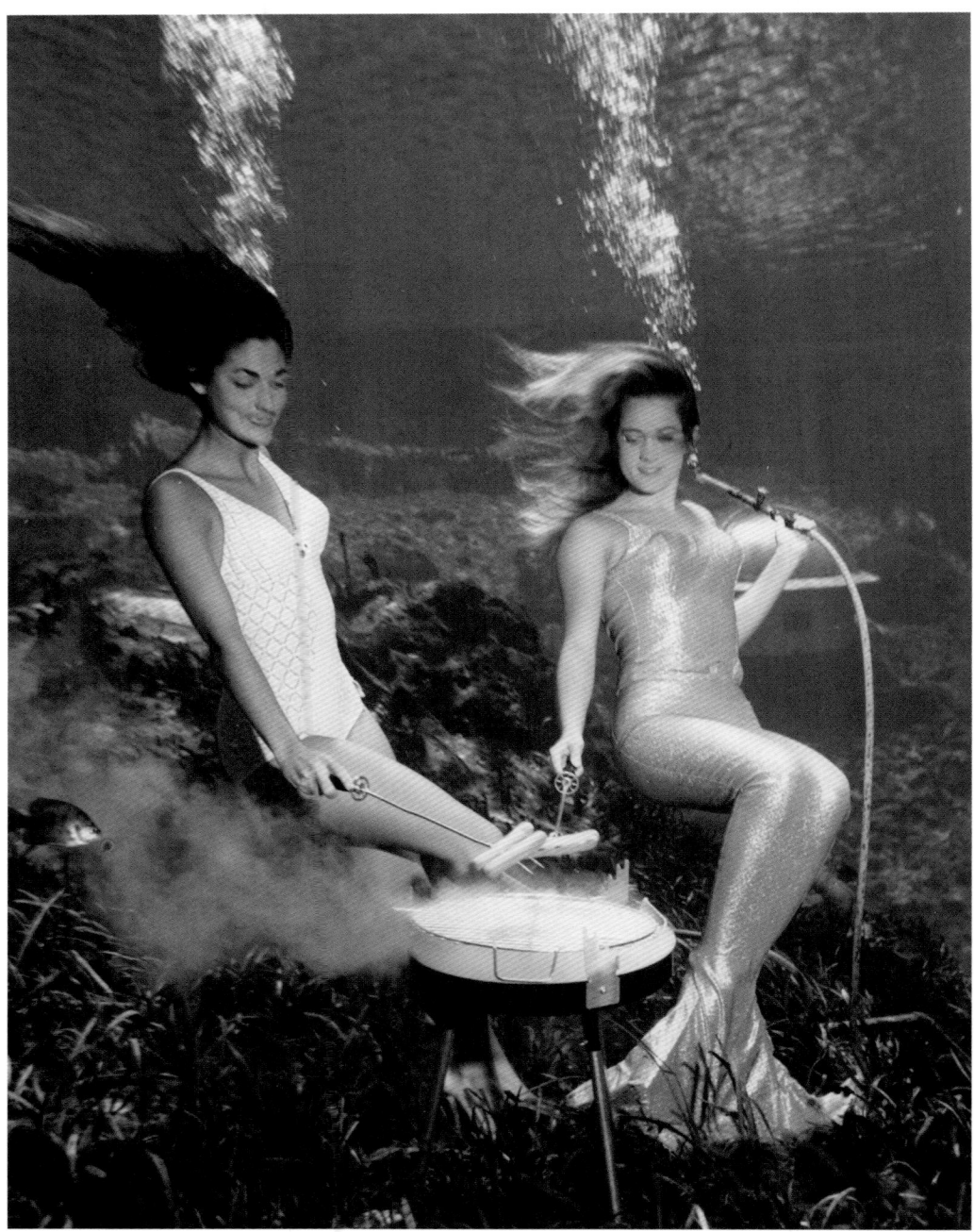

Above: Marianne Hope brings the tail to this mermaid tailgate party with Genie Young. Even though they are underwater, they have no trouble keeping the coals hot, 1969–70. By permission of Genie Young.

Facing page: Shinko Akasofu Wheeler strikes a pose in this 1970 public relations photo. By permission of Genie Young.

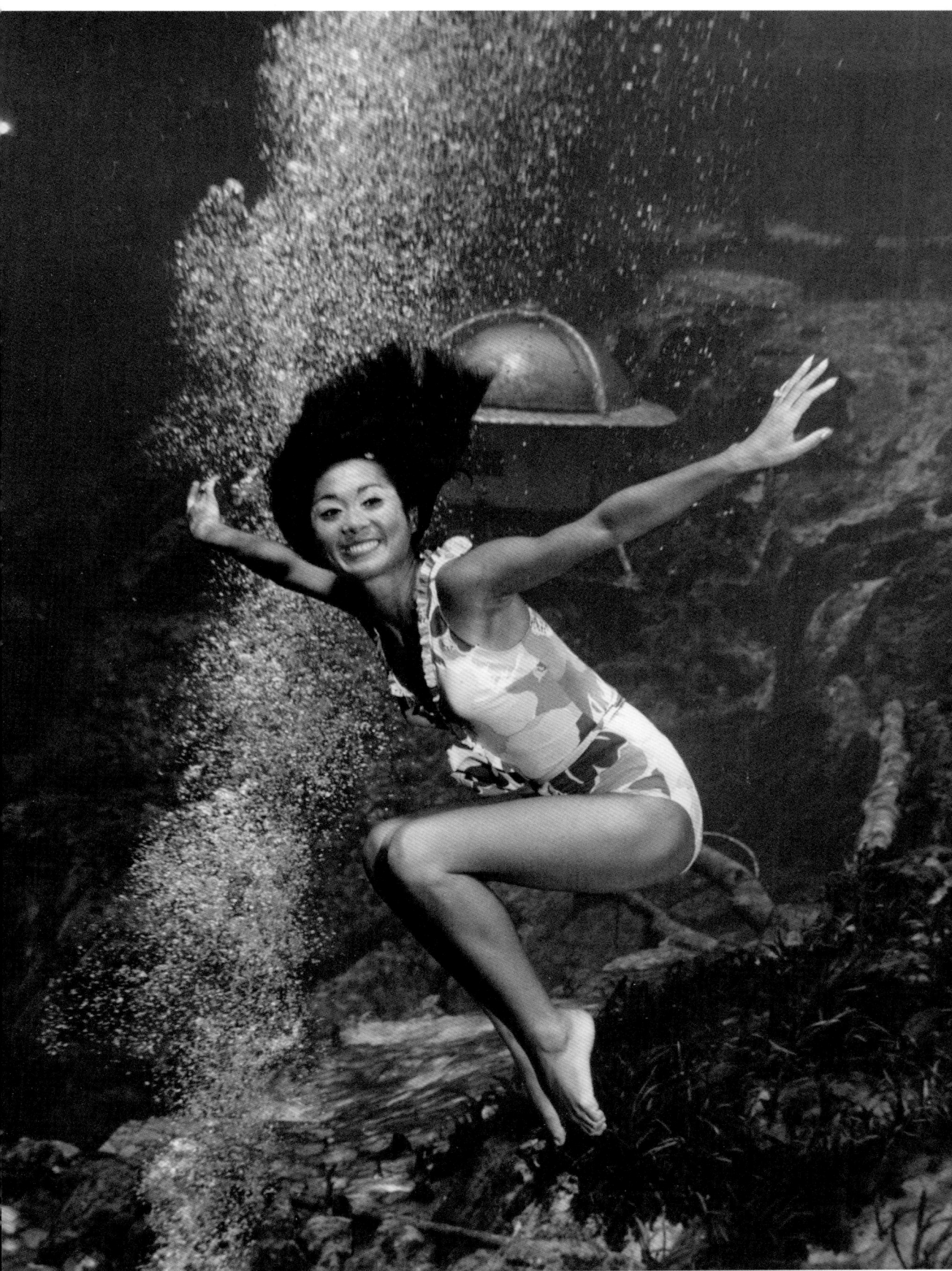

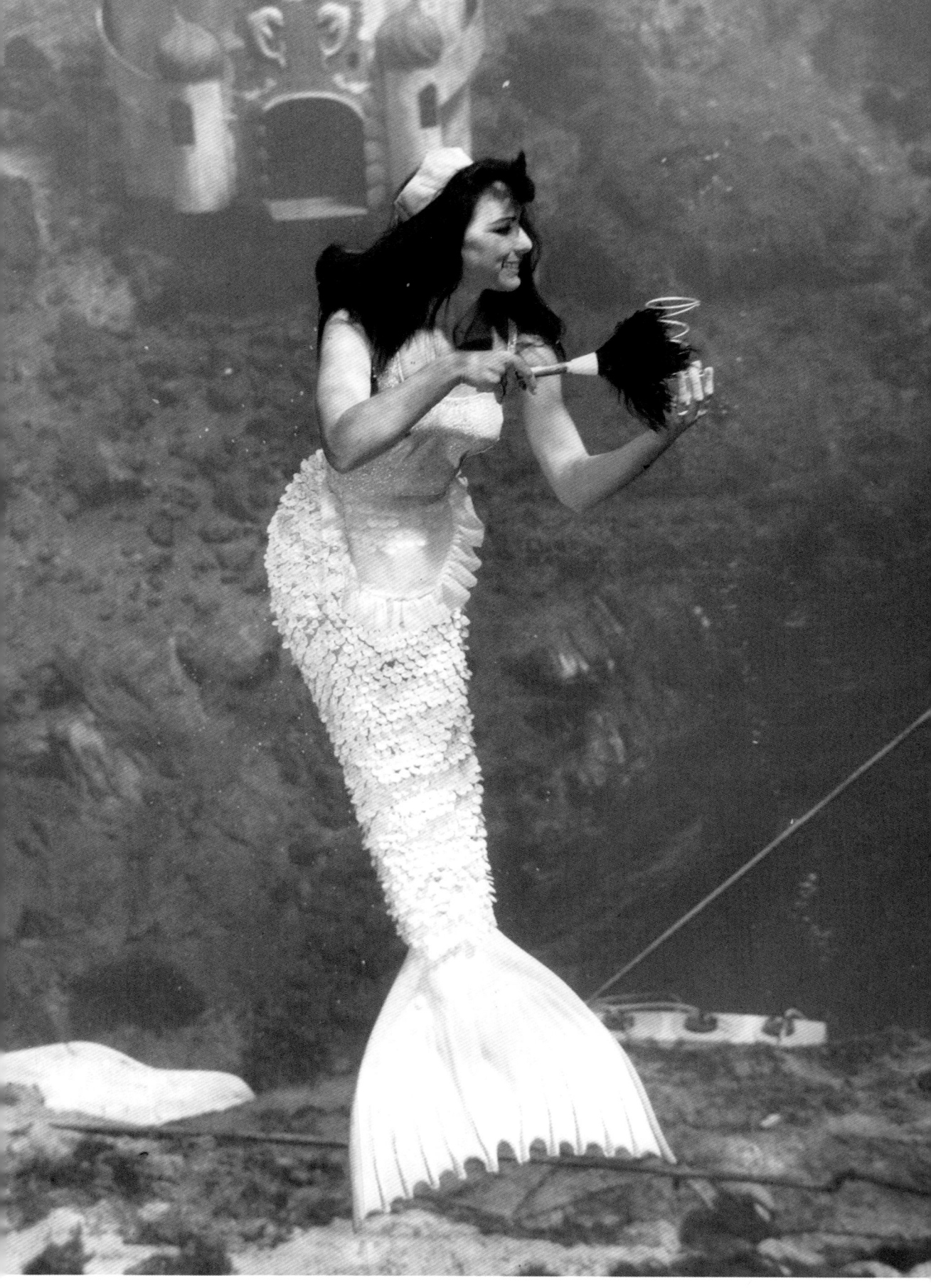

Bonnie Georgiadis donned a frilly apron to
do a little spring cleaning in this promotional
photograph, 1967. Photo by Sparky Schumacher. By permission of Bonnie Georgiadis.

No bubbles? No air hose? Pat Cleveland shows how effortless it is to hold her breath underwater, 1975. By permission of Pat Cleveland.

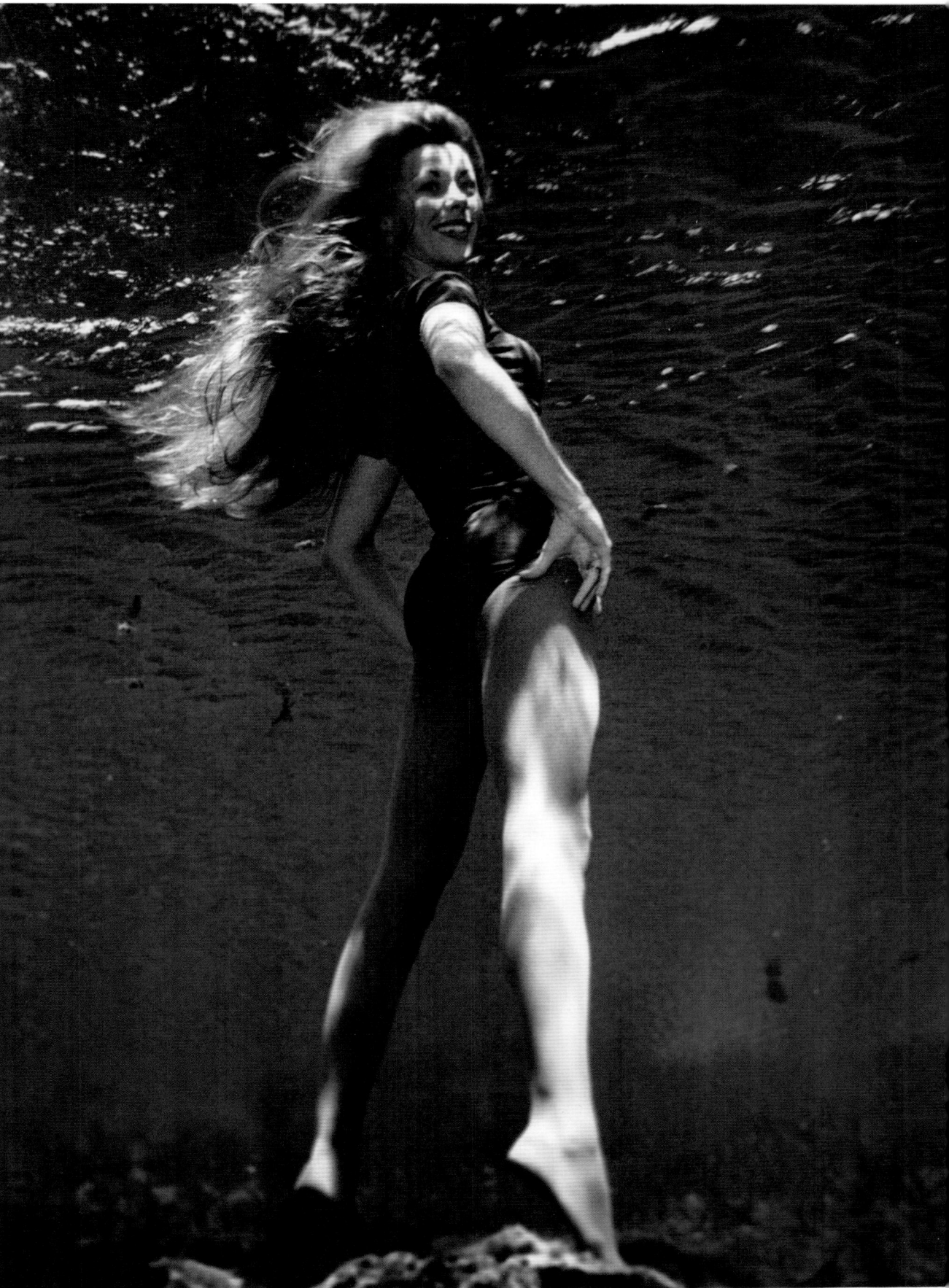

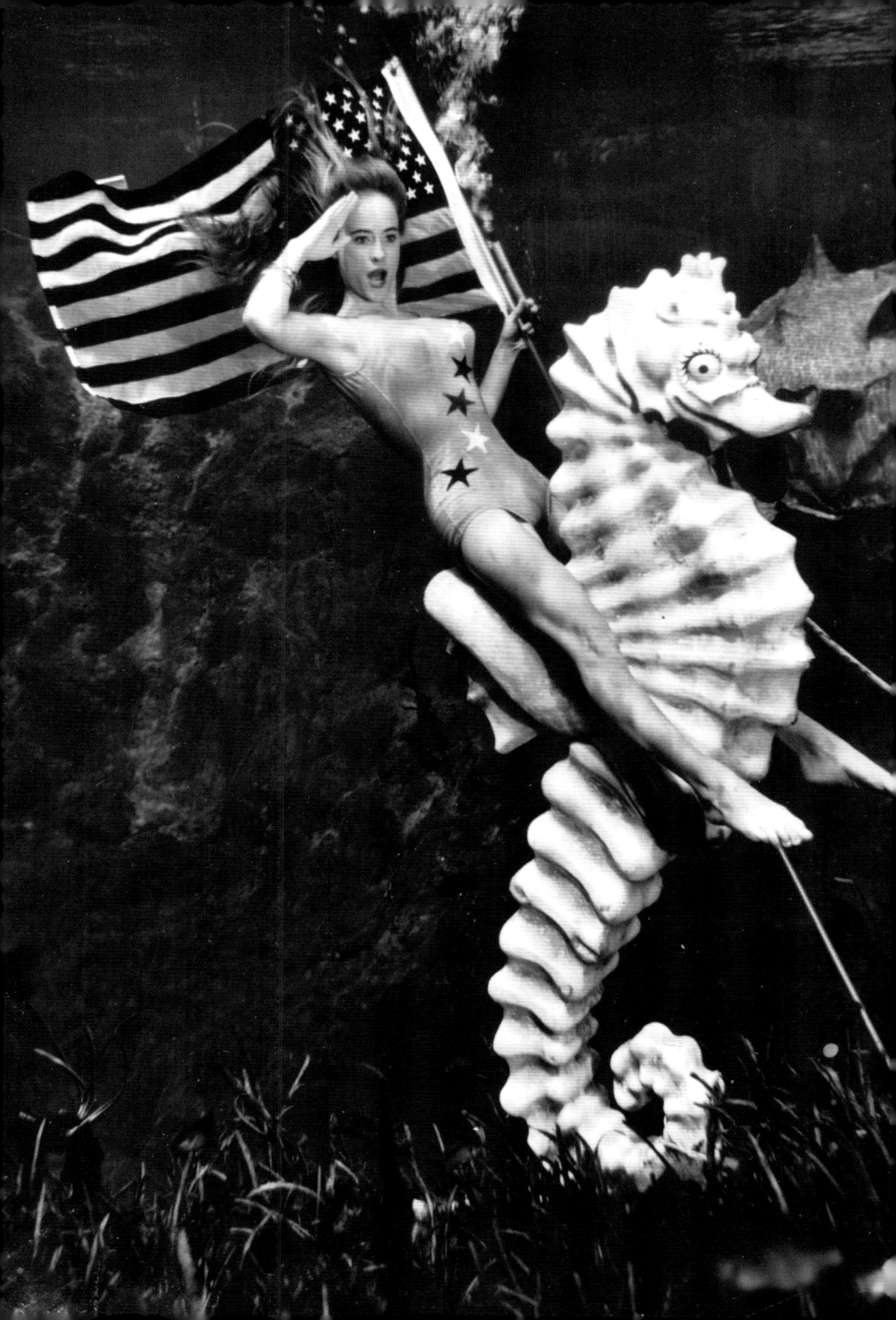

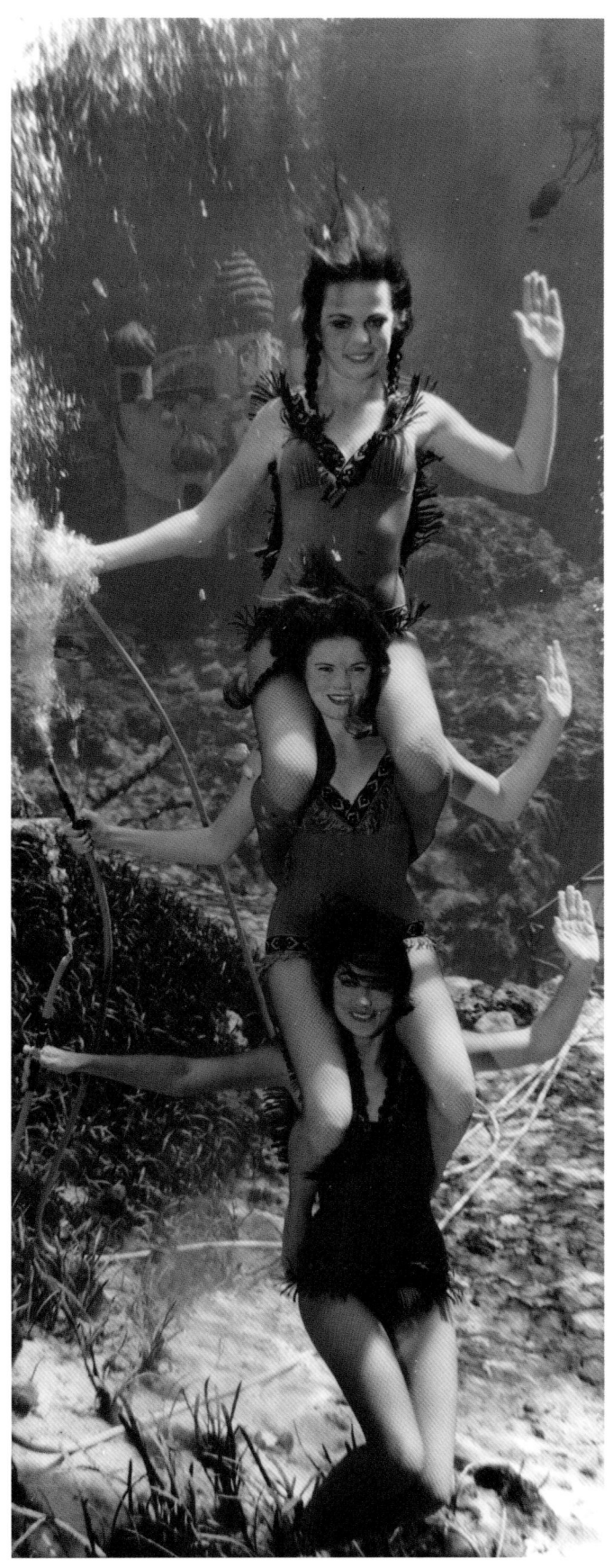

Facing page: Terry Hamlet takes a ride on Bubbles the Seahorse to celebrate the "Spirit of '76." By permission of Bonita Colson.

Left: Uuga, Uuga, Wig Wam! Peter Pan's Indian friends (Dawn Douglas, *top*, Beverly Sutton, *middle*, and Genie Young, *bottom*) perform a tribal totem dance, 1971. By permission of Bonita Colson.

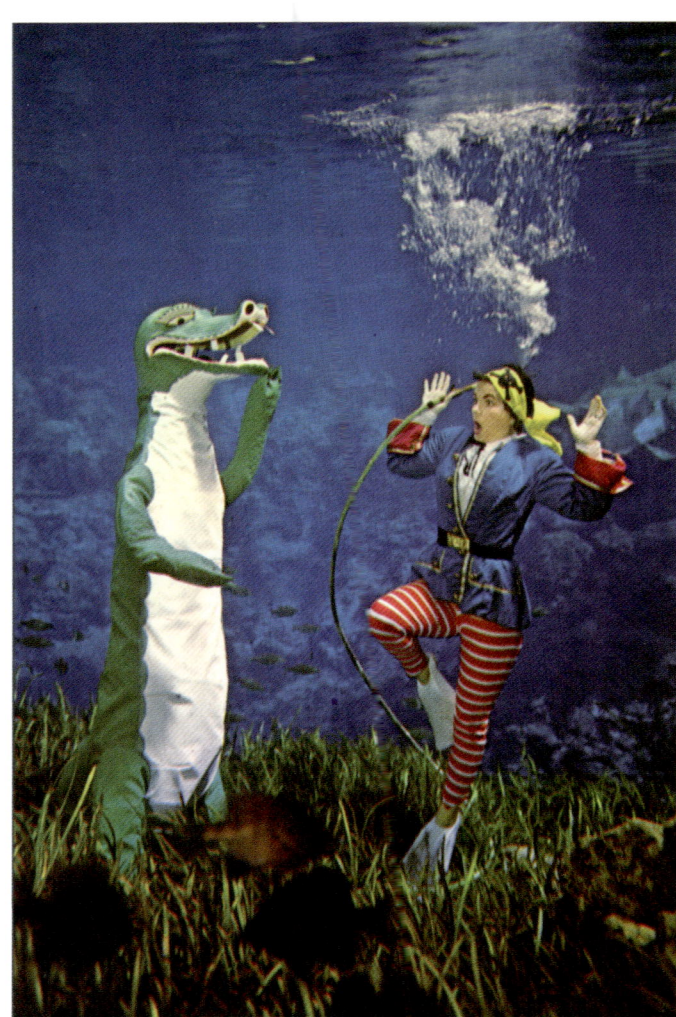

Left: Shirley Walls looks frightened of the crocodile in this scene from *The Mermaids and the Pirates*, 1962. Photo by Sparky Schumacher. By permission of Bonita Colson.

Below: Cheryl Rhodes (*left*) and Bonnie Georgiadis ride a bicycle built for two in the *Underwater Follies* of 1963. Note the blue air tanks tied to their backs. Photo by Claude Long. By permission of Genie Young.

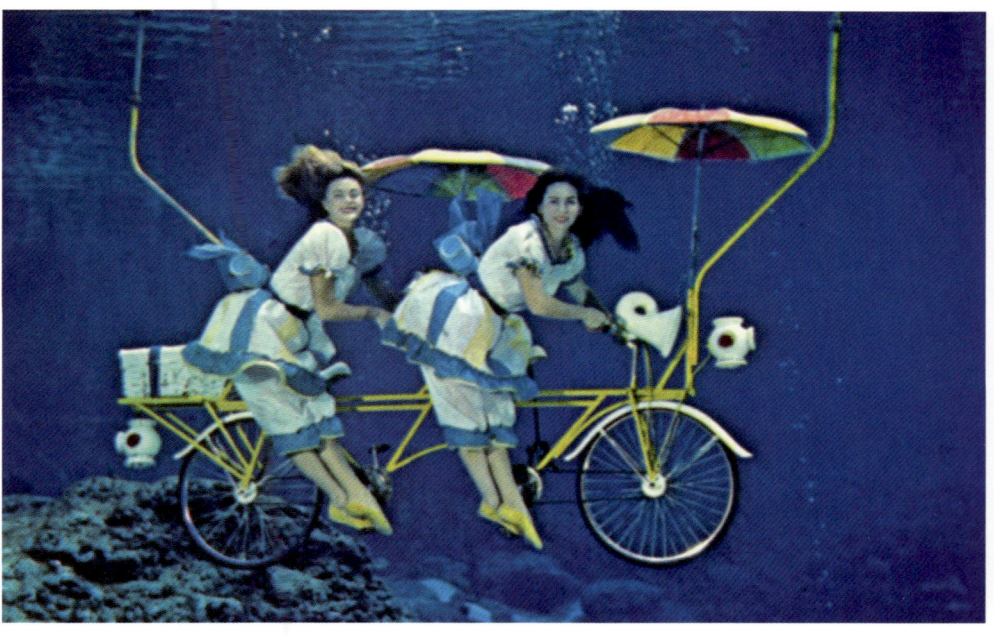

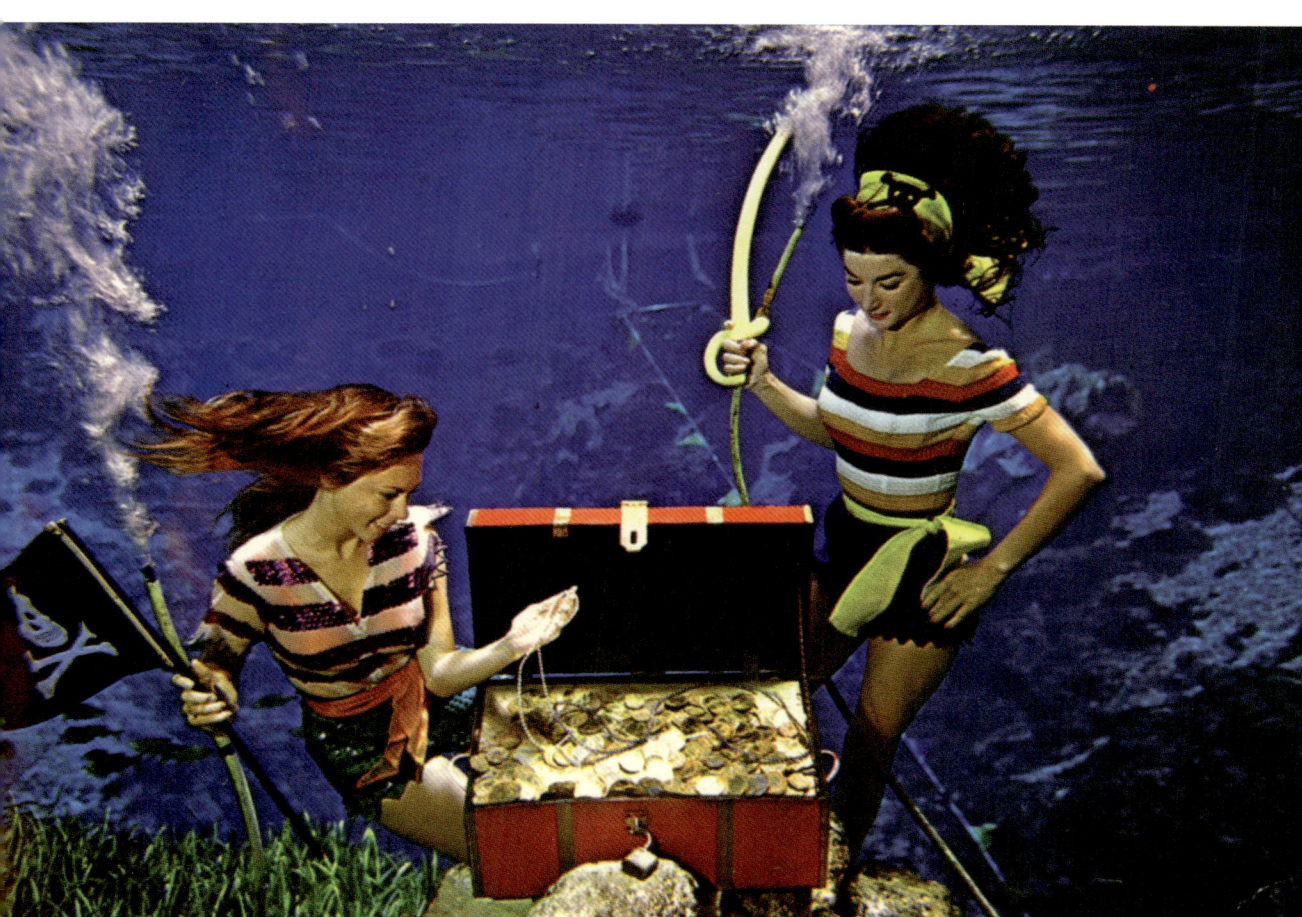

Diane (Danny) Halbrook (*left*) and Nancy Harkness have discovered a pirate's weekly pay in *The Mermaids and the Pirates*, 1962. Photo by Sparky Schumacher. By permission of Bonita Colson

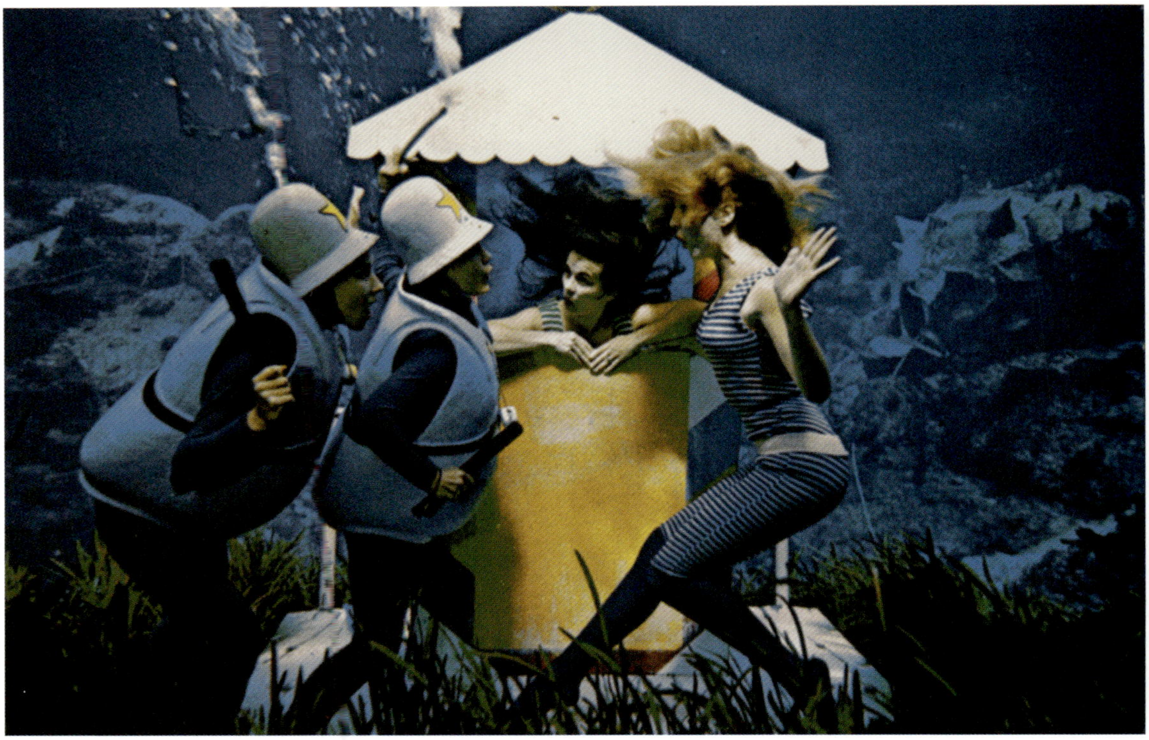

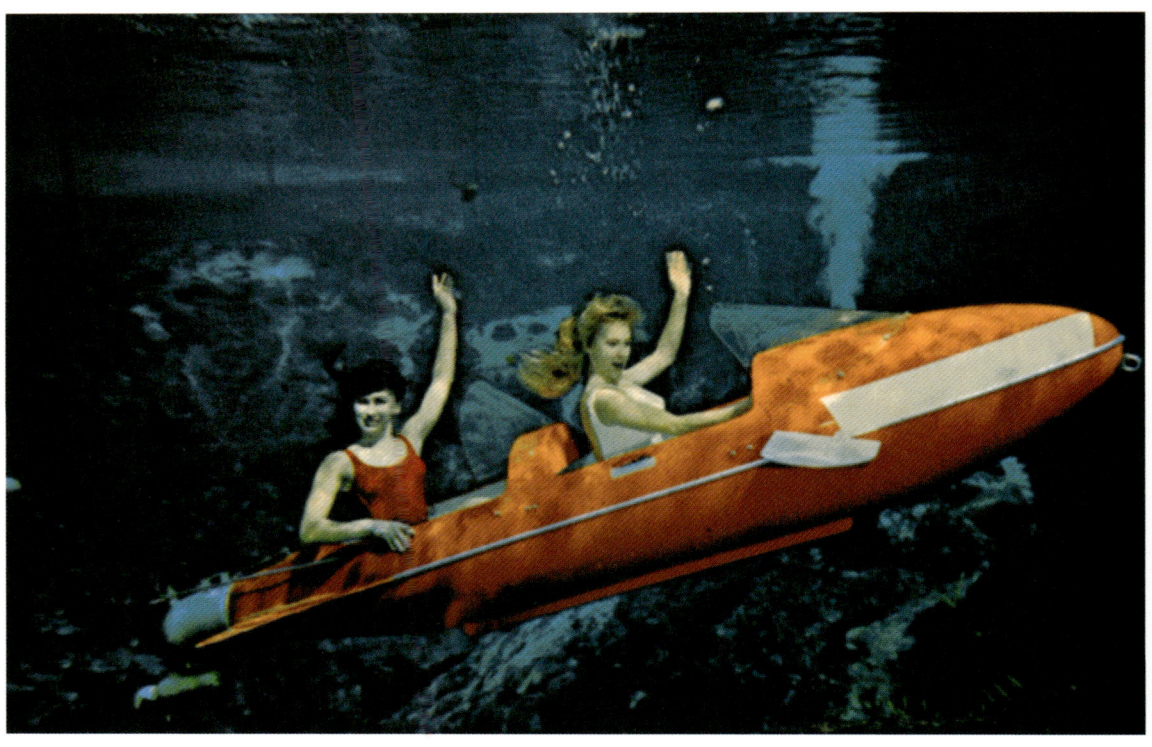

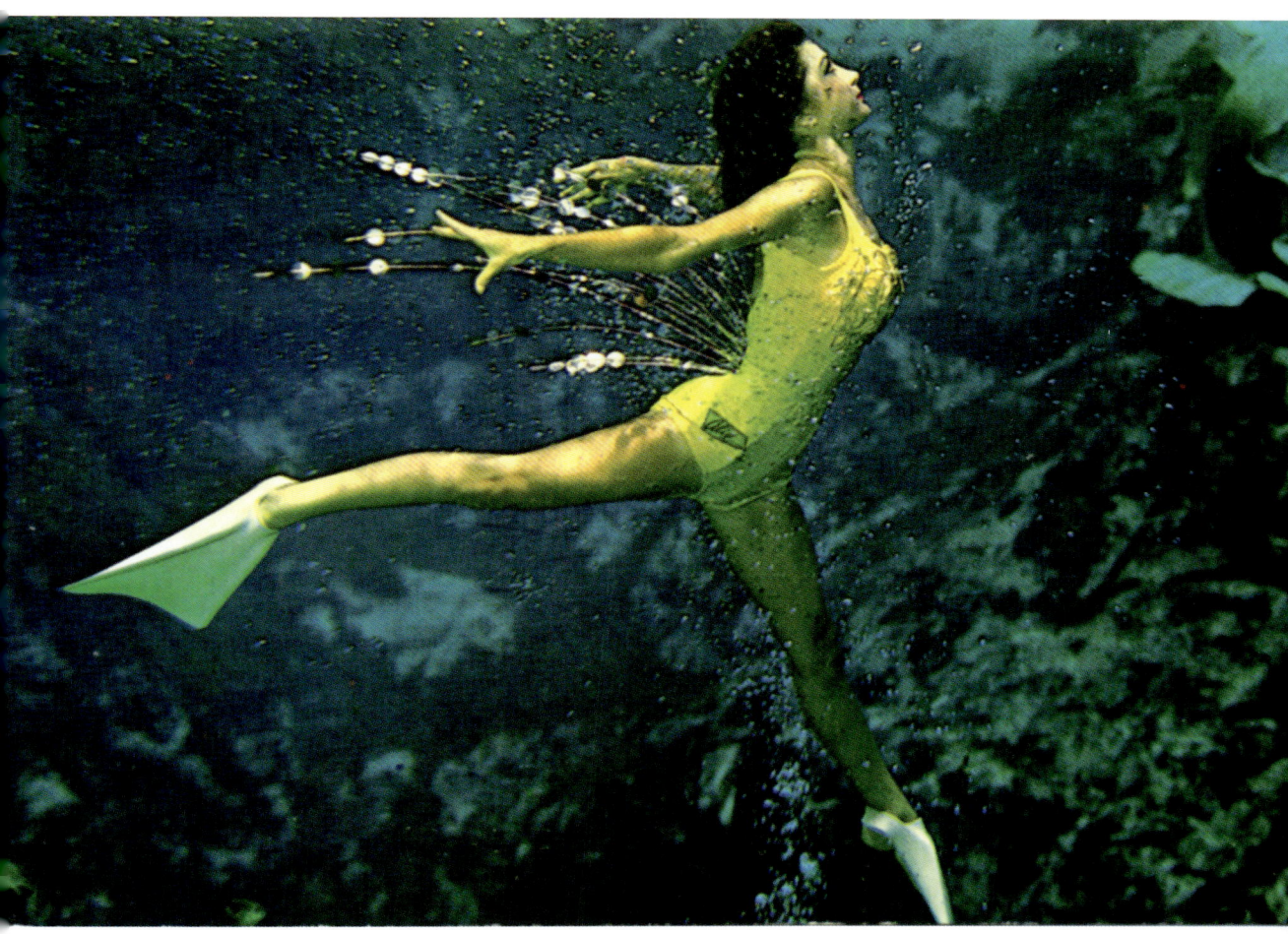

Facing page, top: In this scene from *Underwater Follies*, Keystone Cops Bonnie Georgiadis (*left*) and Debby Poore, arrest flappers Shirley Wall and Barbara Bates (*right*), 1963. Photo by Sparky Schumacher. By permission of Bonita Colson.

Facing page, bottom: For this shot the space-aged scooter was held in place with strong fishing line tied to anchors. Then, Bonnie Georgiadis (*left*) and Terry Hamlet took a deep breath at the surface and dropped into their seats for a quick pose, 1964. By permission of Genie Young.

Above: Nancy Harkness performs a bird arabesque. The sparkling "tail feathers" were easy to swim with unless your long hair got tangled in them. The first tail was made with peacock feathers, but they wilted when they got wet, 1963. Photo by Ted Lagerberg. By permission of Bonita Colson.

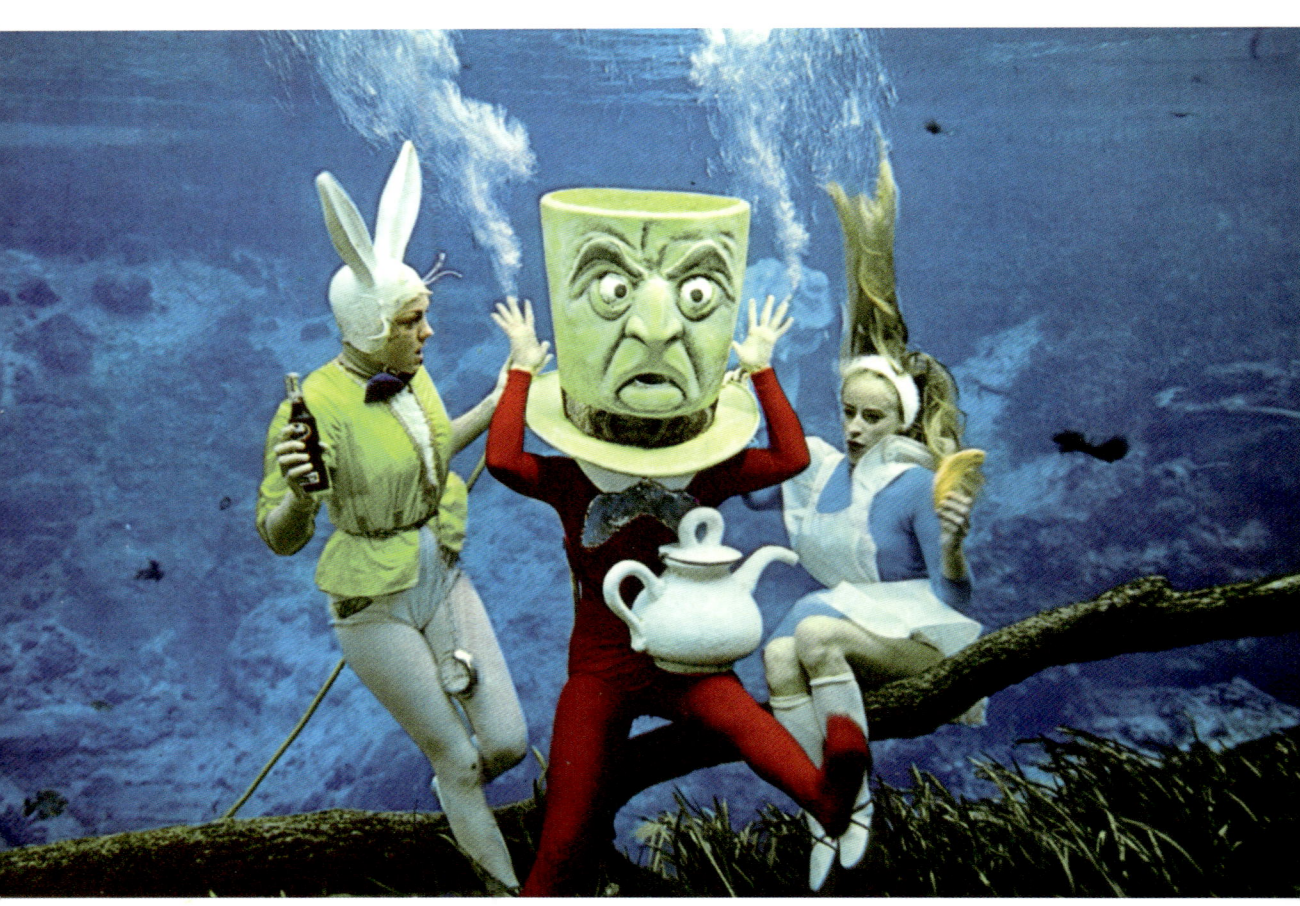

Prop designer Skimp Cumber does it again with this fiberglass and rubber Mad Hatter worn by Dede Parmer at the tea party for Alice (Terry Hamlet) and the March Hare (Vera Huckaby), 1964–65. By permission of Bonita Colson.

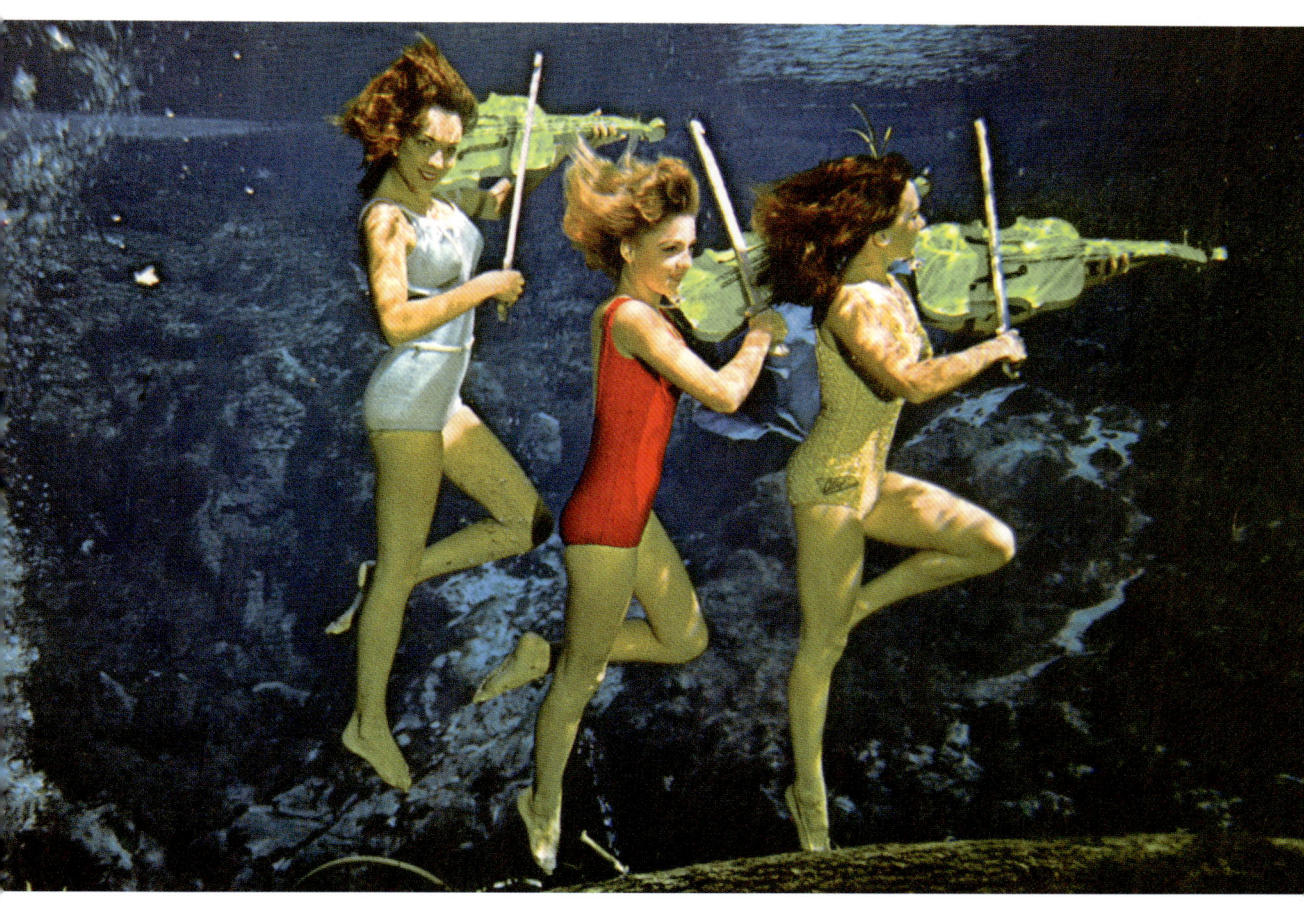

Mermaids Kay Hokstra (*left*), Vera Huckaby
(*center*), and Bonnie Georgiadis never had a
single violin lesson, but it didn't matter because their instruments had no strings, 1964.
By permission of Bonita Colson.

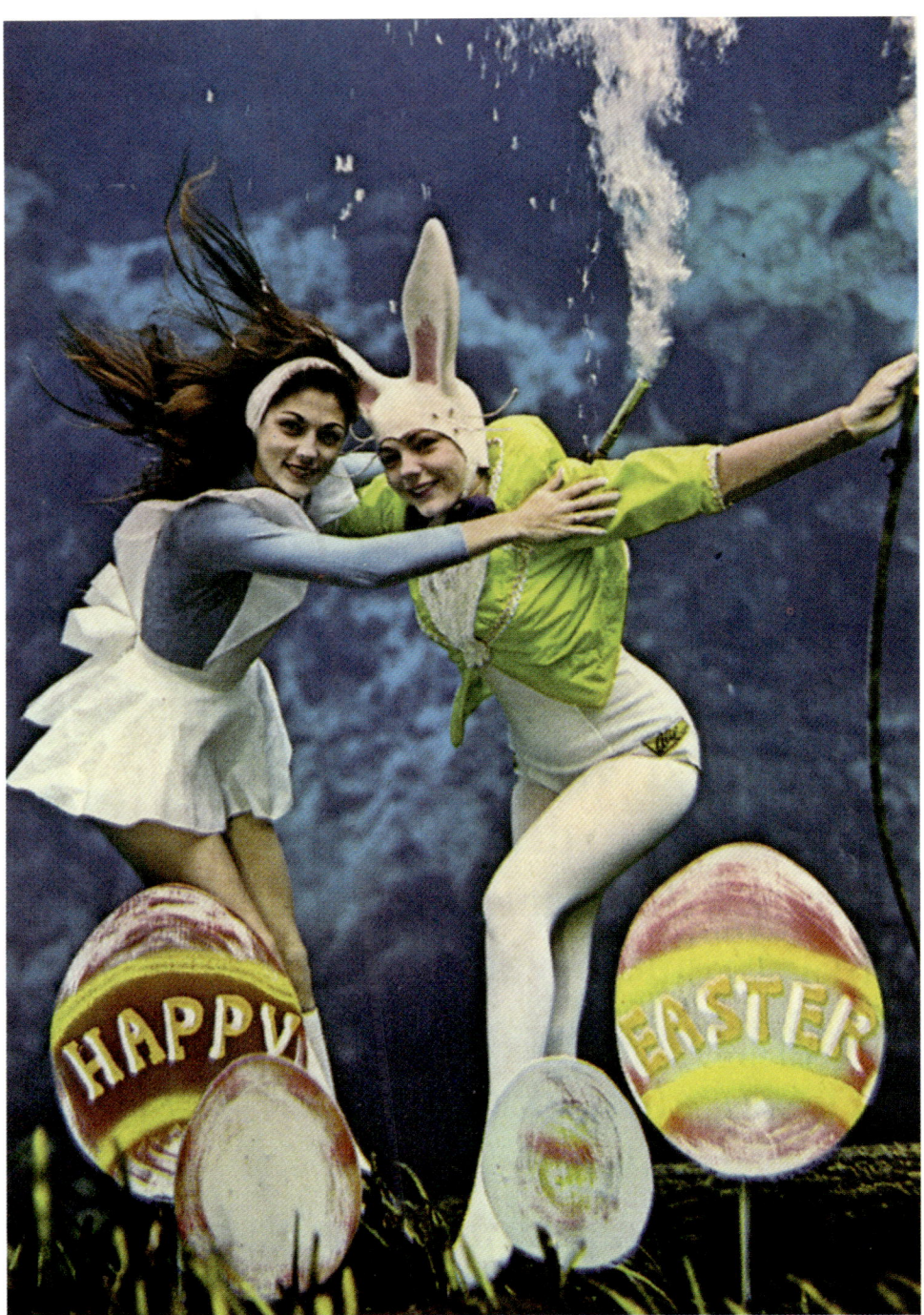

Alice in Waterland stars Genie Young (*left*) and
Nancy Brun show their support for Easter
in this promotional shot, 1964–65. Photo by
Sparky Schumacher. By permission of Sparky
Schumacher.

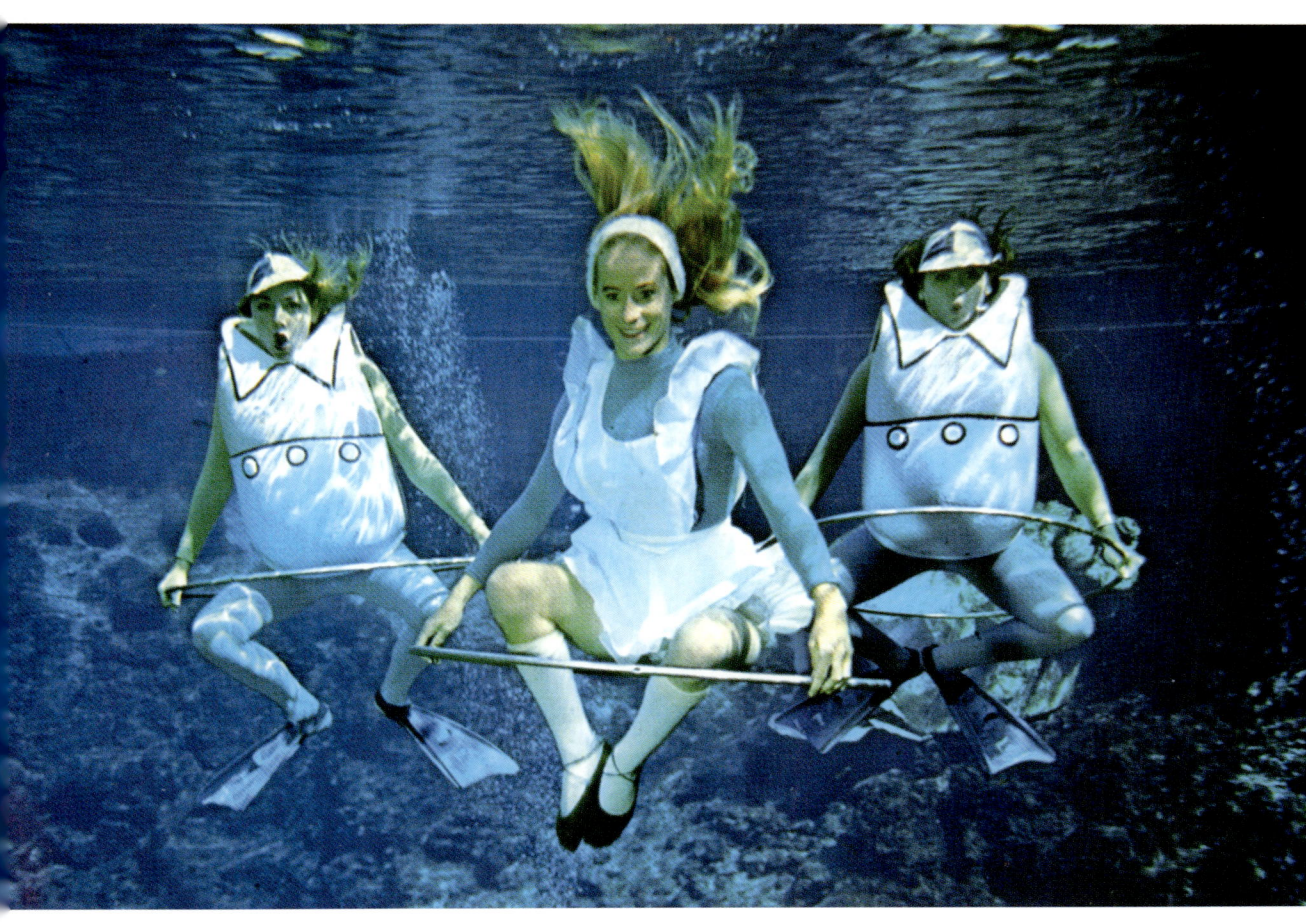

Alice (Terry Hamlet) whoops it up in *Alice in Waterland* with Tweedle Dee, played by Susan Sweeney (*left*) and Tweedle Dum, played by Tammy Craig, 1964–65. By permission of Bonita Colson.

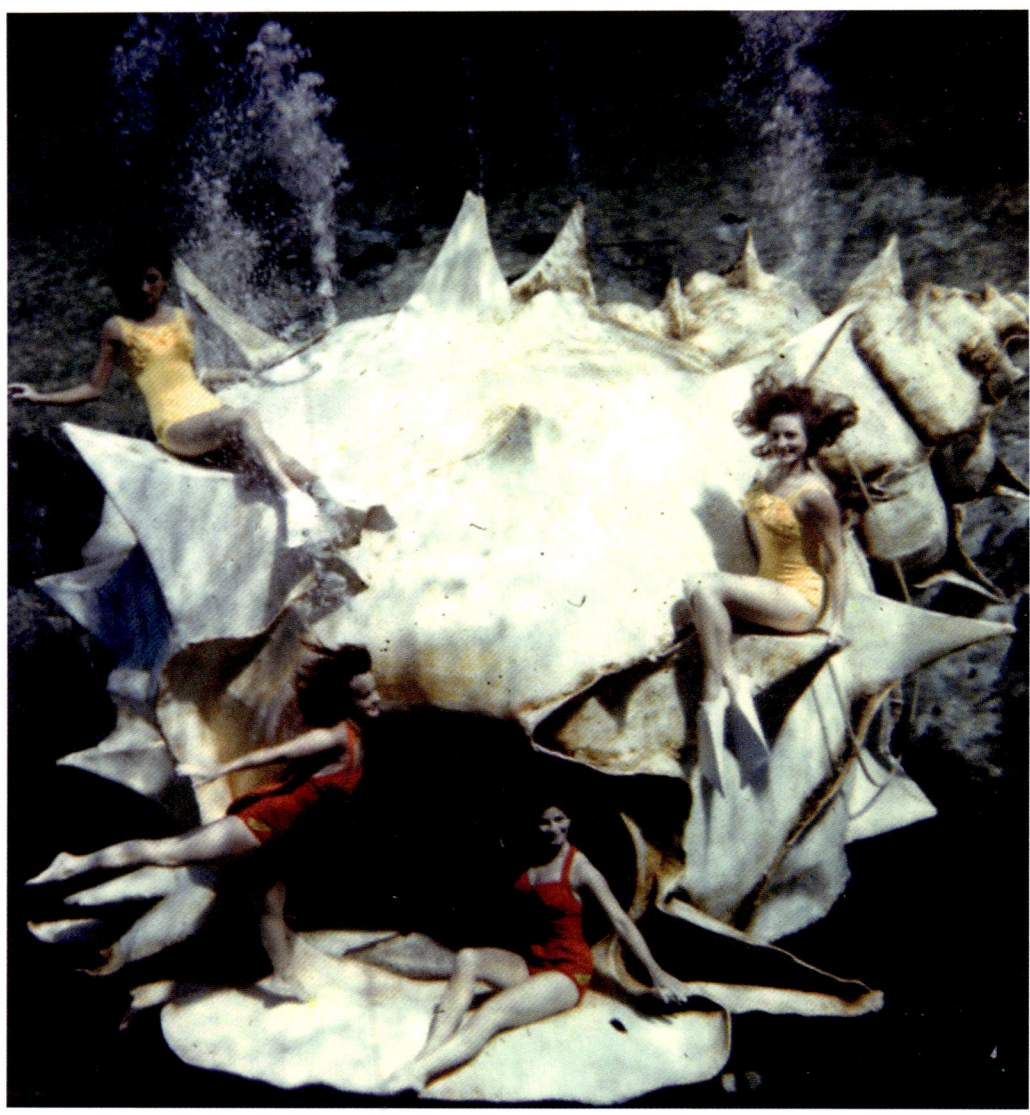

Above: Adorning the beautiful conch shell (the airlock is inside) are mermaids Nancy Harkness (*top left*), Shirley Walls (*bottom left*), Lou Spikes (*bottom right*), and Thea Whitehead (*top right*), 1964–65 By permission of Bonnie Georgiadis.

Facing page: We're late! We're late! For a very important date! The March Hare (Bonnie Georgiadis) tries to hurry Alice (Carol Parrish) along, 1964–65. Photo by Sparky Schumacher. By permission of Bonnie Georgiadis.

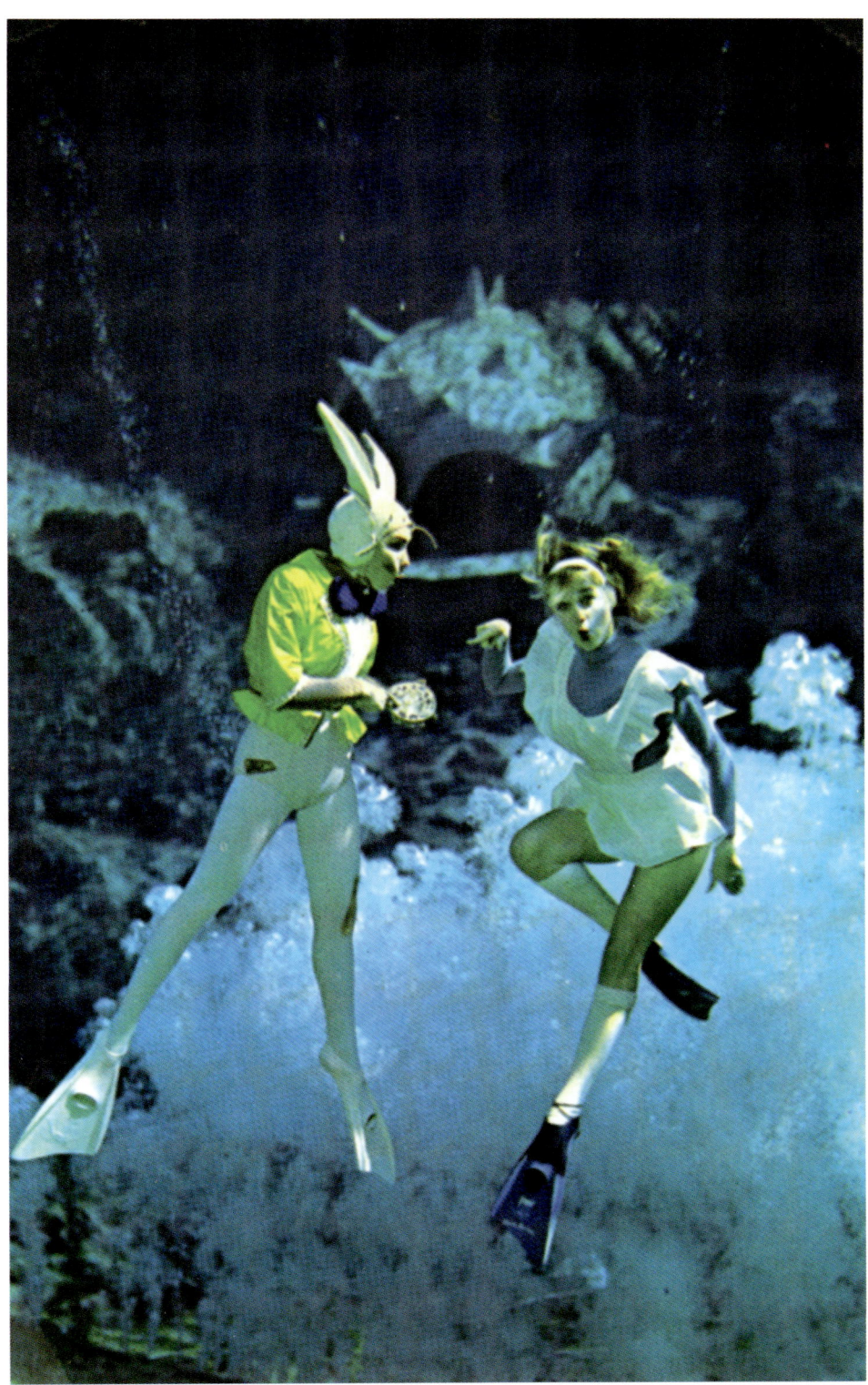

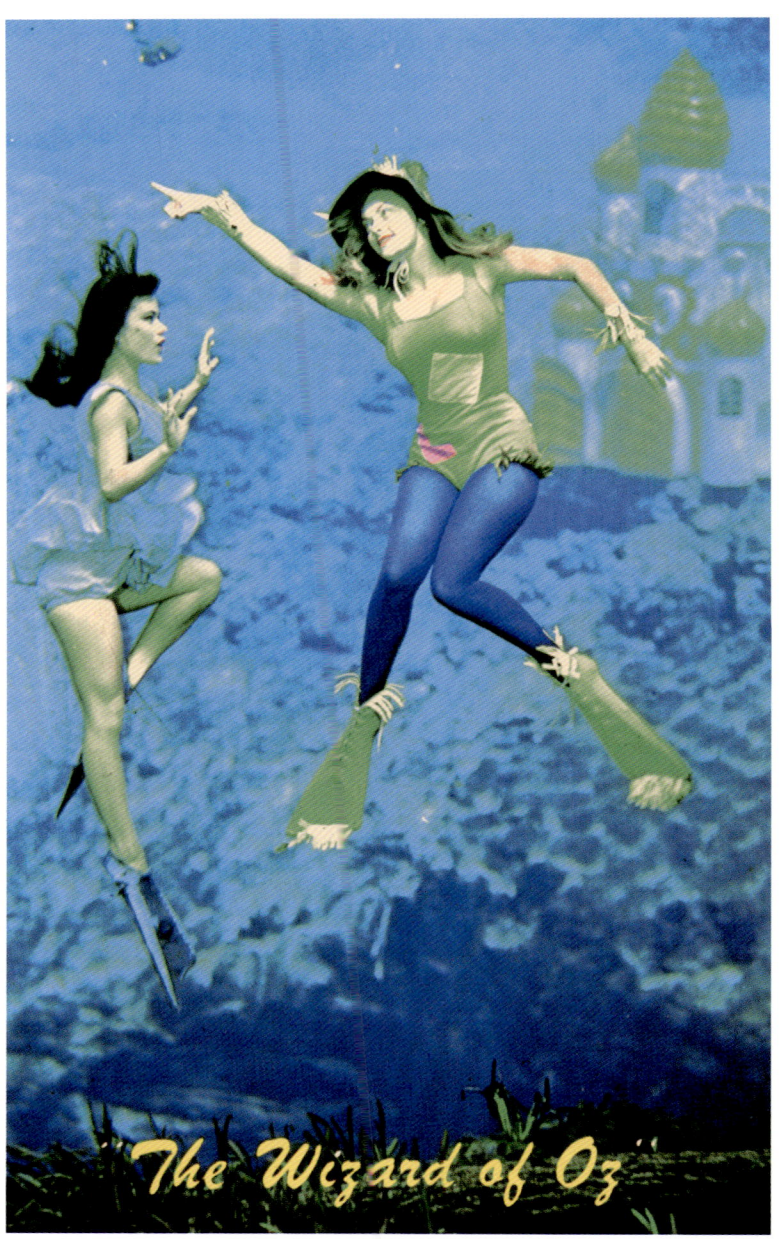

Above: From 1966 to 1967, the mermaids performed an underwater version of *The Wizard of Oz*. Rita McKenna played Dorothy to Cheryl Rhodes's Scarecrow. Guess the scarecrow didn't need to worry about fire in this version of the story. By permission of Bonita Colson.

Facing page: Sometimes it even rains underwater. Pat Cleveland (*left*) and Barbara Wynns are ready for all weather, 1968. By permission of Bonita Colson.

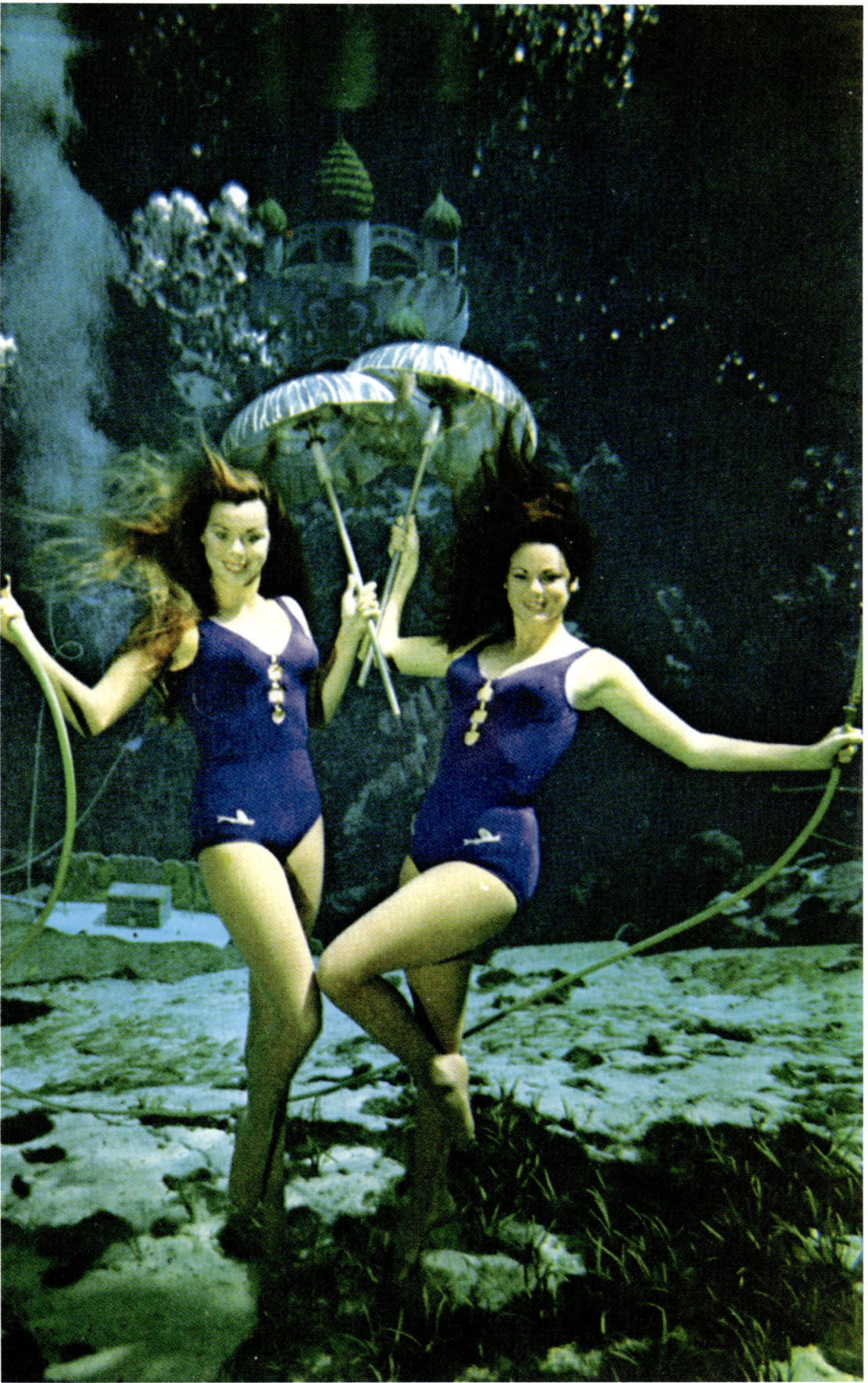

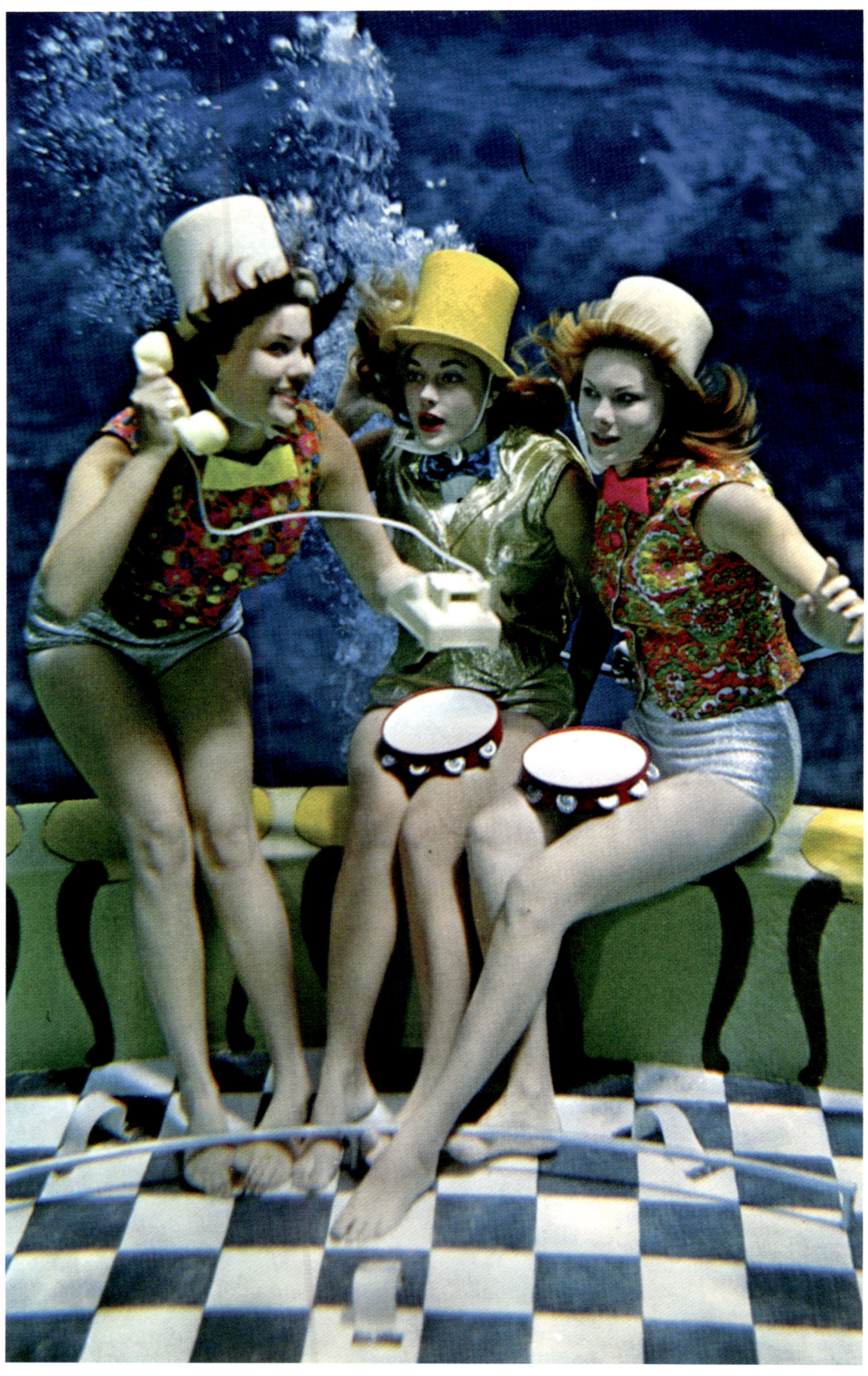

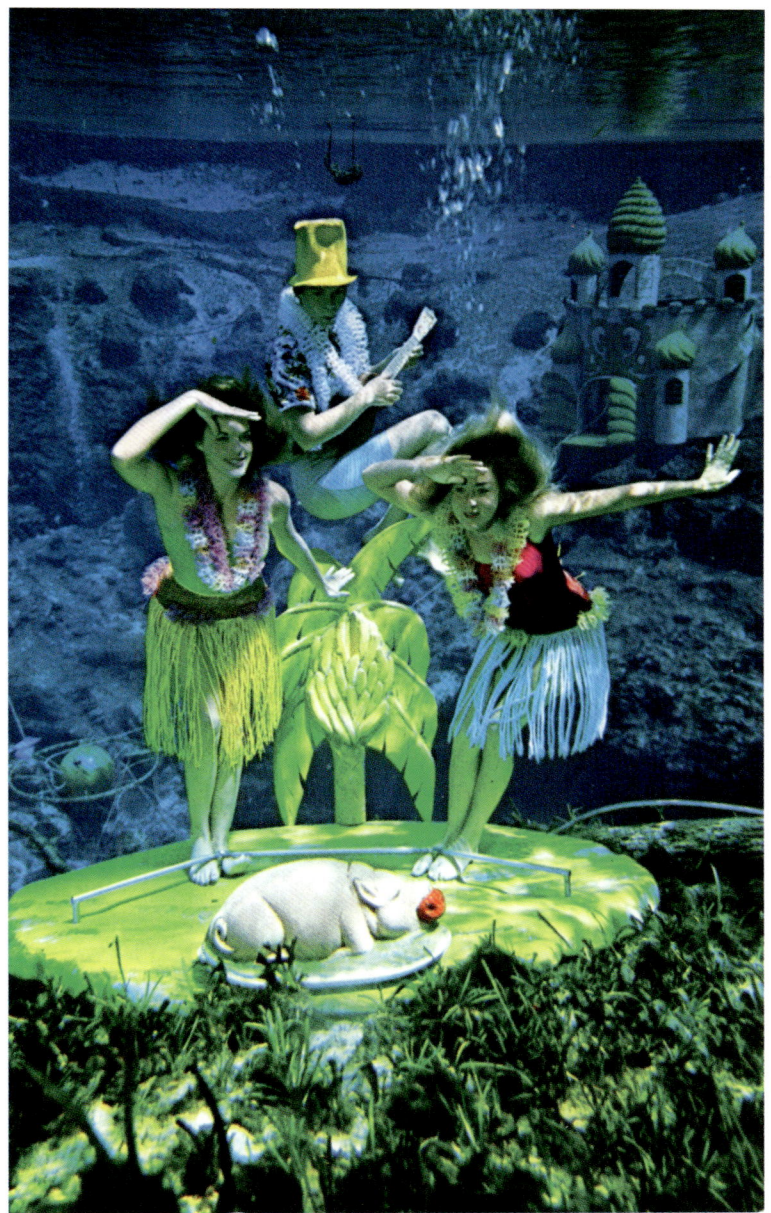

Facing page: Mary Kyle Bartholomew (*left*), Cheryl Rhodes (*center*), and April Johns, perform "Oh Dem Golden Slippers" in *Underwater Dream Girls,* 1967–68. Photo by Claude Long. By permission of Bonita Colson.

Above: From 1967 to 1968, the mermaids performed *Underwater Dream Girls,* a variety show. Susie Spencer (*left*) and Wendy Johnson (*right*) donned hula skirts, then looked for guests to invite to their luau. By permission of Bonita Colson.

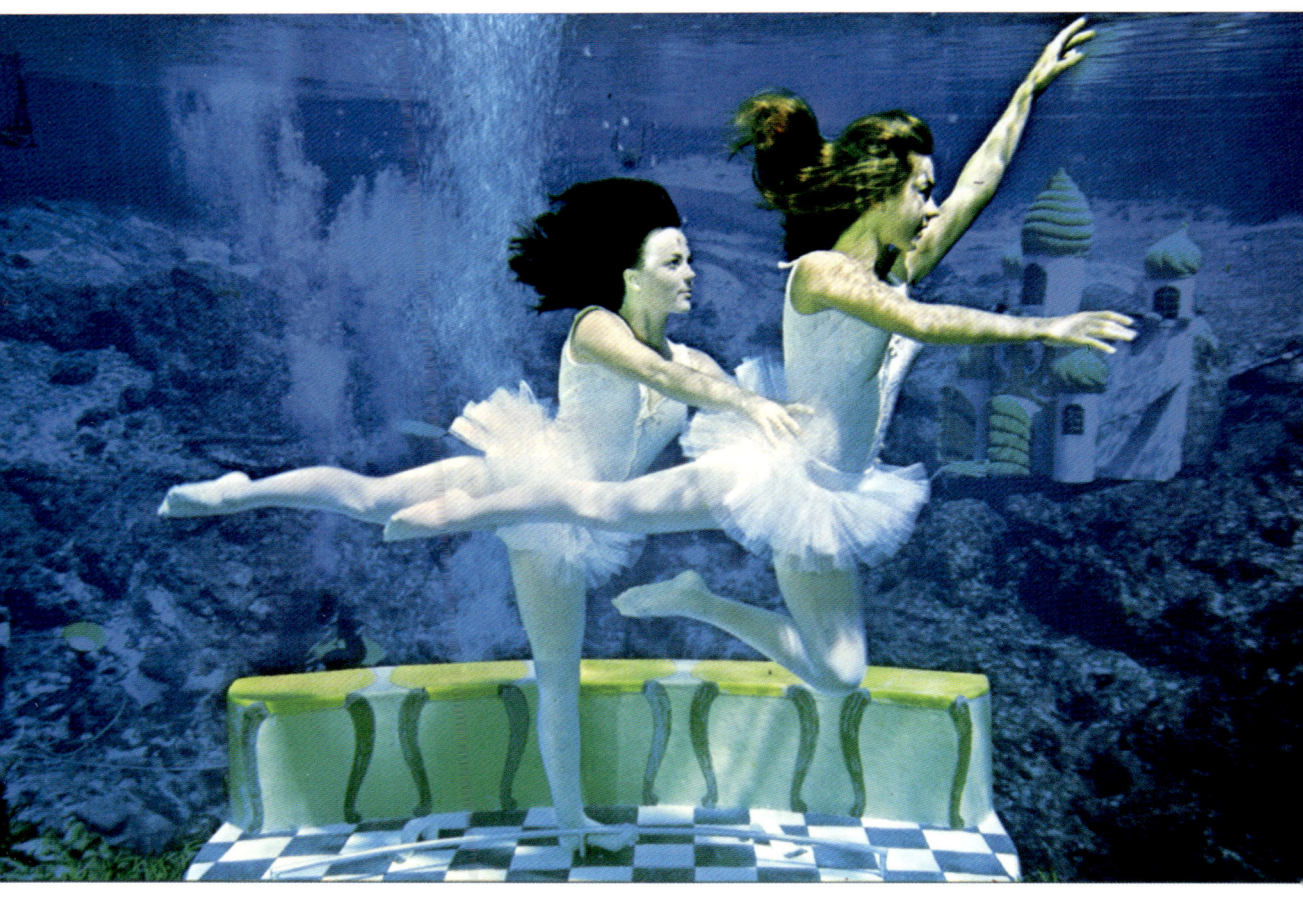

Pam Rose (*left*) and Karen Drapp execute a
graceful dance move from *Swan Lake* in this
scene from *Underwater Dream Girls*, 1967–68.
By permission of Bonita Colson.

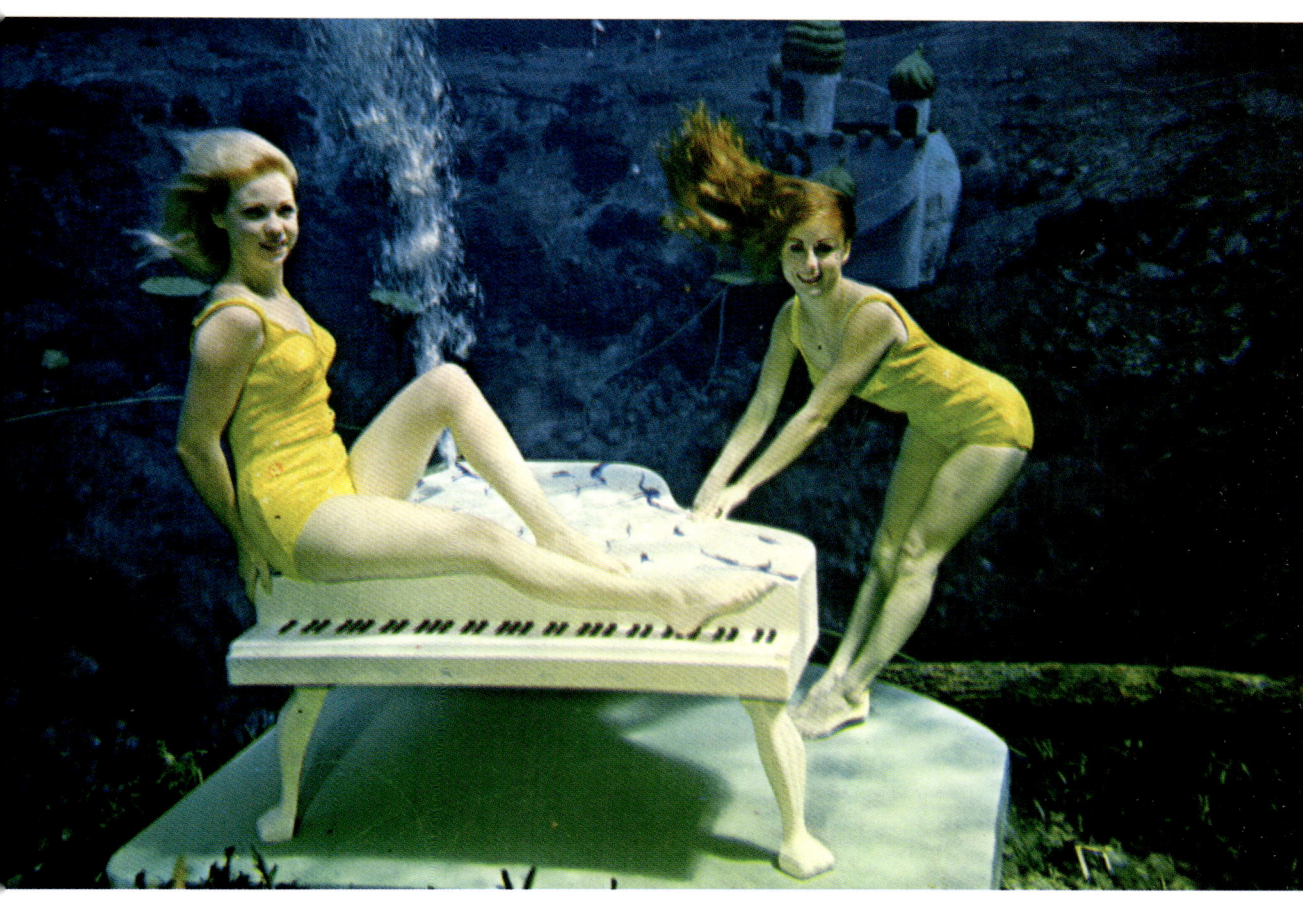

"Hey Trudy, the keys are up front." Dianne
Wingate (*left*) and Trudy Bannow perform to
"As Long as He Needs Me," the famous torch
song from the musical *Oliver,* 1967–68. By
permission of Bonita Colson.

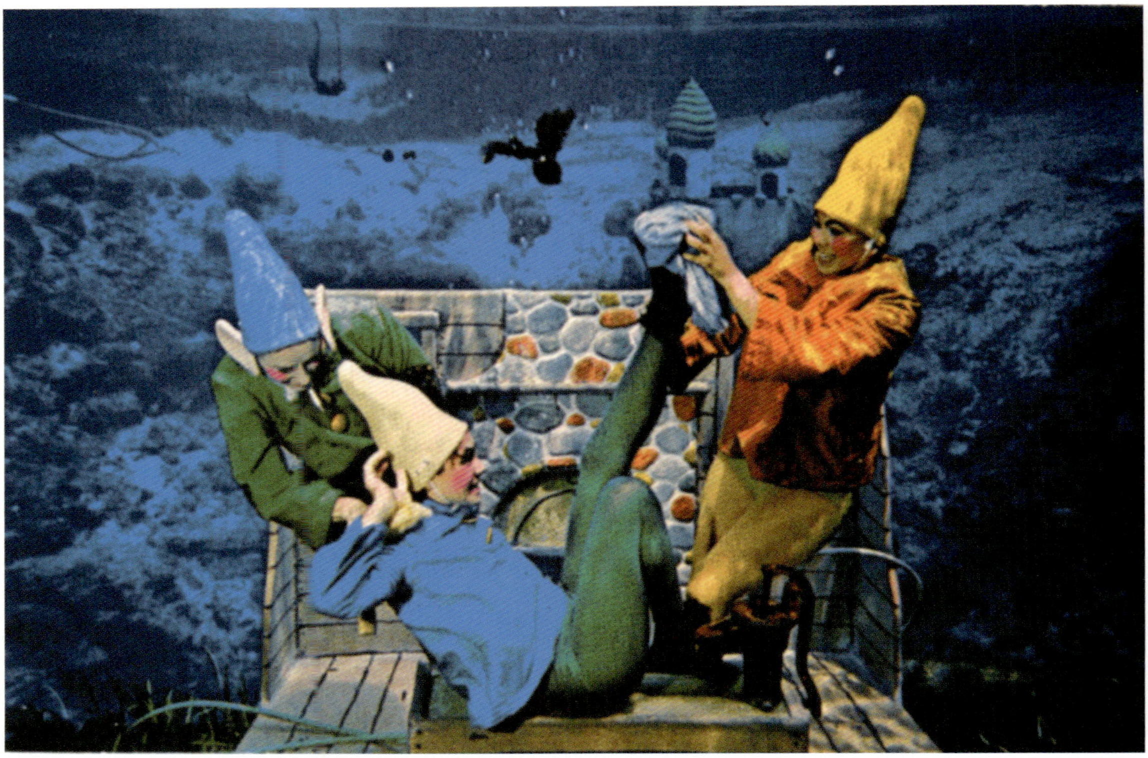

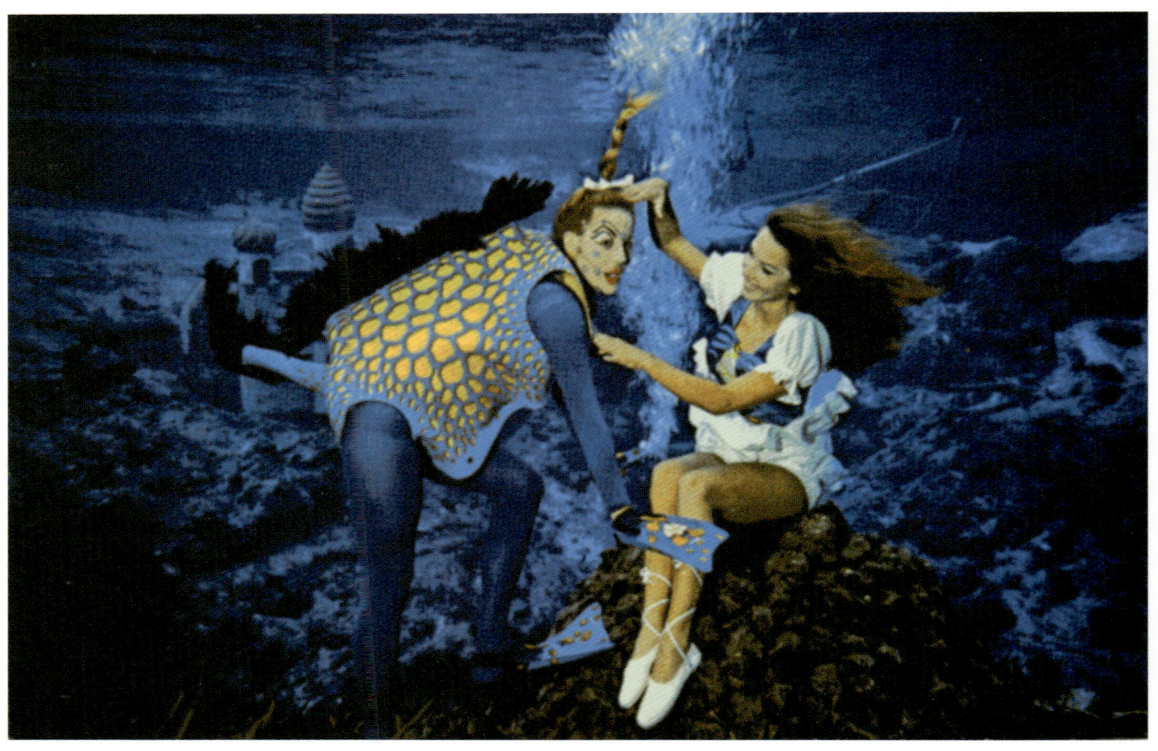

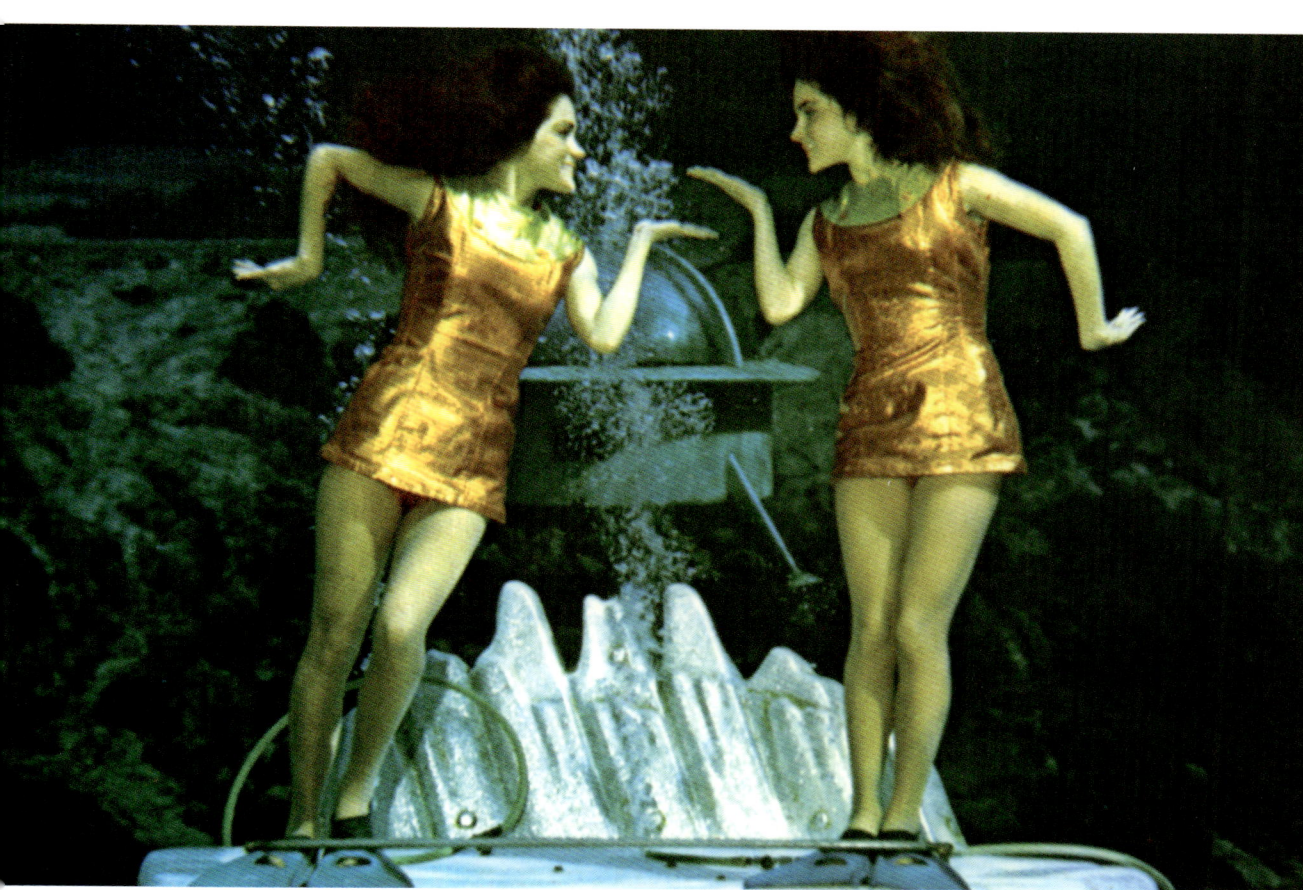

Facing page, top: Three of the seven dwarves, Trudy Bannow (*left*), Peggy Westmoreland (*center*), and Linda Mashburn, ham it up during the "Hi Ho" number in *Snow White*, 1968–69. By permission of Genie Young.

Facing page, bottom: Thea Whitehead is subdued by Snow White (Kerry Drapp) in this scene from *Snow White*, 1968–69. By permission of Genie Young.

Above: Twins Holly and Dolly Harris perform the robot routine in this scene Bonnie Georgiadis choreographed for *Mermaids on the Moon*. Their spaceship (the airlock in disguise) awaits them beyond, 1969–70. By permission of Bonita Colson.

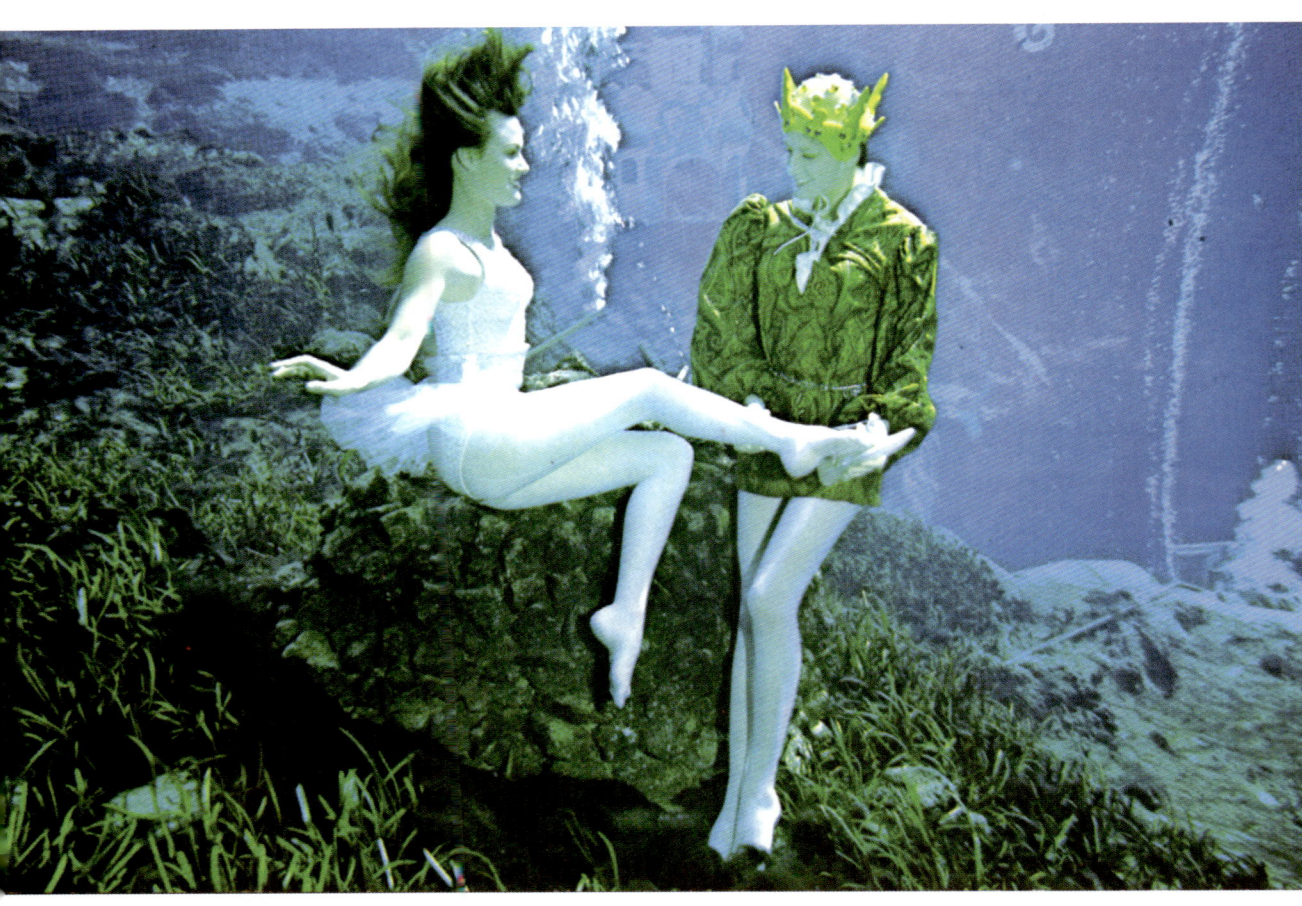

Susan Sweeney pretends to be Prince to Yvonne Chorvat's Cinderella in the underwater version of the classic fairy tale, 1970–71. By permission of Bonita Colson.

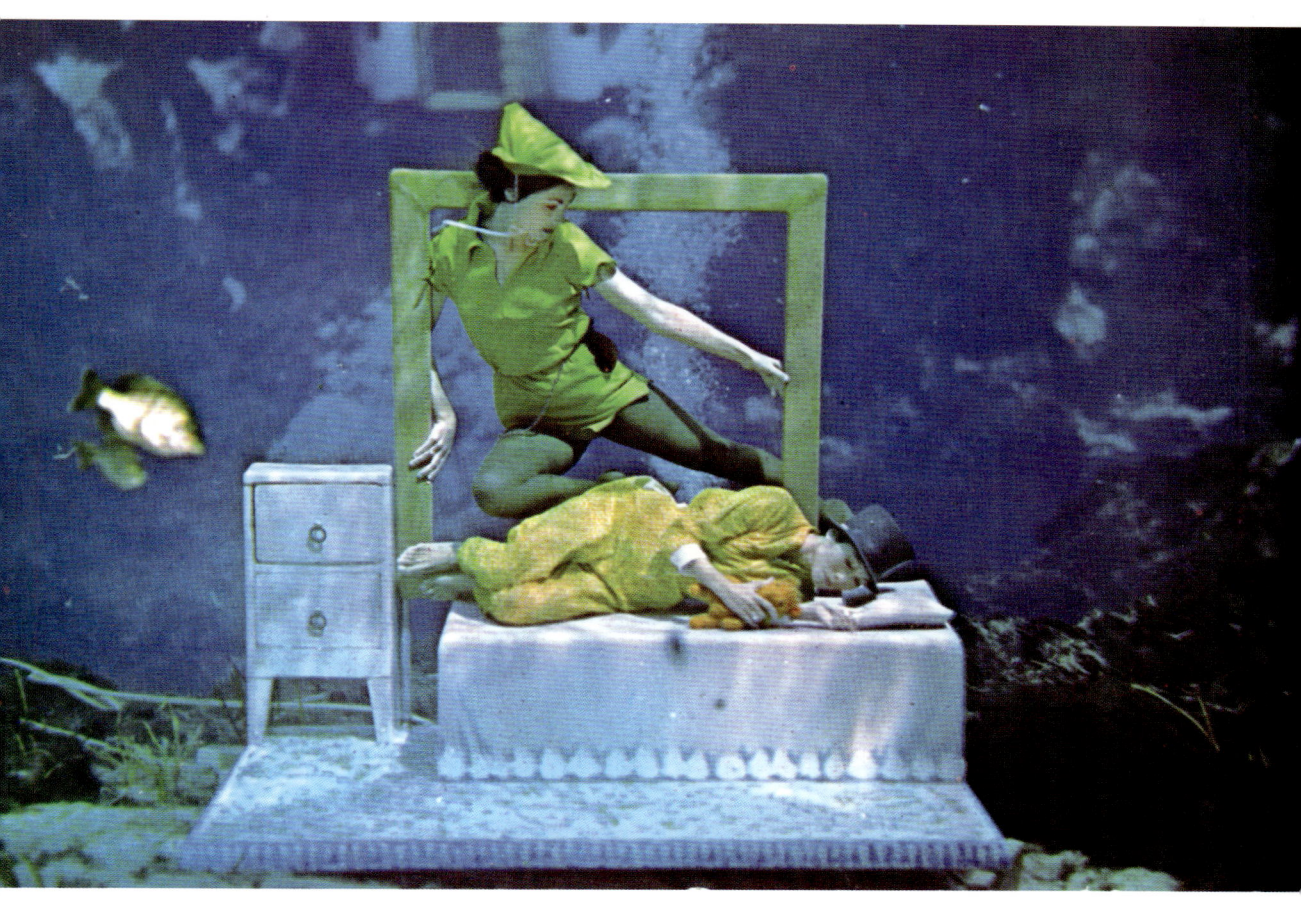

Peggy Westmoreland as Peter Pan climbs through the window to spy on a sleeping Michael played by Shinko Akasofu Wheeler, 1971–72. By permission of Bonita Colson.

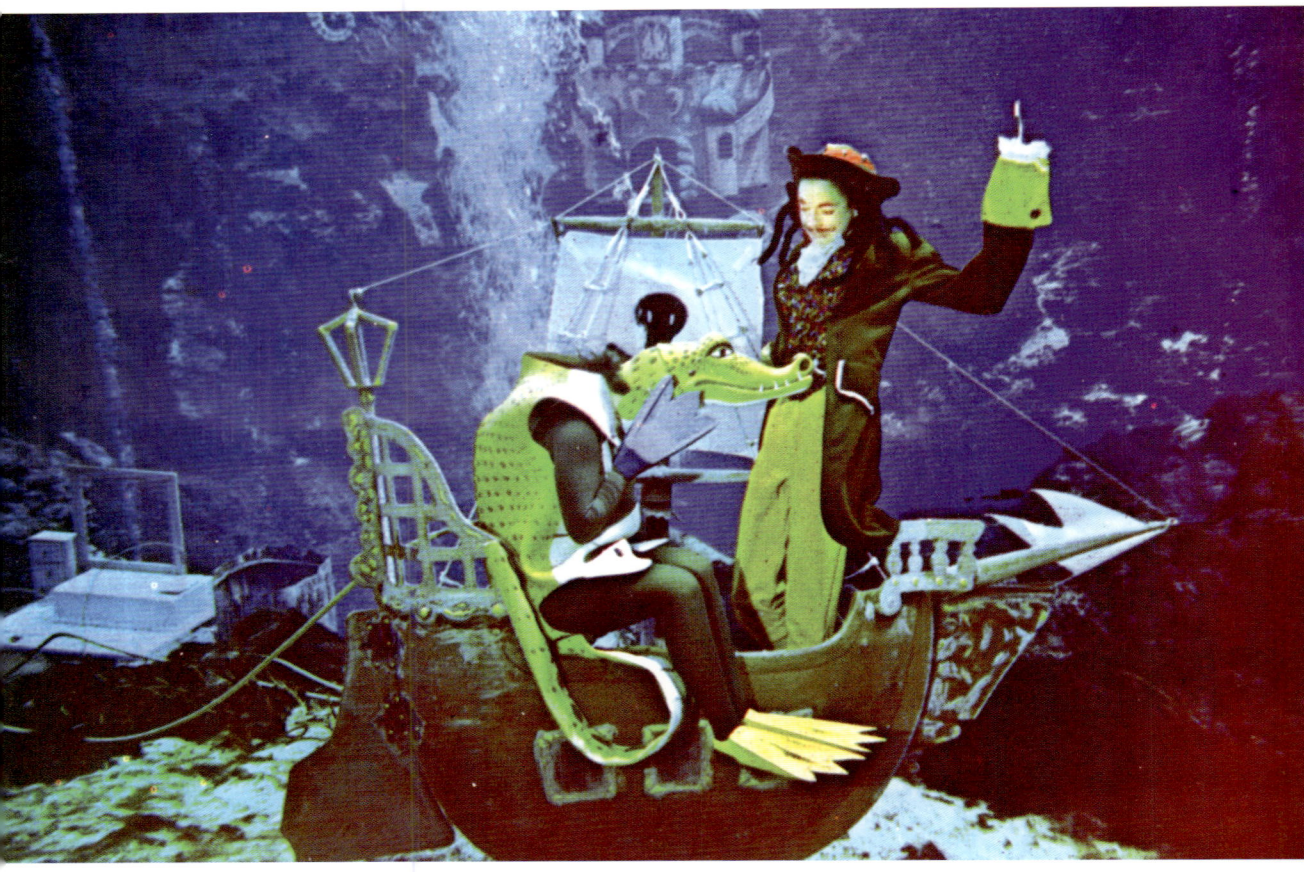

Above: Trust me. Captain Hook (Marianne Hope) is done for. The crocodile is about to do him in, 1971. By permission of Bonita Colson.

Facing page: The deed is done! Captain Hook (Marianne Hope) has captured Wendy (April Johns) as Peter Pan (Karen Sikes) comes to the rescue, 1971. By permission of Bonita Colson.

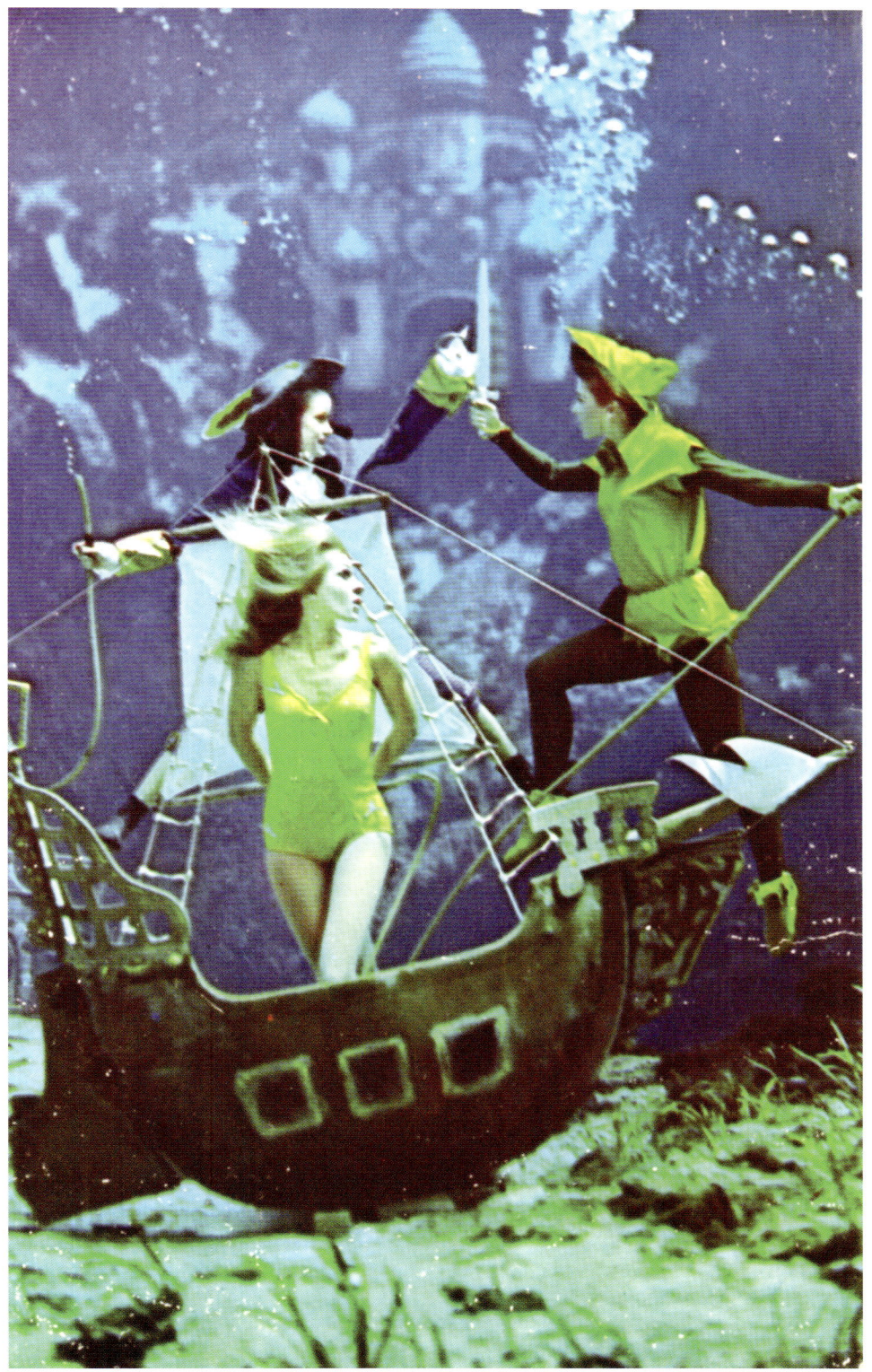

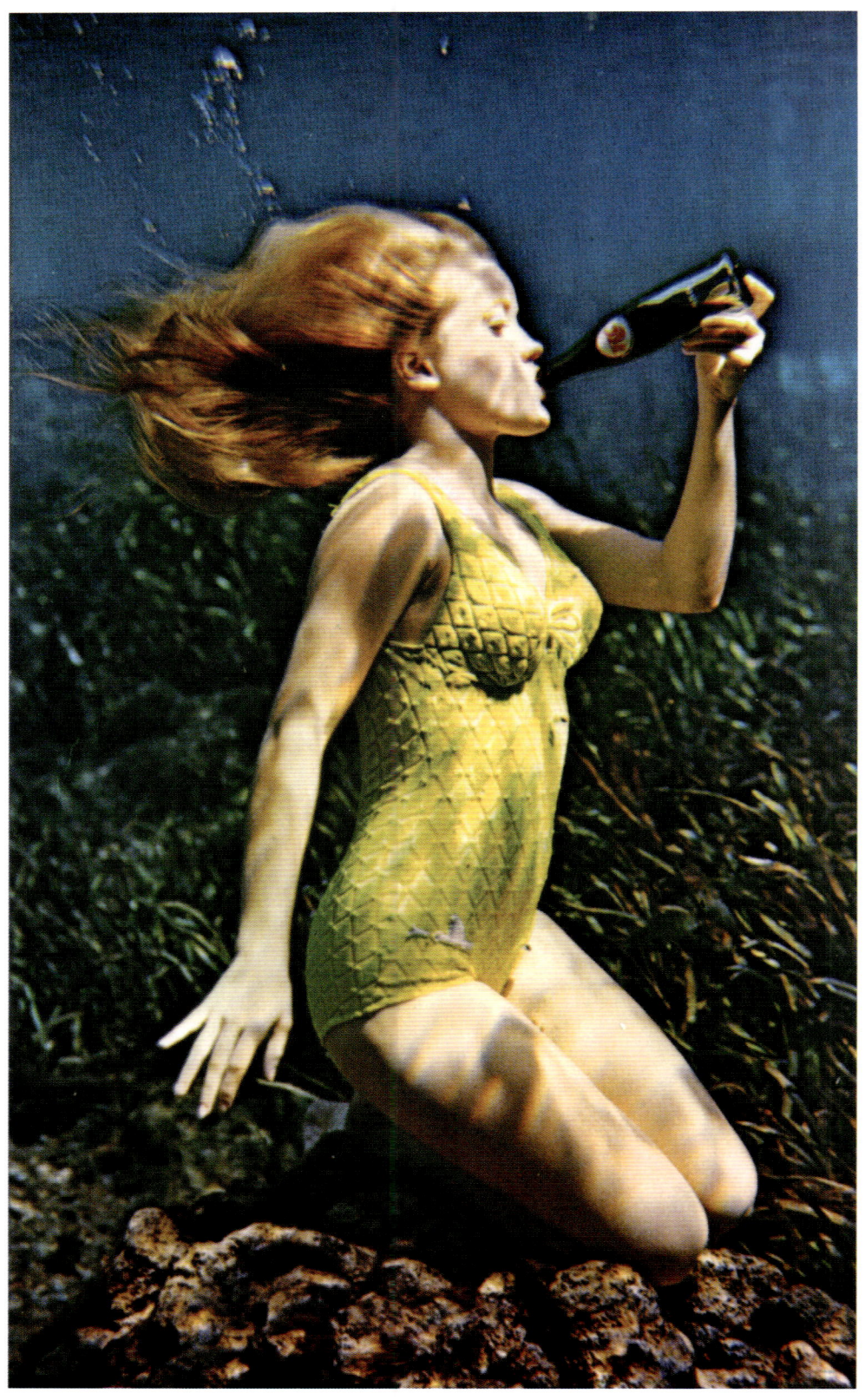

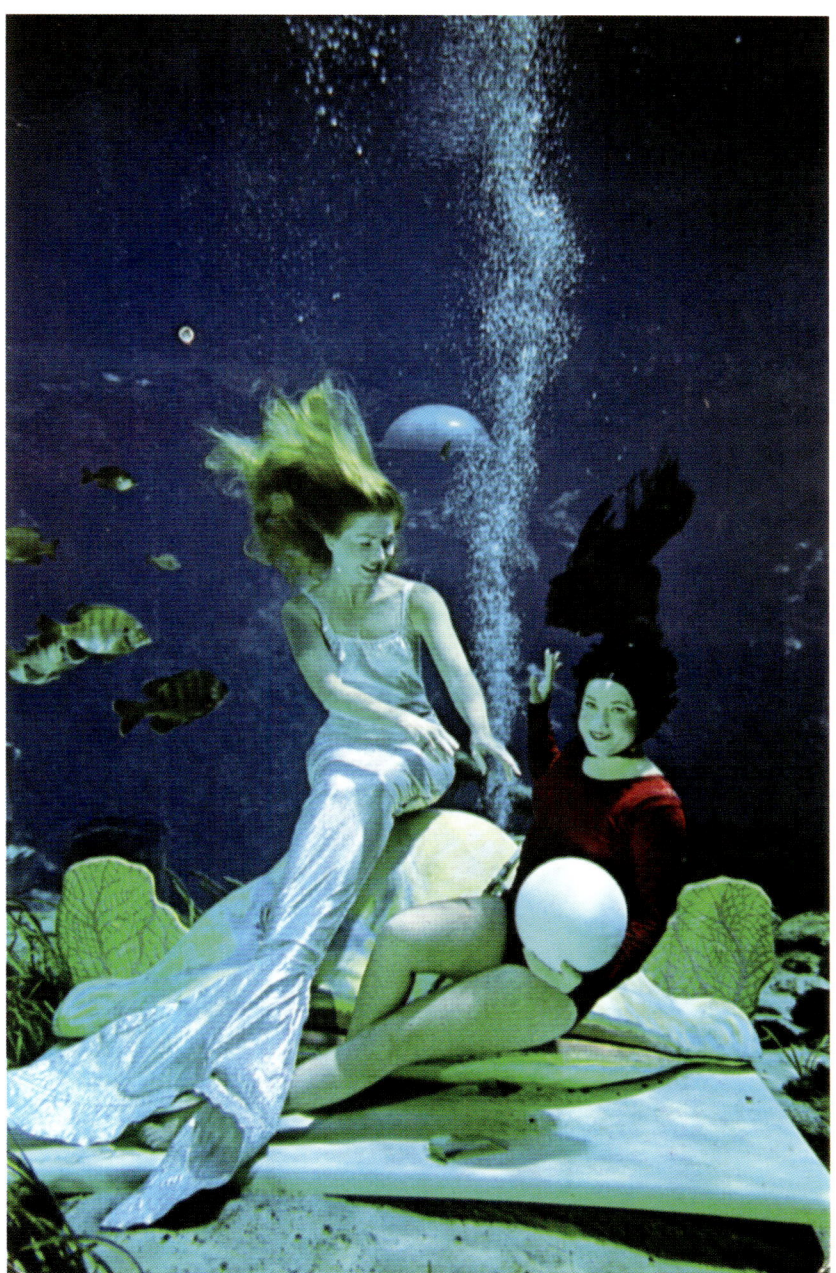

Facing page: The mermaids drank Grapette in the early years, then Coca-Cola, then RC Cola. Marianne Hope shows how the trick is done, 1972. By permission of Bonita Colson.

Above: Mermaid Barbara Bates wants the pearl held by Marianne Hope in this scene from *The Littlest Mermaid, ca.* 1972–73. By permission of Genie Young.

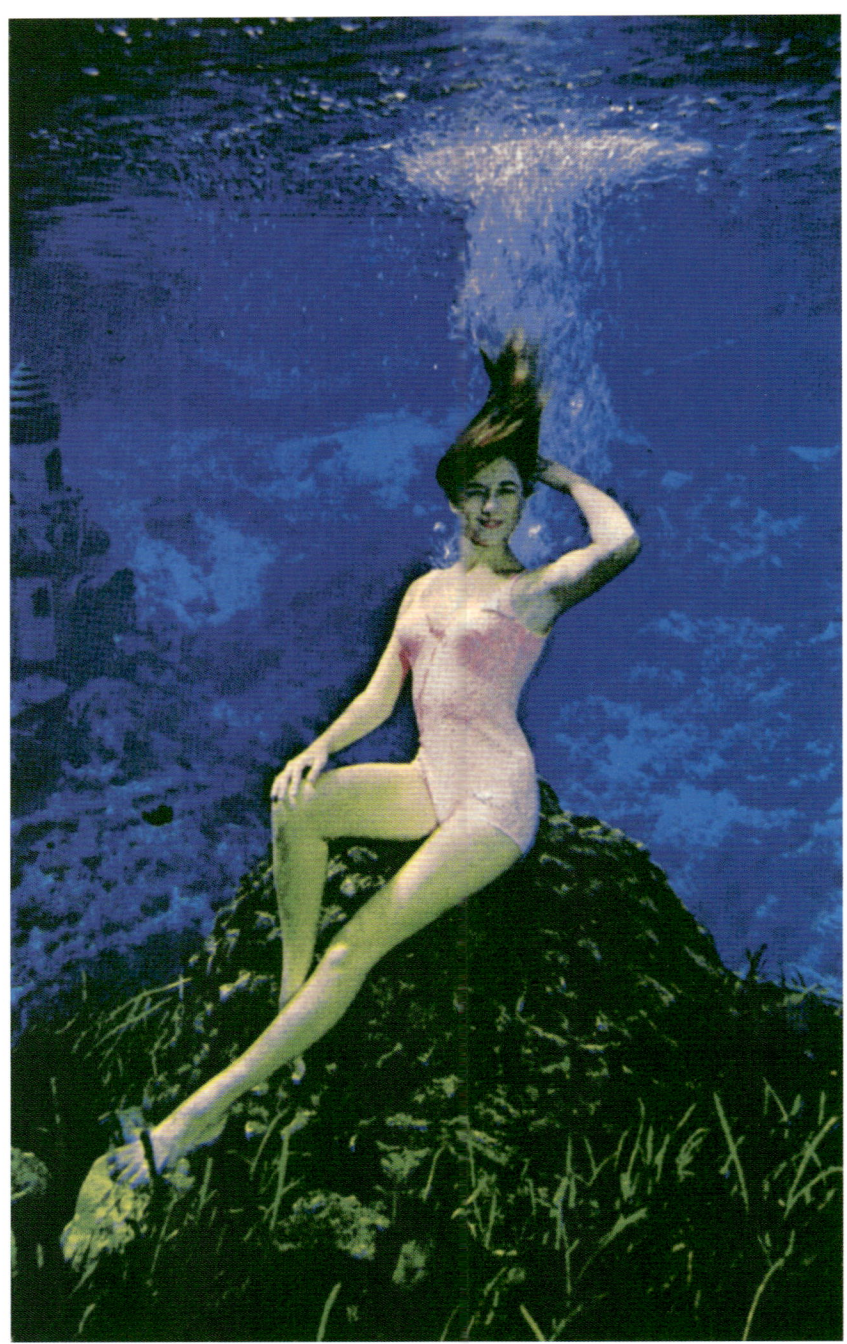

Above: Susan Sweeney makes sitting underwater look easy, 1971. By permission of
Genie Young.

Facing page: Shinko Akasofu Wheeler performs a classic swan, 1972. By permission of
Genie Young.

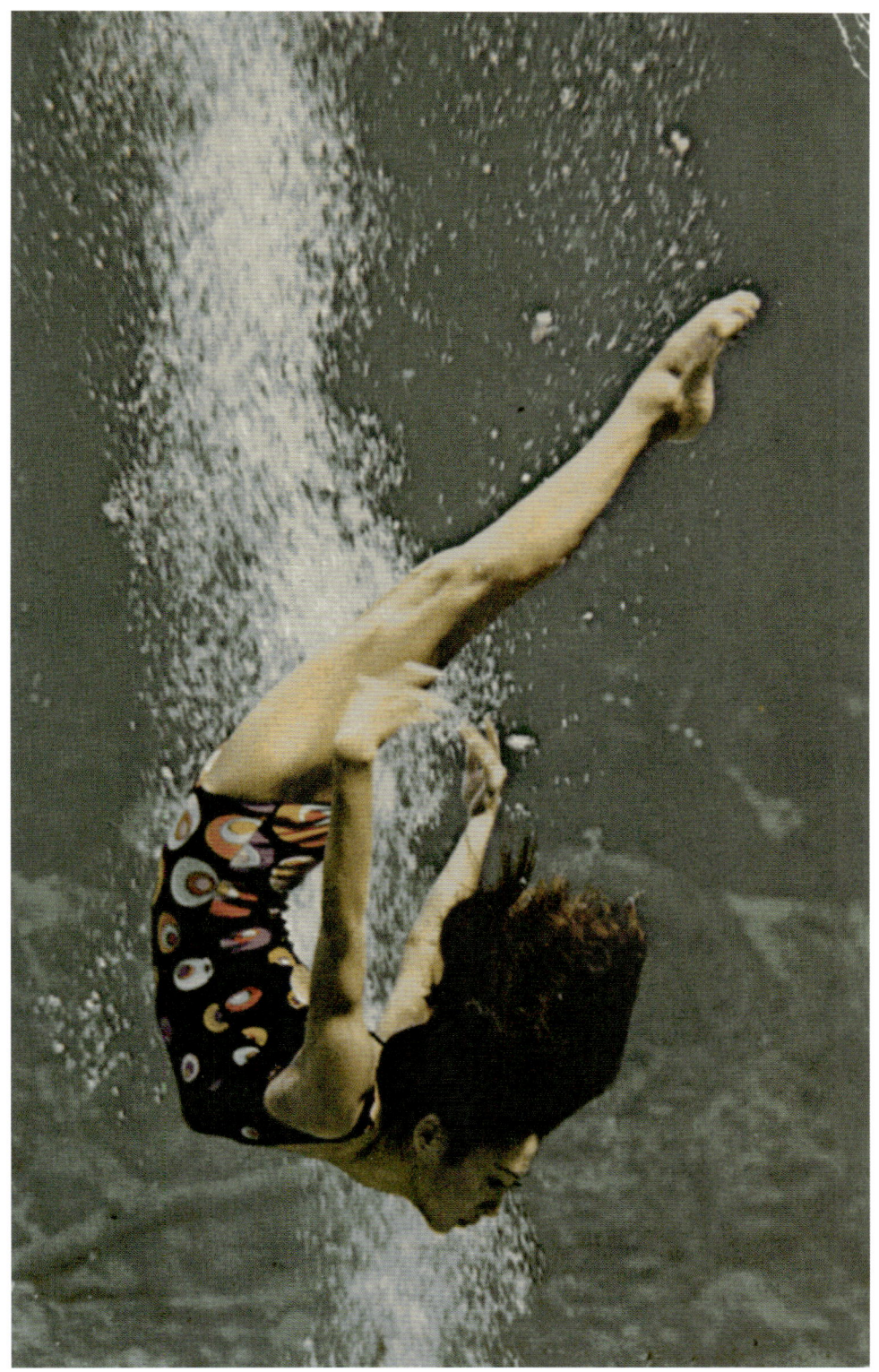

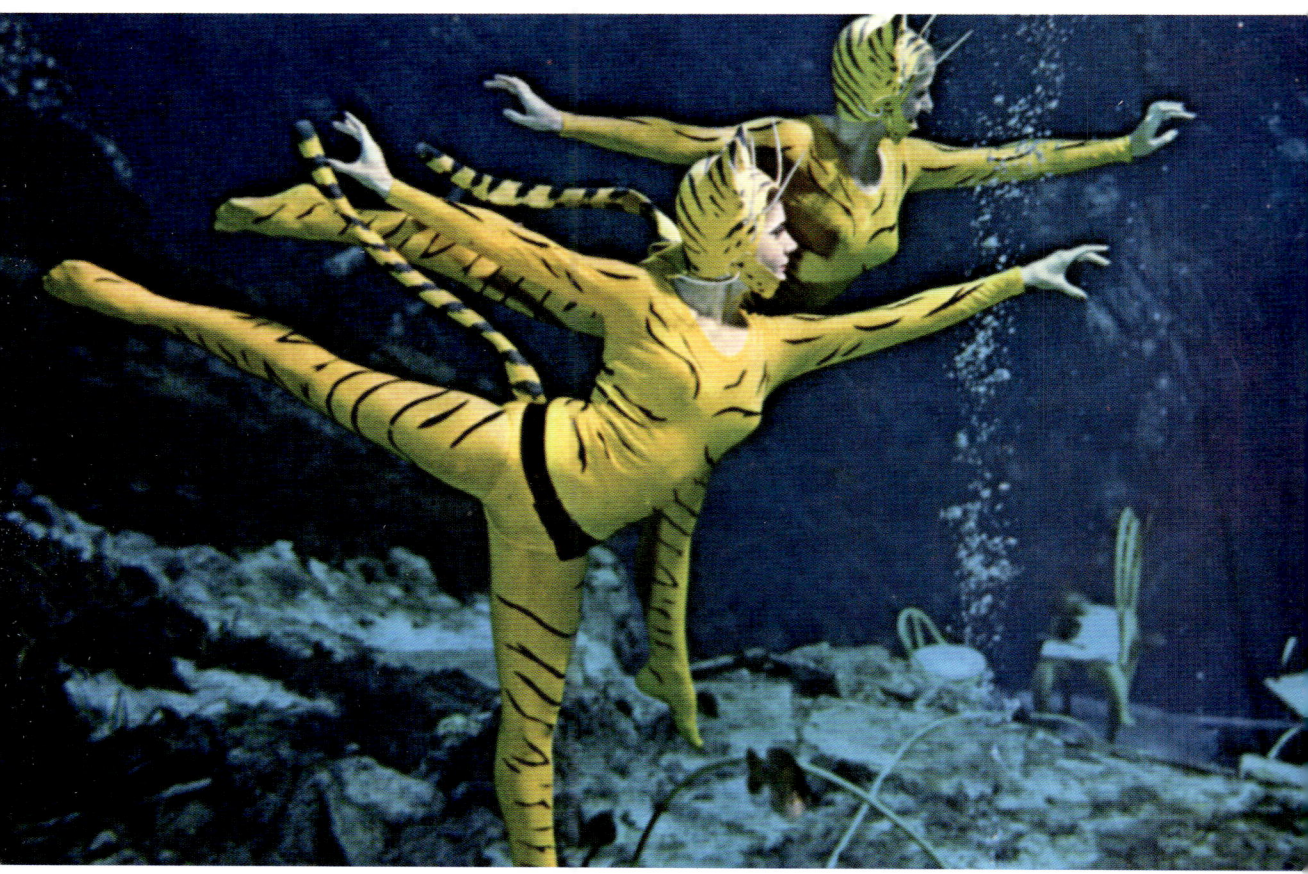

Above: Carol Bates (*left*) and Becky Stahlhut perform "What's New Pussycat?" in *The Best of Everything*. To hold this pose, they have taken a breath of air, then dropped their hoses, 1974. By permission of Bonita Colson.

Facing page: Pat Cleveland shows why long hair was a must for mermaids in this 1976 publicity shot. Photo by Sparky Schumacher. By permission of Sparky Schumacher.

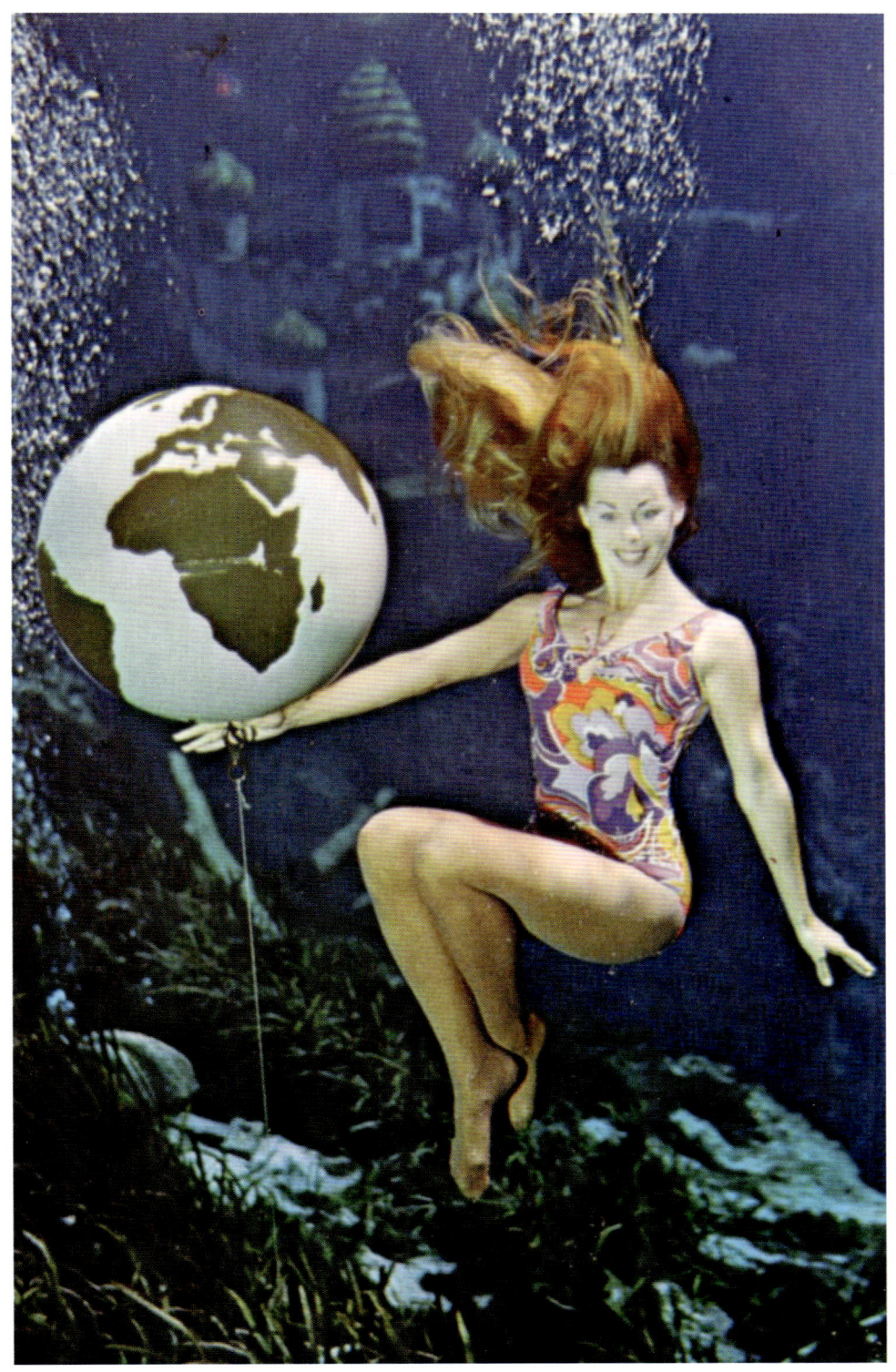

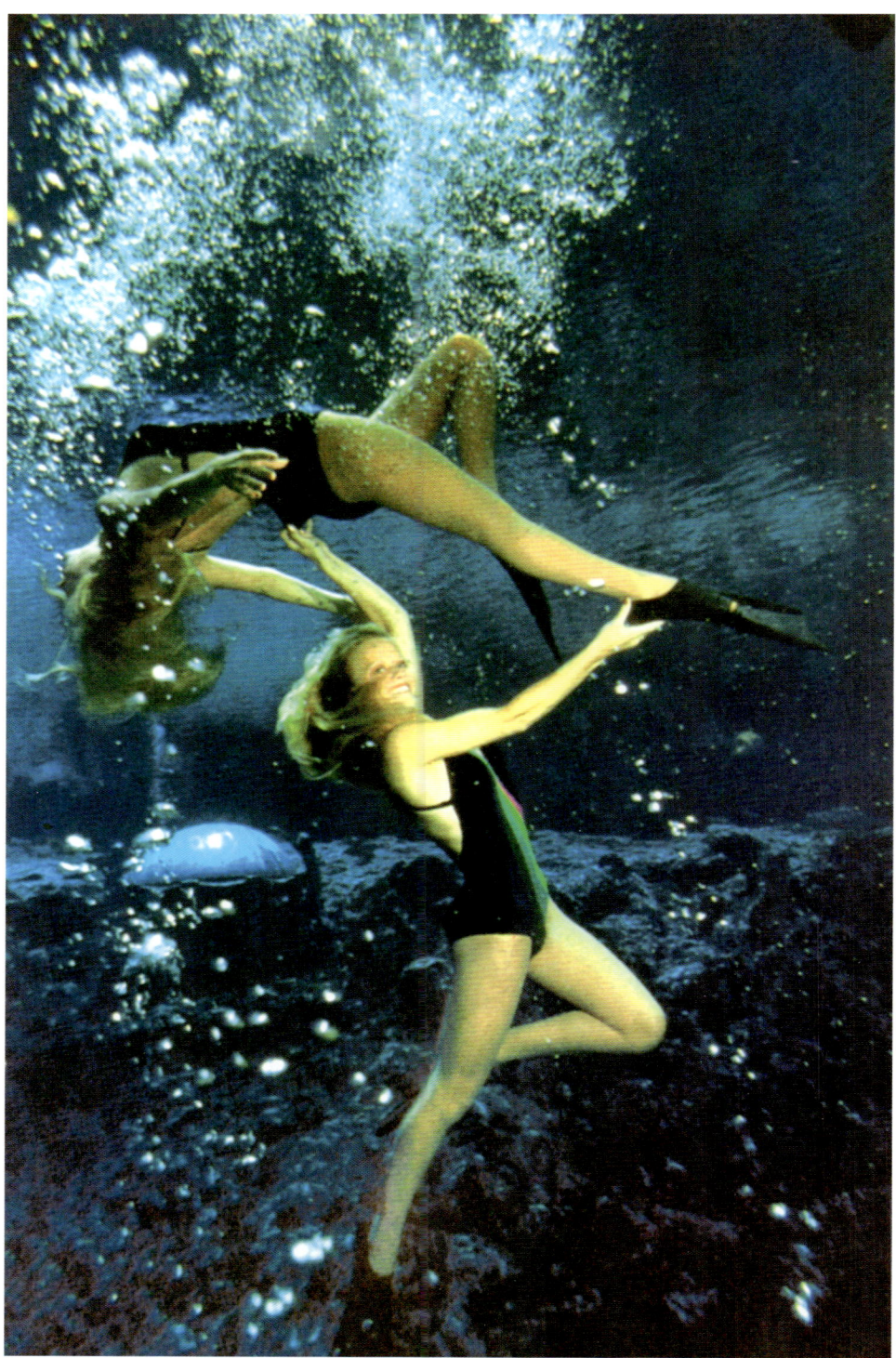

More than thirty years after the adagio's creation, twins Melody (*top*) and Melinda Harding perform Weeki Wachee's iconic pose, 1977. By permission of Bonita Colson.

We would like to thank the following people for generously sharing their photographs, stories, and moral support: Eileen Perry Hogshead, Nancy Tribble Benda, Mary Darlington Fletcher, Dianne Wyatt MacDonald, Ginger Stanley Hallowell, Sparky Schumacher, Terry Ryan Hamlet, Dawn Douglas, Alan Scott, Vera Huckaby, Genie Young, Pat Cleveland, Kay Finney, Vicki Vergara Smith, Kevin Griffin, Carl Ludwig, and Meri Culp. Special thanks to Bonita Colson—we couldn't have completed the book without her assistance. Thanks to Pam Ball, Elias and Samuel Cherrier-Vickers, Shani Angela Hervey, Gary Monroe, and Tim Hollis for feedback on the manuscript. Thanks also to Larry Leshan and Michele Fiyak-Burkley.

"just like a Broadway musical": Weeki Wachee program brochure, ca. 1960s.

"can trace its history": Jean Marbella, "Picture Perfect Florida Was Made for Postcard Posing," *Fort Lauderdale News/Sun-Sentinel*, September 2, 1985, http://articles.orlandosentinel.com/1985-09-02/lifestyle/0320400144_1_postcards-boca-raton-flagler.

"According to the legend": Tracy J. Revels, *Sunshine Paradise: A History of Florida Tourism* (Gainesville: University Press of Florida, 2011), 5.

"Weeki Wachee was a hauntingly beautiful": Michael Garvey, "Authentically Fake," *Commonweal*, September 14, 2007.

"composed of vanishing tourist attractions": Joel Achenbach, "Three Floridas: The Authentic, The Fake, The Authentically Fake," *Chicago Sun-Times*, December 15, 1991.

"backwater Eden": Michael Garvey, "Authentically Fake," *Commonweal*, September 14, 2007.

William Henry Jackson: Charlotte M. Porter, "Natural History and Early Tourism in Florida," *Florida Naturalists*, The Florida Museum of Natural History, http://www.flmnh.ufl.edu/naturalists/tourism01.htm.

"selected the bright colors": Charlotte M. Porter, "Natural History and Early Tourism in Florida," *Florida Naturalists*, The Florida Museum of Natural History, http://www.flmnh.ufl.edu/naturalists/tourism01.htm.

"popularized the Florida tourist trail": Kathryn E. Holland Braund and Charlotte M. Porter, eds., *Fields of Vision: Essays on the Travels of William Bartram* (Birmingham: University Alabama Press, 2010), 231.

"development of the tourist industry": Hampton Dunn, *Wish You Were Here: A Grand Tour of Early Florida via Old Post Cards* (St. Petersburg: Byron Kennedy and Co., 1981).

By the mid-1940s, visitors to Florida: "Postcard Business a Thriving One, Survey Reveals," *Evening Independent*, July 29, 1948. Google News Archive, http://news.google.com.

"Persons shop for postcards": Ibid.

"Florida can thank the amazing growth": Ash Wing, "Weekiwachee's Underwater Ballet," *Brooksville Sun*, undated clipping, collection of Delee Perry.

"flood of postwar tourists": Gary Mormino, *Land of Sunshine, State of Dreams: A Social History of Modern Florida* (Gainesville: University Press of Florida, 2008).

"It took Florida": "Newt Perry's Mermaids Provoke Wirephoto Battle," *St. Petersburg Evening Independent*, April 28, 1948.

"getting away from the glass-bottom boat": Ash Wing, "Weekiwachee's Underwater Ballet," *Brooksville Sun*, undated clipping, collection of Delee Perry.

"Many people said": "Interview with Mr. Newton Perry," September 11, 1974, Samuel Proctor Oral History Program, Department of History, University of Florida, http://ufdc.ufl.edu/UF00007993/00001.

"One time this woman was sitting": Nancy Tribble Benda, interview by Lu Vickers, October 10, 2004.

Terry Hamlet, who performed: Terry Hamlet, interview by Lu Vickers, August 2011.

"They look as though": "Newt Perry's Mermaids Provoke Wirephoto Battle," *St. Petersburg Evening Independent*, April 28, 1948.

"Florida kids take to the water": "Underwater Babies," *Spokane Daily Chronicle*, April 27, 1948. *Newspaper Archive*, http://www.newspaperarchive.com.

In the late 1800s: Simon Louvish, *Man on the Flying Trapeze: The Life and Times of W. C. Fields* (New York: Norton, 1999), 47

In the early 1900s: John Lucas, "Making a Statement: Annette Kellerman Advances the Worlds of Swimming, Diving and Entertainment," *Sporting Tradition* 14, no. 2 (May 1998): 25–35.

By 1917, when she returned: Ibid.

"Hollywood may be": Homer Gramling, "You Can Call Him Mister Underwater," *Miami Herald*, 1964.

Hullam Jones fitted: "Learn about Our Heritage," http://www.silversprings.com/heritage.html.

Phillip Morrell later built: Richard A. Martin, *Eternal Spring: Man's 10,000 Years of History at Florida's Silver Springs* (St. Petersburg, Fla.: Great Outdoors Publishing, 1966).

"seen through the glass-bottom boat": O. E. Meinzer, "Large Springs in the United States," U.S. Geological Survey Water-Supply Paper 557, Washington, D.C., 1927.

"was not unlike the interest": Wendy Adams King, "Through the Looking Glass of Silver Springs: Tourism and the Politics of Vision," *Journal of American Popular Culture (1900 to Present)* 3, no. 1 (Spring 2004), http://www.americanpopularculture.com/journal/articles/spring_2004/king.htm.

"The underwater scenery": Ibid.

"There the transparent depths": "Along the Ocklawaha," *Fitchburg Daily Sentinel*, Jan. 22, 1916. *Newspaper Archive*, http://www.newspaperarchive.com.

"DEVIL'S KITCHEN": Undated brochure from Silver Springs.

"Paramount News came down": "Interview with Mr. Newton Perry," September 11, 1974, Samuel Proctor Oral History Program, Department of History, University of Florida, http://ufdc.ufl.edu/UF00007993/00001.

British Pathé newsreel: "Watery Ways," *British Pathé*, http://www.britishpathe.com/record.php?id=10485.

just a couple of years after: Delee Perry, interview by Lu Vickers, November 15, 2004.

"by the remarkable clarity": Richard A. Martin, *Eternal Spring: Man's 10,000 Years of History at Florida's Silver Springs* (St. Petersburg, Fla.: Great Outdoors Publishing, 1966).

"We've spent fortunes": "Nature Furnishes Better Facilities Than Hollywood," *Daytona Beach Morning Journal*, March 3, 1939. Google News Archive, http://news.google.com.

90 percent of all underwater: Richard A. Martin, *Eternal Spring: Man's 10,000 Years of History at Florida's Silver Springs* (St. Petersburg, Fla.: Great Outdoors Publishing, 1966).

"Mermaid of the Springs": Dan Guido, "Tarzan Stunts, Mermaid Magic Remembered," *Ocala Star Banner*, July 22, 1983.

"The best place in America": "One Way to Take Your Best Girl For A Ride," *American Weekly*, 1938. *Newspaper Archive*, http://www.newspaperarchive.com.

"I should've been born": Eileen Perry Hogshead, interview by Lu Vickers, fall 2011.

"The ordinary diver breathes": "Leads Life of Mermaid Posing for Underwater Pictures," *Hartford Courant*, May 24, 1936, G1. *Newspaper Archive*, http://www.newspaperarchive.com.

"seasoned performer": Ibid.

"I would squint my eyes": Nancy Tribble Benda, interview by Lu Vickers, August 2011.

"such movie magic": "The Wonder of Underwater Movies," *Popular Mechanics*, June 1941.

"to swim in unison": Ibid.

"One Way to Take": "One Way to Take Your Best Girl For A Ride," *American Weekly*, 1938. *Newspaper Archive*, http://www.newspaperarchive.com.

"best known inland": Harris Sims, "Down Florida's Bright Trails," *New York Times*, January 15, 1939.

"There was only a barrel": Bruce Mozert, interview by Lu Vickers, August 13, 2004.

"Newt's influence": Ginger Stanley Hallowell, interview by Lu Vickers, November 15, 2004.

"Newt was actually": Bruce Mozert, interview by Lu Vickers, August 13, 2004.

"Instead of looking down": Ernie Pyle, "Scenic Wonder for Tourist's 'Must' List; View at Silver Springs Has Pyle Goggle-Eyed," *St. Petersburg Times*, Feb. 22, 1934. Google News Archive, http://news.google.com.

"the man who swims underwater": "Interview with Mr. Newton Perry," September 11, 1974, Samuel Proctor Oral History Program, Department of History, University of Florida, http://ufdc.ufl.edu/UF00007993/00001.

"I could get whatever": Eileen Perry Hogshead, interview by Lu Vickers, fall 2011.

"Just as good as": Allen Skaggs, "Tarzan Johnny Weismuller Disports Self at Wakulla," *Tallahassee Democrat*, June 12, 1941.

"gags we want to work out": Jack Eaton to Newt Perry, Feb. 28, 1941, collection of Delee Perry.

"reel on how underwater": Ibid.

"swimmers' filling stations": "Underwater Air Trap Is New Device," *Panama City News-Herald*, May 13, 1941. *Newspaper Archive*, http://www.newspaperarchive.com.

"a thriving center of": Ibid.

"Very early, Newt started": Nancy Tribble Benda, interview by Lu Vickers, October 10, 2004.

"We had a beauty contest": Nancy Tribble Benda, interview by Lu Vickers, October 10, 2004.

"From Wakulla Springs": "Bathing Beauties," *The History Channel website*, http://www.history.com/videos/bathing-beauties.

"What's the use of": Frederick Simpich, "How We Use the Gulf of Mexico," *National Geographic* 85, no. 1 (January 1944): 24.

"I just happened to be there": "Tallahassee Woman Featured in National Geographic," WCTV, February 25, 2003, http://www.wctv.tv/news/headlines/234101.html.

"It was literally just": Nancy Tribble Benda, interview by Lu Vickers, October 10, 2004.

"he put all the mermaids": Nancy Tribble Benda, interview by Lu Vickers, October 10, 2004.

"They wore the full rig": Ricou Browning, interview by Lu Vickers, September 24, 2004.

"Weekly Washing": John Reese Jr., "At Weekiwachee Springs It's All Done Underwater," *St. Petersburg Independent*, November 21, 1947.

"'submarine photo lounge'": "$100,000 Playground Development Planned at Weekiwachee Springs," *St. Petersburg Times*, June 28, 1946.

"The Mountain Underwater!": "Weekiwachee, The Mountain Underwater," undated press release, collection of Delee Perry.

"had spent almost as much": John Reese Jr., "At Weekiwachee Springs It's All Done Underwater," *St. Petersburg Independent*, November 21, 1947.

"He can produce photos": Ibid.

"I couldn't believe the": Ricou Browning, interview by Lu Vickers, September 24, 2004.

"That whole first summer": Nancy Tribble Benda, interview by Lu Vickers, October 10, 2004.

"The Mountain Underwater!": "Weekiwachee, The Mountain Underwater," undated press release, collection of Delee Perry.

"That photograph was taken": Nancy Tribble Benda, interview by Lu Vickers, October 10, 2004.

"Take Pictures Like This Yourself": "Weekiwachee, The Mountain Underwater," undated press release, collection of Delee Perry.

"water show on top": Dianne Wyatt McDonald, interview by Frederick Olsen Jr., January 18, 2003.

"We did not use air hoses": Dianne Wyatt McDonald, interview by Frederick Olsen Jr., January 18, 2003.

Mary Dwight Rose and her sister: Dianne Wyatt McDonald, interview by Frederick Olsen Jr., January 18, 2003.

"Florida will soon be known": "Underwater Theaters State's Latest Promotion to Lure Visitors' Dollars," *St. Petersburg Times*, October 19, 1947.

"There is an ethereal beauty": Claire Lui, "The Wacky World of Weeki Wachee," American Heritage Magazine.com, May 31, 2007.

"I swam three shows": Eileen Perry Hogshead, interview by Lu Vickers, fall 2011.

"take fashion models out": *New York Times*, article 12—no title, November 6, 1977.

"Only once has a young": "Lady in the Lake," *Sports Illustrated* 13, no. 3 (July 18, 1960): 33.

Despite what the caption: Kay Finney, interview by Lu Vickers, August 2011.

"And if we made it": Mary Darlington Fletcher, interview by Lu Vickers, February 13, 2000.

"For the first time": "Melon Cutting Under Water Draws Newsreels," *The Evening Independent*, June 5, 1948. Google News Archive, http://news.google.com.

"replica of Weekiwachee": "And Now, about Women: Parties and Personals," *St. Petersburg Times*, November 16, 1948, 8.

"The underwater boys": Allen Scott, interview by Lu Vickers, April 24, 2005.

Sometimes the underwater boys: Susan Sweeney Hopkins, interview by Lu Vickers, April 23, 2005.

"Tired of feeding fish": "Underwater Theater," *Independent Record* (Helena, Montana), October 6, 1948. *Newspaper Archive*, http://www.newspaperarchive.com.

According to the local paper: Lil Burrus, "Tarpon Springs Girls Lend Beauty to Weekiwachee Springs Water Show," *St. Petersburg Times*, June 28, 1948.

"To say that my heart": Newt Perry to Bob Gilham, August 15, 1950, collection of Delee Perry.

"Father of Underwater Swimming": Grantland Rice to Newt Perry, October 1, 1951, collection of Delee Perry.

"The tourists would use flash": Sparky Schumacher, interview by Frederick Olsen Jr., October 27, 2002.

"make Weeki Wachee one": "Famous Naturalist at Weeki Wachee Springs," *Brooksville Sun-Journal*, June 2, 1960.

Lauretta Jefferson: Paul Wilder, "Manager of the Mermaids," *Tampa Tribune*, October 9, 1960.

"The performers are masters": C. E. Wright, "Florida Taps A Spring As Tourist Attraction," *New York Times*, May 15, 1960, XX20.

"You blink your eyes at girls": "Mermaids Perform at Weeki Wachee," *The Miami News*, September 9, 1962. Google News Archive, http://news.google.com.

"The base of the material": Genie Young, interview by Lu Vickers, March 7, 2005.

Terry posed for so many: Terry Hamlet, interview by Lu Vickers, August 2011.

She couldn't remember actually: Terry Hamlet, interview by Lu Vickers, August 2011.

"The more people the": Dawn Douglas, e-mail interview by Lu Vickers, July 10, 2011.

"We sold half a million": Sparky Schumacher, interview by Frederick Olsen Jr., October 27, 2002.

"A collection of scenic cards": Marjorie Dent Candee, "And Be Sure To Send Us A Postcard," *New York Times*, November 23, 1952, X27.

"We'd send the photos": Sparky Schumacher, interview by Frederick Olsen Jr., October 27, 2002.

"Posing with Maverick": Vicki Smith, e-mail interview by Lu Vickers, July 11, 2011.

"My yellow bird": Vicki Smith, e-mail interview by Lu Vickers, July 11, 2011.

"The one promotional pose": Vicki Smith, e-mail interview by Lu Vickers, July 11, 2011.

Lu Vickers has published numerous essays and short stories in magazines such as *Salon.com* and *Apalachee Review,* and she has received three Individual Artist's Grants for fiction from the Florida Division of Cultural Affairs. In addition to her novel *Breathing Underwater,* she has published two books on Florida history, *Weeki Wachee, City of Mermaids: A History of One of Florida's Oldest Roadside Attractions* and *Cypress Gardens, America's Tropical Wonderland.*

Bonnie Georgiadis dived into mermaiding in 1953 when she was seventeen. She held her breath and stayed wet for fifteen years, then produced/choreographed seven underwater shows before drying out. She is now retired in Tarpon Springs not far from water.

The University Press of Florida is the scholarly publishing agency for the State University System of Florida, comprising Florida A&M University, Florida Atlantic University, Florida Gulf Coast University, Florida International University, Florida State University, New College of Florida, University of Central Florida, University of Florida, University of North Florida, University of South Florida, and University of West Florida.